To, Dear Cath,

Love & Blessings.

E Donovan

CW01456739

The Science Called
Hinduism

ॐ

Sri Ganeshaaya Namaha!

Salutations to Lord Ganesha!
Who removes and overcomes all obstacles,
And grants success in every endeavour.

Ganashtakam

Bharat Mata

ॐ

Vishvasmai Namaha!

The Science Called Hinduism

The Play of the Divine in the Form of the Rishis

Narrated by

Vanamali

Aryan Books International

New Delhi

The Science Called Hinduism

ISBN: 978-81-7305-462-4 (HB)
978-81-7305-463-1 (PB)

© Vanamali Gita Yogashram, 2013

All rights reserved. No part of this book may be reproduced
or transmitted in any form or by any means, electronic
and mechanical, including photocopy, recording or any
other information storage and retrieval system or otherwise,
without written permission from the publisher.

Published in 2013 by

Aryan Books International
Pooja Apartments, 4B, Ansari Road, New Delhi-110 002 (India)
Tel.: 23287589, 23255799; Fax: 91-11-23270385
E-mail: aryanbooks@gmail.com
www.aryanbooks.co.in

Designed and Printed in India at
ABI Prints & Publishing Co., New Delhi.

ॐ

Dharmaaya Namaha!

Dedicated to

My dearest brother, friend and companion

MOHAN

With deep gratitude for the innumerable ways he
has served Vanamali for so many years. Without him
Vanamali Ashram will not function.

BHARAT MATA

Awake O Mother!
The time has come to assert your rights!
To open the veil of ages,
To disclose your eyes,
Filled with the wisdom of the ages,
Your children are crying to Thee,
Why are you silent?
Queen of Beauty!
Queen of Wisdom!
Queen of the world!
Uplift us who have fallen so low,
As to put artha before dharma,
Who have renounced moksha
And embraced kama.
Help us O mother!
Deliver us from the greed that seems to bind us,
Allow us to raise our heads once again,
And proclaim to the world,
This is our land!
The Holy Land!
The land of the sages!
The land of martyrs!
The land which has given the world,
The knowledge of our Immortal Self,
The knowledge to free us,
From the thraldom of ignorance.

ॐ

Contents

ॐ

List of Illustrations

Jacket design and all illustrations done by Anjali Kamat
    Jacket cover:
    front - Shiva Nataraja.
    back - Ancient map of India with Aum superimposed.

ॐ

Essentials of Hinduism
by Pujya Swami Bhoomananda Tirtha Maharaj

Is Hinduism or Hindu Dharma a religion, as such? Religion generally denotes a system of morality based on the concept of God. Hindu Dharma is not something exclusively like that. The dharma of Hindus evolved in the Gangetic plains in the prehistoric times, when the world had not seen or heard the word 'religion' at all. To speak then of Hinduism or Hindu Dharma as a religion is, to say the least, preposterous. But sometimes such references and statements do creep into the minds of people, and it becomes difficult to redress them.

This does not mean that no mending efforts should be made. In fact, any society remains vibrant and creative only when it hosts thinkers, who go into the wrongs, violations and delusions of people from time to time and administer redress measures effectively. We cannot blame any society for its wrongs. But it is inexcusable indeed if its thinking members do not take stock of the situation and strive to remedy the wrong plights by instilling the right introspection and corrections whenever required.

Dharma does not have an English equivalent. Righteousness can be an approximate word to convey what dharma stands for. Dharma denotes the power or process of sustaining human life in all situations, in fortune and misfortune, favour and disfavour, prosperity and adversity. This power is truly applicable to the mind and intelligence, not to anything else in the human personality.

The word Hindu also calls for a discreet analysis and assessment. Barhaspatya Samhita defines the land lying between Himalayas on the north and Indusarovara on the south. Indusarovara has since been under the sea. The relevant verse reads thus:

हिमालयात्समारभ्य यावदिन्दुसरोवरम् ।
तद्देवनिर्मितं देशं हिन्दुस्थानं प्रचक्षते ॥

Beginning from Himalayas extending to Indusarovara, the land created by the Lord is called Hindusthanam, the word being derived from the first letter of 'Himalaya' and the last letter of 'Indu'. Those who belong to Hindusthaanam are called 'Hindu'.

Hindu, thus, is not a religious name. It is a territorial or geographical reference, denoting the people who lived and still live in a specific area of the earth. Whatever new religion or cult they belong to does not matter at all. They are all ethnically Hindus, having been born in and continuing to live in this blessed land.

The concept, process and pursuit of righteousness were evolved by the dwellers in Hindusthanam, who lived and spread in the plains, graced by the perennial flow of the holy river. We cannot say when the thought process and culture first began. Hence they derived the status of 'anaadi', meaning beginningless. As we are not able to trace any point of time when this transpired, it naturally becomes beginningless.

Over the ages, based upon the Vedas, many a literature has evolved on the theme of Dharma. This gradually became an amazing assortment. Even now all the scriptural writings on Hindu Dharma are not traced at all. The fact that these are too numerous to be identified, is clearly revealed by a proverbial statement:

अनन्तशास्त्रं बहु वेदितव्यं
स्वल्पश्च कालो बहवश्च विघ्ना: ।
यत्सारभूतं तदुपासितव्यं
हंसैर्यथा क्षीरमिवाम्बुमिश्रम् ।।

Scriptural compositions are endless. There is a great deal to be known. The obstacles are many, but the time available is short. Therefore, the essence of all these must be discerned and pursued vigorously, like swans separating milk mixed with water.

Swan has the unique capacity of separating milk from water and drinking it exclusively. Such is the art and process of discrimination the dharmic votary must have, in approaching the countless scriptures Hindu Dharma encompasses.

Over the ages many have tried to present the Dharmic thoughts and practices of this land in various forms. It is such presentations that help and guide the people from time to time to get to the ocean of Hindu scriptures and understand with relevance their fundamental tenets and pursuits. Efforts like these should continue. Only then the newer generations will have the opportunity to know the continuing relevance of this most ancient spirituo-philosophical analysis of human life, and the resultant guidance as to how it has to be led to success, peace and fulfilment.

Sage Valmiki's *Ramayana*, Vyasadeva's *Mahabharatam*, *Srimad Bhagavatam* and so many other such writings have come to be evolved thus to serve the same purpose of presenting the thoughts with a renewed concern and relevance to life. Over time, these have come to occupy a place and importance similar to those of Vedas and Upanishads. *Bhagavadgita*, a portion of the epic *Mahabharatam*, is itself considered a commentary on the Upanishads. Brahmasutras are an aphoristic rendering of the various Upanishadic thoughts and findings.

This is so far as the age and vastness of Hindu Dharma are concerned. The uniqueness of Hindu Dharma is that in every form of its practice, you will find the basic spiritual and philosophical notes. At the same time, it is also empirical in every way.

COMPREHENSIVE SCRIPTURAL VISION
ABOUT LIFE AND SOCIETY

The whole dharma has two phases, *achara* and *vichara*. *Achara* denotes various kinds of practice relating to individual, family, society and the administration that governs them. *Vichara* denotes truthful introspection on these and allied matters. The intention is to begin with *achara*, which alone will be possible for children and young minds, and as one grows, take to meaningful introspection, and elevate the practices from sensory level to the mind and intelligence. If the sensory practice has say 1 unit effect, oral has 100 units, the mind has 1000 units and the intelligence carries 100,000 units. Such is the difference. In the human, the mind and intelligence are the causal in all activities, and are the highest.

The entire Dharmic practice is phased in such an effective manner that it takes the practitioner from the bodily and sensory level to the higher ones as early as possible. This progress and evolution can be facilitated, if the right exposure is had and the right guidance sought and gained. People generally lack this. All the dharmic exponents strive to bridge this gap and bring as many people as possible to the right exposure and assessment.

Thus Hindu Dharma has always remained a subject of exposition by an assortment of exponents. Public discourses and publications are the usual means for this great mission. This is how spiritual and philosophical discourses form part of the Hindu culture and tradition. Enlightening discourses are widely attended both by the erudite and common people, young as well as old.

Despite the vast nature of Hindu literature on the subject of Dharma, the concept as well as pursuit of the whole Hindu Dharma can be condensed in three sets of four words each – a total of twelve words:

1. Four Varnas – Brahmana, Kshatriya, Vaishya and Shudra
2. Four Purushaarthas (human pursuits) – Dharma, Artha, Kama and Moksha
3. Four Ashramas – Brahmacharya, Garhasthya, Vanaprastha and Sannyasa

FOUR VARNAS

Varnas refer to the fourfold inner classification, which rules the activities and proclivities of humans. The varna variety is preserved by Nature. Variety is an inevitable expression of Nature. We have no option in the matter. Instead, we should understand, assess and be governed by it properly and lead our life and aspirations to the destined goals.

The first of the four divisions, brahma svabhava, refers to the calm and self-restrained qualities of a person. The second denotes the chivalrous qualities adorning an individual. The third implies the tendencies and skills needed to take up agriculture, trade and commerce, indispensable for societal wellbeing. And the fourth points the predilections, which make one ready and willing to serve others, using his bodily resources and skill.

These are necessary for the society's cohesion and welfare. Because these are invisible, each is explained with its identification marks. For instance, regulation of desire, control of senses, austerity, cleanliness, tolerance and straightforwardness are the traits that make the brahmana group. Brahmanas are generally calm and given to lead a life of self-restraint, inner excellence and joy.

The kshatriya group is extrovert in nature, but chivalrous. They have such qualities and inspirations that keep societal behaviour under check and balance. Heroism, valour, will, skilfulness, not retreating from the warfront, being given to ample charity, gifting, the feeling of lordliness – these are the traits of kshatriya, the warrior group.

Agriculture, rearing cows, dealing in trade, commerce and industry, are the predilections of the vaishya group.

FOURFOLD PURUSHAARTHAS

Belonging to these groups by birth, what should be the goal to be achieved by each during one's tenure upon earth? Hindu Dharma has very clear thoughts and assessments. Our dharmic proponents have evolved the fourfold human pursuit, viz. Dharma, Artha, Kama and Moksha.

By Dharma is meant the code of righteousness, which should govern the life and activities of every one. All the disciplines, inspirations, restraints and obligations are necessary to blend and fuse individual life with the societal one, to make them a beautiful whole.

With such a righteous life, every one should find and develop his own monetary resources by self-effort. Thus the second object is artha, meaning pecuniary sufficiency. Wealth earned by one's own effort is the best, most desirable. That gained from patrimony comes next. The one derived from marriage in the form of dowry and the like is derogatory.

By self-earned wealth, one must try to fulfil his legitimate desires, kama. Stinginess or miserliness is detestable. Frugality is the ideal, the right option. The true objective of wealth is to gain dharma, for that alone will lead to inner spiritual enlightenment, bestowing peace, wisdom and freedom in the end.

When dharma, artha and kama are pursued in their right order and measure, the fourth object, moksha, becomes relevant, facile and meaningful. Moksha denotes the release from the suffocating shackles of the mind and intelligence. With such release, redemption, one becomes an heir to immortality and inner ecstasy. This is to be achieved while living here and now. Everything about dharma is thus relevant to our life, to be pursued wholesomely here and now. It enriches, empowers, enlightens and fulfils human life.

Hindu Dharma is called Sanatana for two reasons. *Sanatanam karoti iti sanatanah.* It makes its votary feel and realize that his personality is, in truth, immortal. He is not the body. He only has his body, like his house or car. The 'presence and power' that animate the body is not physical, but spiritual. Different from matter and energy, which constitute the body, he is actually unborn, undying, eternal and everywhere present. The inner consciousness that he verily is, makes him immortal.

Equally so, Hindu dharma is sanatana, eternal, because it relates to the mind and intelligence of the human, which have not changed over ages. The ancient human had the same emotional mind and rational intelligence, which alone his modern counterpart also has. Values which relate to these changeless constituents of the human personality are naturally eternal.

As for the scientific nature of Hindu Dharma, it rests upon the observations our senses make, and the inferences the mind and intelligence arrive at on the basis of such observations. In fact, these are the two canons on which all objective sciences also subsist. That the objective science uses instruments like the telescope and microscope makes no difference to the fundamental nature and validity of both, namely science and spirituality. What employs the instruments are the senses in oneself. And it is the mind and intelligence within that employ the senses. Thus the grounds on which objective science and Hindu dharma, the subjective science, rest are exactly the same. As is any other science acceptable, the Hindu dharma also is.

Sanatana Dharma lays down a set of common disciplines for all people, despite their bodily or inner differences. They are:

अहिंसा सत्यमस्तेयं शौचमिन्द्रियनिग्रहः ।
एतत्सामासिकं धर्मं चातुर्वर्ण्येऽब्रवीन्मनुः ॥

Non-hurting, not to speak of non-killing, truthfulness, non-stealing, cleanliness and sensory control, are the common disciplines and values meant for all categories of people.

You will find all these are ethical and mind-intelligence based. Cleanliness is both physical and inner.

FOUR ASHRAMAS OR STAGES IN LIFE

To gain the fourfold purushartha, our Dharmic exponents had evolved a four-phased life-pattern. Brahmacharya, celibacy, devoted solely for learning, is the first phase, where the student lives in the residence of the teacher and pursues learning wholesomely. At the end of this phase, he has the freedom to return home, get married and raise a family, to perpetuate the lineage. He has also the choice, depending upon the degree of dispassion and earnestness he gains, to pursue spiritual wisdom exclusively, take directly to ascetic life, sannyaasa.

But the household life is not an all-time pursuit. At the age of 55 or 60, when the children become adults, one should entrust the household to them and adopt the vanaprastha way of life, the third phase, devoted to truthful introspection leading to inner refinement and expansion. This can be done along with one's wife, if she so desires and is ready to take up the same inner refinemental mission.

If the incumbent succeeds in fulfilling this phase, he can adopt the last phase called sannyaasa, renunciation, which is the climax and crowning glory of human life. Sannyaasa is a sequel to one's realizing his own Imperishable Self. *Jnanadeva kaivalya-praaptih*, so goes the aphorism. From wisdom alone dawn the joy and fulfilment of inner spiritual freedom.

Thus the 12 words, taken together, become the synopsis of Hindu Dharma. No matter what tendencies one has, there is a way of changing them for the better, by adopting and practising the higher disciplines and values. Practice makes one perfect. In fact, the sole object of human will, ingenuity, is to change, correct and improve oneself, so as to become what one verily aspires for.

All the four varnas have equal freedom and opportunity to adopt the four phase-life and reach the climax of fulfilment, though by nature all do not do so. Failure does not invalidate the concept of fourfold purushartha, and the sure way of achieving it.

KNOWLEDGE – THREE CATEGORIES

Vedanta ascertained ages ago that knowledge is of three kinds – pratyaksha, paroksha and aparoksha. Pratyaksha is that, which is gained by the sensory organs. Paroksha is what is arrived at by the intelligence, through inference. In these, either senses work or the mind-intelligence works.

There is another level and kind of knowledge called aparoksha. It is beyond the realm of senses (pratyaksha) or intelligence (paroksha). Yet there is full comprehension.

For instance, how do we know that we slept and did not know anything at all? In sleep, we are unaware of the body, mind, intelligence and even the ego. Yet we wake up to say we were, and we slept. Naturally that knowledge is beyond and different from the one perceived through senses, mind and intelligence.

The aparoksha concept about knowledge is something unique to Sanatana Dharma.

It is always good to remember the fundamental principle, namely rationality, which governs Hindu Dharma, in every step.

युक्तियुक्तं प्रगृह्णीयात् बालादपि विचक्षण: ।
अन्यत्-तु तृणवत्त्याज्यं-अप्युक्तं पद्मयोनिना ॥

The wise one should accept whatever is reasonable, told even by a child. Anything otherwise, even if stated by Brahma, the Creator, is to be summarily rejected like a blade of grass.

If this is the basic premise governing Hindu Dharma, is there a question or doubt as to whether it is rational, scientific and logical? In fact, three are the tests for any dharmic statement or revelation. It should be enunciated in the ageless scriptures (Shruti); it must have the support of reason (yukti); and it should also be experiential to oneself (anubhava). Only when these three together confirm a proposition, it can be accepted and followed.

WHY HINDUS WORSHIP SO MANY GODS

Though Hindu Dharma is primarily and ultimately philosophical and spiritual, it does comprehend religious thoughts and needs of the assorted humanity, thereby catering to their varied tendencies and predilections. As in the matter of food, dress and residences, in religious and devotional relish also, there is need for ample variety. On this basis, Hindu pantheon also arrays a variety of Gods and Goddesses, each of whom is imbued with a specific set of qualities, which are, in fact, the desire, choice and affinities of the human mind. Nevertheless, our Dharma clarifies, emphasizes and confirms in unambiguous terms that God is but one, omnipresent, having no physical form or shape.

Such a God naturally becomes unthinkable and inaccessible to the ordinary minds. At the same time, they cannot be denied the freedom and scope to worship God and derive the resultant benefits. This is how various deities, together with the specific qualities associated with them, have come to be evolved, sought and spread among the people. It is more a socio-psychological compulsion than otherwise!

To give one instance, Hanuman is a pet Lord of a large multitude of people. There is something called *Hanuman Chaleesa*, forty hymns on Hanuman, daily sung by millions of people. By reciting this composition with fervour and piety, what verily happens is that the singer gets infused with the qualities – courage, resolve, fidelity to the Master, wisdom, robust health, sensitiveness, dexterity in speech and the like. Those seeking these qualities piously sing the *Chaleesa*, thereby imbibing the essence of what they sing. In fact, all devotional practices are like this, self-enriching and self-empowering!

The best explanation about worship and its scientific background is in *Srimad Bhagavatam*, a full authority on Devotion and God, where young Prahlada praises Lord Narahari, after He encountered Hinranyakashipu (Prahlada's father) and killed him. This is one of the most cherished hymns of the great holy Text:

नैवात्मन: प्रभुरयं निजलाभपूर्णो
मानं जनादविदुष: करुणो वृणीते।
यद्यज्जनो भगवते विदधीत मानं
तच्चात्मन: प्रतिमुखस्य यथा मुखश्री: ॥

Srimad Bhagavatam 7.9.11

You, the Lord of entire creation, are always all-fulfilled by virtue of your own nature and glory, and hence do not need any adoration, praise or offering from any one. Those who praise and make offerings to you, do so out of their own ignorance. And you seem to accept all this solely because of your own mercy. Whatever praise, worship or adoration is showered on you, all that conduces to the worshipper's own development, as is the case with the anointment done to the reflected face on oneself, whom the mirror reflects.

A question may arise as to why then so much of worship is done for the Lord. Whatever the ignorant people do in the nature of adoration and offering brings about their own enrichment and elevation. We cannot live without the mirror. The mirror is made by us. It is hung on the wall or mounted suitably to serve our purpose. By looking into it alone we can see our face and decorate it variously. Whatever we do to the face in the mirror, does not touch the mirror at all. Instead all of it verily falls on one's own face. Likewise, any praise, worship or similar acts done to God verily enrich, empower and elevate the worshipper himself, not God!

An impersonal, formless presence cannot be accessed by the ordinary human mind. At the same time, the mind wants to give vent to its feelings and affinity for the Lord. Hence the Idol and various methods of worship are evolved.

It is significant that at no time or place, the worshipper addresses the stone idol or the painted picture. Sitting in its front, he thinks about, speaks to and tries to interact with the Lord, the omnipresent. "O Lord, the omnipresent", is how the devotees think, speak and address.

THE PRESENT WORK

Swamini Vanamali, the author of this book, has been an ascetic living in the Himalayan slopes in Rishikesh for many years. Hinduism always insists upon and exhorts people to take up austerity and asceticism, as a natural culmination of spiritual life and pursuit. Generally the ascetic and the austere alone have lived the true spiritual life and disseminated spiritual wisdom in this holy land. True philosophers have always been ascetic and austere.

Naturally when someone like this speaks and writes about Hindu Dharma, it will have an additional note of experiential vision and maturity. Such writing will always be distinct from the rest. Swamini Vanamali is not a new writer. Her earlier books are there to speak about her and her writing. In the background of her earlier publications, this book on the scientific nature of Hinduism has its distinct place and relevance. May this be well understood, and the effort bring its destined fruition.

The society always will need enlightenment and hence the efforts towards this should be consistent in every generation. May Swamini Vanamali's effort have its distinct contribution and effectiveness in this direction.

My love, appreciation and blessings for the author as well as the readers.

Antaraatma
Swami Bhoomananda Tirtha
Narayanashrama Tapovanam

ॐ

Bhutatmaaya Namaha!

Introduction

I boldly proclaim Hinduism the greatest in the world.
Hinduism's venerable age has seasoned to maturity. It is the
only religion, to my knowledge, which is not founded on a
single historic event or prophet, but which itself precedes
recorded history. Hinduism has been called the "cradle of
spirituality" and the "mother of all religions," partially because
it has influenced virtually every major religion and partly
because it can absorb all other religions—honour and embrace
their scriptures, their saints, their philosophy.

Sivaya Subramuniyaswami

India has maintained the longest, unbroken continuity of
civilization in the whole world.

The Upanishad says,

Satyam eva jayati naanrutam,
Truth alone shall prevail, not falsehood.

What is Truth and how is it to be known? Time alone is the
touchstone of truth. However much one tries to stamp out Truth,
it shall not be overcome. Hence, Hinduism, which is based on
Truth, can never be stamped out and has existed from the dawn
of time. The universe exists on Truth and anything that is not

founded on Truth is automatically deleted by Time. Many religions and many cultures have come and gone. One by one, they have been mown down by the relentless scythe of Time. Hinduism alone has remained. This is because it is based on the eternal verities—*satyam, ahimsa* and *dharma*, truth, non-violence and righteousness. This is the cosmic *dharma*—the law of eternal justice by which this cosmos has been created, sustained and destroyed. That is why Hinduism is known as "Sanatana Dharma", the ancient law of righteousness. It is a living relic of the ancient past of not just India but the past of the whole history of humanity and thus it follows that Hinduism is the oldest religion. Much of the forms of Hindu culture today are the same as they were more than ten thousand years ago. The ancient world never died in India. It still remains and can be contacted everywhere.

Actually, the word Hinduism is a misnomer. It was the name given by the westerners to those who lived below the Indus River. The actual name of Hinduism is the Sanatana Dharma or the way of Eternal Righteousness. The ideas and beliefs of Hinduism have existed from time immemorial. It has the ability to evolve with the changing times and this is the reason for its continued existence. Anything which is static and stagnant will eventually decay and die. Just as water has to flow in order to keep itself free of impurities, so also every religion must have the ability to grow. Many of the ancient religions of countries like Egypt and Mesopotamia, which were really highly evolved, have been wiped off the face of the earth with the passage of time, whereas Hinduism has continued to exist. Western religions can be compared to a monolithic iron pillar, which is incapable of bending or giving way or changing. Hinduism, on the other hand, can be compared to a banyan tree which has spreading branches reaching out with ever more new shoots and more ideas. That is why we find more religions within the Hindu faith than there are in the rest of the world put together. Though its fundamental concepts are ancient, it is capable of accepting and even welcoming all new ideas which are consistent with *dharma* or righteousness.

There was no antagonism between science and religion in India as there was in the west since the religion is based on scientific truths. In the *Isavasya Upanishad*, the great sage Yajnavalkya says that there are two types of understanding, *vidya* and *avidya*. Usually we take *avidya* to mean ignorance. However, he gives a different interpretation. *Vidya* is eternal, experiential, spiritual knowledge or *para vidya*, while *avidya* is external, experimental, material knowledge or *apara vidya*. We should make use of the second to guide our lives so that it leads us to the first. Unless both these types of knowledge are integrated into our lives, we will end up being blind or lame as Einstein put it. He who believes that science alone can take away all the miseries of our life is like a blind man entering a dark room. However, he who believes that it is only by chanting *mantras* in the solitude of a cave, is also entering blinding darkness. Hinduism has never held that blind faith can lead to liberation or that science alone can give you a Utopian life. Both are necessary for a fulfilled life.

Every time the Sanatana Dharma showed signs of declining, God Himself took an incarnation to revive it. As Lord Krishna told Arjuna in the *Bhagavad-Gita, Yada yada hi dharmasya glanirbhavati*, Whenever this *dharma* declines O Arjuna, I incarnate myself *dharma samsthapanarthaya sambhavami yuge yuge*, in order to re-establish this ancient *dharma*. Thus, our country has had many *avataras* as well as great sages who have incarnated themselves in every age in order to uplift the Sanatana Dharma and that is how it has retained its pristine glory for countless ages.

The westerners who came to India in the early part of the last century were totally incapable of appreciating the wonders of this ancient knowledge. This is because Hinduism is a most obscure and difficult religion to understand. What is generally exposed to the common eye is only the scum on top of the deep pond which contains a treasure of gems which are not easily available to the cursory glance. Hinduism is as difficult for the un-initiated to understand as quantum physics to the layman. In fact, it has great similarities to quantum physics, hence the title of this book is "The Science called Hinduism".

The object of writing this book is to try and make everyone understand and appreciate the great depth and beauty of this religion which has survived the test of time and withstood the onslaughts and challenges of countless other cultures which have tried to cast scorn on it and reduce it to nothing.

People have asked me how I dared to write about physics, which is an alien subject for me. My answer it that it is only my in-depth knowledge of Hinduism that has made it easy for me to understand quantum physics. The first time I read the *Tao of Physics* by Fritjof Capra, I was struck with wonder for I instinctively understood what the physicist was trying to say. Many of the abstruse points in the *Bhagavad-Gita* suddenly became crystal clear to me. Later, when I went through the Puranas, I was again struck at the amazing ways in which the great saints of the Puranas—Vyasa and Valmiki—had woven great scientific truths into their stories. These scientific truths are not what the ancient western world believed to be true but the truths of the most modern kind—that of quantum physics.

This fact hit me like a sledge hammer—that right from the Vedas to the Puranas, everything was completely scientific. For obvious reasons the sages did not expose this fact to the common eye. If we of the modern age who are quite used to so many technical facilities, which we accept as common-place, find it impossible to understand quantum physics, how much more would it have been impossible for people to understand what the sages were trying to say at that age and time when even things like ordinary matches was unheard of!

Since Hinduism is more a way of life than what is normally thought of as a religion, it is also a fact that the methods of leading a *dharmic* (relating to the laws of righteousness embedded in nature) life, is slowly creeping into other cultures even though they do not realise that the foundation of such ideas come from Hinduism. For instance, words like *yoga, dharma, karma, lila* and so on have become common parlance in western cultures. However, for some reason, westerners don't like the idea of admitting that these words have a Hindu basis. The Semitic concept that the body is as important as the soul and that this body and soul have only one birth is also slowly being replaced by the Hindu concept of re-incarnation. The Semitic religions believe that it is essential to preserve this body which will rise up along with the soul at the end of time so it is always buried, wearing fine clothes or preserved in crypts and graves. The Hindus, however, believe that this body is only one of hundreds which the soul takes to achieve certain purposes of its own and thus the body is always cremated. The increasing number of people in the west who are opting for cremation rather than burial is a sure sign to show that people are slowly veering to the Hindu view of re-birth and reincarnation, which of course is much more scientific.

The scientists of this culture were known as *rishis*. The entire credit for ensuring that this culture never died goes to them. They were both philosopher-saints and scientists and existed from the dawn of the Indian civilisation, which is the dawn of time. The sages desired that this country should progress not just materially but through a constant inner renewal of the cosmic law of righteousness, guided by the wisdom embedded in our scriptures. So they were the ones who gave us many paths called *yogas,* which are all scientifically based which would lead the human being to discover his blissful inner self. I had wanted to write a book about the *rishis* but after a number of futile attempts, I realised that they preferred to remain anonymous and wanted me to write about the Sanatana Dharma which was their particular offering to humanity.

I conclude this introduction by offering my total and whole-hearted prostrations at the feet of those *rishis*—Vasishta, Vishvamitra and many others—who were the great *gurus* of our land as well as to the sages, Vyasa and Valmiki, who alone have inspired and given me the courage to write this book.

> The Creator is perfect,
> He possesses perfect power,
> Whence is created perfect Nature.
> The perfect universe derives life,
> From the perfect Creator.
> Let us comprehend this perfect power,
> That bestows life on all beings.
>
> *Atharva Veda*

Loka Samasthath Sukhino Bhavantu!

ॐ

Vishvaaya Namaha!

CHAPTER I

The Sanatana Dharma

After a study of some forty years and more of the great religions of the world, I find none so perfect, none so scientific, none so philosophic, and none so spiritual as the great religion known by the name of Hinduism. The more you know it, the more you will love it; the more you try to understand it, the more deeply you will value it. Make no mistake; without Hinduism, India has no future. Hinduism is the soil into which India's roots are struck, and torn of that she will inevitably wither, as a tree torn out from its place. Many are the religions and many are the races flourishing in India, but none of them stretches back into the far dawn of her past, nor are they necessary for her endurance as a nation. Everyone might pass away as they came and India would still remain. But let Hinduism vanish and what is she? A geographical expression of the past, a dim memory of a perished glory, her literature, her art, her monuments, all have Hindudom written across them. If the Hindus do not maintain Hinduism, who shall save it? If India's own children do not cling to her faith, who shall guard it? India alone can save India, and India and Hinduism are one.

Annie Besant

These were indeed prophetic words that Annie Besant wrote at
the time of the British Raj. Perhaps she realised what her own
people were doing to the deep-rooted faith and culture of the
land they had conquered. The British never went out overtly to
destroy temples or desecrate Hindu art. Their attempts were
more subtle and the unfortunate part was that this attempt was
aided by the Hindu intelligentsia who were desperate to impress
and get into the good books of their conquerors. The 19th
century saw more harm being caused to classical Hinduism than
any other century, including the Mogul conquest. It is imperative
for all Indians to save Hinduism and its culture, for without it,
India itself would not exist as Annie Besant said and this would
be a terrible loss not just to India but to the whole world, for
Hinduism is unique in many respects and genocide is a serious
crime. Let us go through the history of the Sanatana Dharma
and thereby allow Hindus everywhere to see what is being done
to their own faith.

The Sanatana Dharma is the name of the most ancient
religion in the world. Hinduism is the name given to it by the
British. It only meant the people who lived below the Indus
River. Hinduism has been called a way of life rather than a
religion and that is why its ancient name is Sanatana Dharma
or the ancient law of righteousness. It is the most tolerant and
the most liberal of all religions. More and more intelligent people
in the world with spiritual leanings are turning away from the
orthodox ideas of a God who lives in his heaven and who
punishes sinners and casts them into eternal hell and blesses the
pious and gives them a place in heaven. One of the aspersions
cast against Hinduism is that it has many gods whereas all
Western religions have only one God.

In this context it must be pointed out that the One God of all Semitic religions is a sectarian god, exclusive to the followers of that particular faith or sect. He has nothing whatsoever to do with those who do not believe in him. They are cast beyond the pale of divine grace.

Hinduism also believes in One God and one divine power. But the One God of the Sanatana Dharma is a universal Being, who transcends all boundaries of time, space and causation. He is not bound to only the Hindus but is available to the whole of creation and not just for human beings. He or IT has existed always and will continue to exist even if no one believes in IT. IT is the Ultimate Truth of everything and everyone.

Hinduism is the most tolerant religion in the world. It is a goal-oriented religion and thus gives us many paths of approach to God. These are known as *yogas* and they cater to different types of personalities. It does not insist that there is only one path and one way to approach the Paramatma or the Supreme. There are many paths and many ways and what we choose is decided by our temperament. Hinduism is accused of being pluralistic but pluralism means freedom—freedom of choice. It has no overall authority which dictates what every Hindu should or should not do. The first charter of human rights and liberties was given by Hinduism to every human being and hence it is imperative that we educate our children in all these facts so that they realize how fortunate they are to be born in the arms of such a loving and tolerant mother. The *rishis* have catered to every type of person. No one is cast out of the loving arms of this divine mother. It is highly tolerant of all other religions. Everyone is given freedom to worship god in his or her own way as suited to his or her own personality. No one is cast out. We can take as many lives as we want but eventually every soul will be liberated. This is the beautifully consoling clarion call of Hinduism. Krishna tells Arjuna in the *Gita, Kaunteya pratijanihi, na me bhakta pranasyati.* "O Arjuna I give you my solemn promise that my devotee will never perish."

This is why Hinduism has always been a religion that has taught tolerance of other valid religious traditions. However, the assertion that we should have tolerance for the beliefs of other religions is a radically different claim from the declaration that all religions are the same. Historically speaking, pre-colonial classical Hinduism never taught that all religions are the same. Of course it is absolutely true to say that Hinduism has always believed in tolerance and freedom of religious thought and expression. But these are two thoroughly separate assertions and should not be taken to mean that Hindu tolerance is synonymous with Radical Universalism (identity of all religions). To maintain a healthy tolerance of another person's religion does not mean that we consider their religion to be the same as ours and that there is no harm in conversion!

Traditional Hinduism has always been the most tolerant, patient and welcoming of all religions. It never persecuted others merely because they had a different theological belief. India is the only country in the world which has never practised slavery. Hindu India has been the sole nation on earth where the Jewish community has never been persecuted even though they have been living here for over 2000 years. Similarly, Zoroastrian refugees escaping the destruction of the Persian civilization at the hands of Islamic conquerors were warmly welcomed in India over 1000 years ago. The Zoroastrian community (now known as the Parsis) has thrived and lived amicably with their Hindu neighbours in peace and mutual respect. Hinduism has always sought to live side-by-side peacefully with the followers of other religions, whether they were the indigenous Indian religions of Buddhism, Jainism, and Sikhism or the foreign religions of Christianity and Islam.

In keeping with the Vedic injunction that a guest should be treated with as much hospitality as one would treat a visiting divinity, Hinduism has always been gracious to the followers of other religions, and respectful of their gods, scriptures and customs. The tolerance and openness of Hinduism has been historically unprecedented in the community of world religions and has been universally acclaimed. But now that very tolerance has been misunderstood and misinterpreted by the Hindu intellectuals themselves.

The mistake that is now being made by modern Hindus, especially those living abroad, is to misunderstand the long-held Hindu tradition of tolerating other religions with the notion that Hinduism encourages us to believe that all religions are exactly the same. We have mistaken Hindu tolerance with Radical Universalism. The leap from tolerance of other faiths to a belief that all religions are equal is not a leap that is grounded in logic. Nor is it grounded in the history, literature or philosophy of the Hindu tradition itself.

Unfortunately, in our headlong rush to devolve Hinduism of anything that might seem to even remotely resemble the close-minded sectarianism sometimes found in other religions, we tend to forget the obvious truth that Hinduism is itself a systematic and self-contained religious tradition in its own right. It is true that Hinduism is not an organised religion. It has no hierarchy of priests or popes or cardinals who impose orders which are obligatory on everyone. However, like every other religion, Hinduism has a distinct and unique tradition, with its own in-built beliefs, world-view, traditions, rituals, concept of the Absolute, metaphysics, ethics, aesthetics, cosmology, cosmogony, and theology. The grand, systematic philosophical edifice that we call Hinduism today is the result of the extraordinary efforts and spiritual insights of the *rishis, yogis, acharyas* and great *gurus* of our religion, guided by the transcendent light of the Vedic revelations, which has stood the test of time. It is a tradition that should be protected and preserved by all Hindus and given respect and admiration by non-Hindus.

Such a realisation and acceptance of Hinduism's unique place in the world does not, by any stretch of the imagination, have to lead automatically to sectarianism, strife, conflict or religious chauvinism. On the other hand, the recognition of Hinduism's distinctiveness is crucial if Hindus are to possess even a modicum of healthy self-understanding, self-respect and pride in their own tradition. Self-respect and the ability to celebrate one's unique spiritual traditions are basic psychological needs and the right of all human beings whether Hindu or non-Hindu.

Unfortunately, we find that the modern Hindu youth, especially those who live abroad, is forced to take a defensive stand against the onslaughts of other religions and has no method of defending themselves since neither they nor their parents know enough to defend their own religion.

It should be impressed on the Hindu modern youth that they have no reason to be uncomfortable or ashamed about their unique spiritual tradition, or to be frightened of asserting their exceptional contributions to the development of global religious thought. This is an obvious, yet all too often forgotten, fact the importance of which cannot be overstated: *Hinduism is its own uniquely independent religious tradition, different and distinct from any other religion on earth.* Hinduism has a distinct tradition.

Adi Shankaracharya

This distinction has been asserted by all our great saints. Every time another faith came to disturb the even tenor of the Hindu tradition, we find that some great religious leader or prophet would rise up in order to keep it on the correct track and uphold the values of the Sanatana Dharma.

The great Hindu saints used to have debates with the protagonists of non-Hindu traditions like Buddhism, Jainism and Charvakins (atheists). The sages of Hinduism met all philosophical challenges with infallible logic and sustained pride in their own tradition, and always succeeded in defeating their philosophical opponents in open assemblies. Adi Shankaracharya, founder of Advaita Vedanta, went all over the peninsula defeating all his learned opponents in open debate. This was known as his "Digvijaya", or "Conquest of all Directions". This indomitable title was awarded to Shankaracharya solely due to his formidable ability to defend the Hindu tradition from the philosophical attacks of non-Hindu schools of thought. Indeed, Shankara is attributed as being partially responsible for the decline of Buddhism in India due to his great ability in debate by which he totally annihilated his opponent's arguments and proved the superiority of the Vedantic doctrines.

The great teacher Madhvacharya, founder of the Dwaita school of Vedanta, is similarly seen as being responsible for the sharp decline of Jainism in south India due to his acute intelligence and great debating skills in defense of the *Vaidika Dharma* (Vedic Dharma). All pre-modern Hindu sages and philosophers recognized and celebrated the singularly unique vision that Hinduism had to offer the world. They clearly distinguished between Hindu and non-Hindu religions, and defended Hinduism to the utmost of their formidable intellectual and spiritual abilities. They did so unapologetically, professionally and courageously. The Hindu world-view makes sense, and will survive only if we celebrate Hinduism's uniqueness today.

India was the richest country in the world till the advent of the British in the 17th century . Robert Clive's personal wealth amassed from the plunder of Bengal was £401,102. The total amount of treasure looted by the British reached one billion pounds by 1901. This was apart from the price of the Kohinoor diamond. Apart from this financial catastrophe, there was another tragic occurrence, during the 19th century, the destructive magnitude of which Hindu leaders and scholars are only dimly beginning to recognise and assess. This development both altered and weakened Hinduism to such a tremendous degree that Hinduism has not even begun to recover from it. During the last century, the classical, traditional Hinduism that had been responsible for the continuous development of thousands of years of a unique culture, architecture, music, philosophy, ritual and theology came under the devastating assault of British colonial rule. This was different from any of the other assaults that Hinduism had to bear in the past. For a thousand years previous to the British Raj, foreign marauders had repeatedly attempted to destroy Hinduism through overt physical genocide and the systematic destruction of Hindu temples and sacred places. Our sages and warriors had fought bravely to stem this anti-Hindu holocaust to the best of their ability, often paying for their bravery with their lives. What the Hindu community experienced under British Christian domination, however, was an ominous form of cultural genocide. It was a subtle yet systematic programme of intellectual and spiritual annihilation. It is easy to defend oneself from the threat of an enemy who tries to kill us physically but much harder to recognise the threat of an enemy who outwardly claims to serve the best interests of the people that it has subjugated but slowly seeks to undermine the authority of its cultural heritage! Thus, you find that all original thought both in the field of science and arts was totally nipped in the bud during and after the British rule.

During the short span of the British Raj, the ancient grandeur and beauty of classical Hinduism that had stood the test of thousands of years came under direct ideological attack. What makes this period of Hindu history especially tragic is that the main apparatus that the British used in their attempts to destroy traditional Hinduism were the British-educated, adopted sons and daughters of Hinduism itself. Seeing traditional Hinduism through the eyes of their British masters, the Anglicized Hindu intellectuals took it as their solemn duty to "westernize" and "modernise" traditional Hinduism to make it more palatable to their new English overlords. One of the unfortunate happenings of this historic period was the fabrication of a new movement known as "neo-Hinduism". Neo-Hinduism was an artificial religious group that claimed to form a bridge between traditional Hinduism and their Christian overlords which would make it more palatable to them. Neo-Hinduism was an effective weapon, used to replace the traditional Hinduism that had been the religion and culture of our people for thousands of years, with a British-invented version designed to make a subjugated people easier to manage and control. Perhaps the British did not quite realise the enormity of the crime they were perpetuating against an ancient culture and heritage which was so far removed from their own religious beliefs, that they were totally incapable of understanding it, far less appreciating it.

Indian intellectuals educated in England and in British public schools in India who were encouraged to read only English classics were an easy prey. The schools and colleges all taught them to admire and appreciate this foreign culture which seemed so delectable to them. If their culture was so admirable then surely their religion must also be great, was their logical conclusion! We learnt to despise our gods and condemn our traditions as superstitious nonsense. Our schools that used to teach *yoga* were replaced by what the British called PT (physical training). We yearned to be considered the equals of our conquerors and bent ourselves backwards in order to change our ancient beliefs to suit the spiritually immature viewpoint of our conquerors. We forgot that our own religion had stood the test of thousands of years and had all the force and strength of the great spiritual giants who had given it to us.

As soon as they came to India, the British recognised that the dignity, strength and beauty of traditional Hinduism were the foremost threat to Christian European rule in India. This is an extract from Macaulay's address to the British Parliament on the 2nd of February 1835.

> I have traveled across the length and breadth of India and I have not seen one person who is a beggar or who is a thief. Such wealth have I seen in this country, such high moral values, people of such caliber that I do not think we would ever conquer this country, unless we break the very backbone of this nation, which is her spiritual and cultural heritage and therefore, I propose that we replace her old and ancient education system and her culture, for if the Indians can be

made to think that all that is foreign and English is good and greater than their own, they will lose their self-esteem, their native culture and they will become what we want them to be, a truly dominated nation!

This is exactly what the British proceeded to do. They systematically destroyed our spiritual wealth, which is the basis of our scientific knowledge, and thus impoverished the whole nation into becoming a set of poor imitators and docile servants of the British Raj. The invention of neo-Hinduism was another diabolically clever method. Had this anti-Hindu programme been carried out only by the British and the missionaries, it would not have met with as much success as it did. Therefore, an Indian facade was used to impose neo-Hinduism upon the Hindu people. The effects of the activities of Indian neo-Hindus were ruinous for traditional Hinduism. The age brought a spate of highly intellectual Indians like Ram Mohan Roy and the Brahmo Samajees who literally played into the hands of their ingenious masters! They brought out a form of watered Hinduism which they felt would find more favour with the British.

Many of the pseudo *gurus* of today are also propagators of neo-Hinduism and the theory of Radical Universalism (all religions are the same), even though they do not realise it. They wear orange clothes and quote liberally from the *Gita* and the *Bible* alike, and try to show the similarity in both teachings and in the lives of Krishna and Christ. Actually they do harm to both religions. The ideas of Radical Universalism have had a paralysing impact on modern Hindu philosophy. It has resulted in killing all Hindu philosophical development since the 18th century and in severely undermining Hindu self-esteem. Its intellectual roots are certainly not to be found in Hinduism, but can clearly be traced back to early Christian missionary attempts to alter the genuine teachings of authentic Hinduism.

The British did their best to suppress the true facts of the historicity of the Hindu gods like Rama and Krishna and even insisted that the Vedas, which are the cornerstones of Hinduism, were actually a graft brought from outside by creating the myth called the Aryan Invasion. The great German Indologist, Max Müller was the first to think of this theory which has no historical basis whatsoever. The Indian historians simply copied him without going to the roots of the matter. The roots of course can be found in the Hindu scriptures. No one thought of investigating the Vedas themselves in order to verify this claim. Indian historians simply swallowed what was given in western historical books and reiterated the myth of the Aryan Invasion. When we look into the Vedas, we find that no mention has ever been made of such an expedition or invasion. According to the Vedas, the whole of the Vedic culture was developed along the banks of the great Saraswathy River, which was the great artery for the whole of north India as the Ganga is today. However, western historians claimed the river to be purely mythical and of course Indian historians repeated this in a parrot-like fashion. It is only today that modern scientific research and photos taken from space have clearly shown the existence of this river which was the very backbone of the Vedic scene and thus of the Hindu culture. Science proves that the Vedic culture is totally indigenous. In fact, now it has been proven that Hinduism has existed right from the great Harappan culture through the Vedic, and right up to the present. The seals found in the Harappan valley have many of the Vedic signs on them like "ॐ", the swastika and the peepul tree. The Vedic culture was developed all along the banks of the great river Saraswati, which has been described as mythical by all the western Indologists who seemed bent on belittling the greatness of this culture for some strange reason of their own. Satellite pictures clearly show the river Saraswati rising in the Himalayas and wending its way to the ocean. Remains of many settlements along the river are also found. The river slowly dried up due to seismic movements and the gradual drying up of her tributaries, giving rise to the Thar Desert. This happened in 1900 BCE. According to the Hindus, part of the river went underground and emerged in Allahabad where it joined the other two great rivers of north India, the Ganga and the Yamuna. This highly spiritual spot is known as Triveni.

The 19th century British-educated Indians had little authentic information about their own Hindu intellectual and spiritual heritage. These Westernized Indians vied with each other to gain acceptance and respectability for themselves from their Christian European audience who saw in Hinduism nothing more than the childish prattle of a primitive people. Many exaggerated stereotypes about Hinduism had been unsettling impressionable European minds for a century previous to their era. Rather than attempting to refute these many stereotypes about Hinduism by presenting Hinduism in its authentic and pristine form, many of these 19th century Anglicized Indians felt it was necessary to remove from Hinduism anything that might seem offensive or barbaric to the European mind. Radical Universalism seemed to be the perfect base on which to construct a "new" Hinduism that would give the Anglicized 19th century Indian intelligentsia the acceptability they so yearned for from their British masters.

The primary dilemma for the Western educated Hindu youth both in India and abroad is that they do not realise that there are really two distinct and conflicting Hinduisms today—Neo-Hindu and Traditionalist Hindu. The Traditionalists, who are the guardians of authentic Hindu Dharma, have not yet found a way of communicating this unadulterated Hindu Dharma, which is the Sanatana Dharma in a way in which the modern mind can appreciate it. Until they do so Hinduism will continue to be a religion mired in confusion about its own true meaning and value until traditional Hindus can assertively, professionally and intelligently communicate the reality of genuine Hinduism to the world.

In order to fully experience Hinduism in its most spiritually evocative and philosophically compelling form, we must learn to recognize, and reject, the concocted influences of neo-Hinduism that have permeated the whole of Hindu thought today. It is time to rid ourselves of the liberal Christian inspired "reformism" that so deeply prejudiced such individuals as Ram Mohan Roy over a century ago. We must free ourselves from the anti-Hindu dogma of Radical Universalism that has so weakened Hinduism, and re-embrace an authentically classical form of Hinduism that is rooted in the actual scriptures of Hinduism, that has been preserved for thousands of years by the legitimate *acharyas* and has stood the test of time. The neo-Hindu importation of Radical Universalism into the Hindu thought may appeal to many on a purely emotional level, but it remains patently anti-Hindu in its origin, and is a highly destructive doctrine to the further development of Hinduism!

Traditional Hindu philosophers continually emphasized the crucial importance of clearly understanding what Hinduism proper was and what non-Hindu religious paths were. You cannot claim to be a Hindu, after all, if you do not understand what it is that you claim to believe, and what it is that others believe. One set of Sanskrit terms repeatedly employed by traditional Hindu philosophers were the words *Vaidika* and *avaidika*. The word *Vaidika* (or "Vedic" in English) means one who accepts the teachings of the *Veda*. It refers specifically to the unique stand taken by the traditional schools of Hindu philosophy, known as *sabda-pramana*, or employing the divine sound current of the *Veda* as a means of acquiring valid knowledge. In this sense the word "*Vaidika*" is employed to differentiate those schools of Indian philosophy that accept the epistemological validity of the *Veda* as a perfect authoritative spiritual source, eternal and untouched by the speculations of humanity, as against the *avaidika* schools that do not ascribe such validity to the *Veda*. In pre-Christian times Buddhism, Jainism and the atheistic Charvaka schools were all known to be *avaidika*—or those who did not accept the *Veda*. These three schools were unanimously considered non-Vedic, and thus non-Hindu. Though they are geographically Indian religions, they are not theologically and philosophically Hindu religions.

Manu, one of the great ancient lawgivers of the Hindu tradition, states the following in his *Manava-dharma-shastra* (XII, 95):

All those traditions and all those disreputable systems of philosophy that are not based on the Veda produce no positive result after death; for they are declared to be founded on darkness. All those doctrines differing from the Veda that spring up and soon perish are ineffectual and misleading, and are of a modern date.

Stated in simpler terms, *Vaidika* specifically refers to those persons who accept the Vedas as their sacred scripture, and thus as their source of valid knowledge about spiritual matters.

Historically speaking, there are six systems of Hindu philosophy which accept the Veda as their main source of valid knowledge. These systems are known as *darshanas*. In Sanskrit, *darshana* means a "point of view" or "a method of looking". It will be interesting to see how scientific many of these ancient systems were. It is important to realize that the founders of these systems were great *rishis* in their own right, who had a deep insight into the workings of nature and hence they can be called scientists. They photographed Truth from various angles as it were, accepting the fact that Truth is many-faceted.

1. The Sage Gautama is the founder of the Nyaya philosophy which deals with logic and reasoning. In fact, all Hindu logic is derived from his work.

2. Kannada is the founder of the Vaisheshika School, which is the first ancient school in the world which dealt with atomism. He decreed that the world is composed of atoms long before the atomic theory was even thought of. He talks of *anus* (atoms) and *paramanus* (molecules). These two schools are closely connected and Vaisheshika makes use of Nyaya logic.

3. The great Sage Kapila is the founder of the Samkhya Philosophy, which postulates Reality as being dual, Prakriti and Purusha or Nature and Spirit. He postulates that the world is made up of the five great basic elements. To these were added many others making up a total of twenty-four cosmic principles. The basics of the Samkhya system were later used by both Yoga and Vedanta.

4. Patanjali, the founder of the Yoga school, was the greatest psychologist known to the world. He taught the various methods of mind control like meditation and breath

control, which is still used by all those who wish to attain
liberation. These will be discussed fully in the chapter
on Patanjali. Samkhya and Yoga are always connected.

5. Mimamsa is differentiated into two schools, one of which
   is known as Purva Mimamsa founded by the Sage
   Jaimini. It stresses the efficacy of that portion of the
   Vedas which advocates *yajnas* and other rituals.

6. Uttara Mimamsa is known as Vedanta, which accents
   the end of the Vedas, or the Upanishads, which contain
   the path of wisdom. There are three schools of Vedanta
   each having its own teacher or *guru*. Adi Shankara is the
   founder of Advaita Vedanta, which is the most famous
   of all the schools. He says that Reality is One alone and
   is called Brahman. This is known as monism and will
   be discussed fully in a separate chapter. Ramanuja is the
   founder of the Visishtadvaita School which is known as
   qualified monism. Madhvacharya is the founder of the
   school known as Dwaita or dualism.

Hinduism is not just a mass of ritual and superstition based
on ignorance as the Westerners have made us believe. It has a
purpose, which is to cater to the human being's aspiration for a
good and happy life. In fact it teaches us our *dharma,* or duties
of righteous behaviour. Apart from the four Vedas, the principles
of Hindu *dharma* are to be found in ten other books. These are
the six Vedangas, or auxiliaries to the Vedas—Shiksha, which
teaches the correct pronunciation of the Vedic hymns, Vyakarna
or grammar, Chandas or metre, Nirukta or etymology, Jyotisha
or astronomy, and Kalpa or procedure. To these ten are added
Mimamsa, the interpretation of the Vedic texts, Nyaya or logic,
Purana or mythology and the Dharma Shastras, which contain
codes of conduct for all human beings. All knowledge and

wisdom are enshrined in these fourteen books. Normally four more books are added to these which are known as Upangas or appendices to the Vedangas. They are Ayurveda or science of life and health, *Arthashastra*, the science of wealth or economics, *Dhanur Veda*, the science of weapons, missiles and warfare, and *Gaandharva Veda* or treatises on fine arts like music, art, dance, drama, sculpture and so on. The Vedangas and the Upangas are all derived from the Vedas and should be studied along with the Vedas so that their meaning becomes clearer.

Let us encourage our youth to go to the source of their religion which have been mentioned above and also to the Itihasas and Puranas in which the great *rishis,* Vyasa and Valmiki, have related the stories of the great incarnations of Hinduism. Only then will they learn to appreciate the greatness of Hinduism and also learn how they can defend themselves from the criticism of other faiths.

> Knowledge, scriptures and discourses cannot disclose the cause of life. Do thou search for the wisdom of existence in the eternal reality that unites life.
>
> *Mundaka Upanishad.*

When the earliest of mornings dawned, the Great Eternal was manifested as the path of light. Now the commands of the *devas* shall be revered. Great is the One source of energy of the cosmic forces.

Rig Veda (3.55.1)

Loka Samasthath Sukhino Bhavantu!

ॐ

Shaswataaya Namaha!

CHAPTER II

The Rishis

India is the cradle of the human race, the birthplace of human speech, the mother of history, the grandmother of legend and the great-grandmother of tradition. Our most valuable and most constructive materials in the history of man are treasured in India only.

Mark Twain

From our Mother, the Dawn, may we be born as the seven seers, the original men of wisdom. May we become the sons of Heaven, the Angirasa seers. May we break open the mountain and illumine the Reality.

Just as our ancient and supreme Fathers, O sacred Fire, seeking the Truth, following the clear insight sustaining the chant, broke through Heaven and Earth and received the radiant Spirit.

Rig Veda IV.2. 15-6

According to modern methods of calculating Time, the Vedas must have been cognised by the *rishis* during that inconceivable past—the dawn of time when the human being was only another animal, hunting for food and digging for roots and fruits. It is very doubtful if he had any method of communicating with others except through guttural sounds and signs. Thus, the Vedas were cognised at a time when the world was still in its infancy, before the creation of language as we know it. Primitive man as conceived by the anthropologists of modern times was surely the last person capable of receiving such types of revelations. Vedic hymns existed well before the time-space calculations of modern times and certainly well before the existence of a well-formulated language. Those were the days when man existed without proper food, clothing or housing and certainly not much of vocabulary. He had no names for the sun, moon or any of the natural phenomena even though he could see them. He was sitting, eating, talking, etc. but had no names for any of these functions. At such a time which to us now seems inconceivable, the divine knowledge of the Vedas was revealed to a set of super-human beings with high receptivity, extraordinary memory and an understanding that was way beyond the intellect of even the most intelligent of modern human beings. Psychologists say that even a most intelligent human being like Einstein used only ten per cent of his brain capacity, what to say of the rest of us. But from this we can guess that these beings were using hundred per cent of their brain power. Naturally, one would suppose that their first duty would be to assign names to all the natural phenomena which were so obvious to the five senses. Hence, the Samhitas or the first portion of the Vedas are filled with names of the natural creations which are all supreme examples of the glory of the divine so they were also divinised and called *devas* or the shining ones. These great souls are called *rishis* in India. They are truly travellers in time who were born centuries ago yet have come to us to this very day, inviting us to go with

them on their Time travels. Even now they keep a watch on us
and look with compassion at us who are still playing with the
toys of our ignorance.

We can imagine that it was only with the revelation of the
Vedas that the concept of communication was manifested in
the world by which the human being could not only converse
with his fellow beings but also forge a link with posterity.
Thousands of years have passed since this divine knowledge was
first revealed to a small group of seers, traditionally named as
Agni, Vayu, Aditya and Angiras. Then came another group of
rishis or seers with stupendous memory who passed on this
knowledge to successive generations. If we but pause a moment
to look at this amazing revelation, we will no doubt be struck
with awe as to the nature of these souls who were the seers of
the Vedas. It was indeed miraculous that in that misty morn of
the universe there existed such beings that appeared to have
attained the fulfilment of all human life which has not been
attained by the majority of humankind even in this age. This
has led to the supposition that the *rishis* had an extra-terrestrial
origin. The reason for choosing the subcontinent of India to
manifest themselves might be because they recognised the
essential spiritual potential of this country. Of course, in India
these great beings seem to have taken birth again and again in
every age to upkeep this *dharma*—The Sanatana Dharma—
which they cognised at the beginning of the world!

Who exactly were these *rishis?* The Hindu tradition
maintains that they were a class of highly evolved souls. India
owes everything to these *rishis,* for they are the ones who gave
us our heritage, our culture and our way of life, which is known
as the Sanatana Dharma—the ancient law of Righteousness.
The word *rishi* is derived from an obscure Sanskrit root "to see",

for they were the seers or the hearers of the Vedic hymns which come from the mouth of Brahma. The word also designates a singer of sacred hymns, an inspired poet or sage, any person who can invoke the deities in rhythmical speech or song of a sacred character. It might also have been derived from the Dravidian word *aric,* meaning "wise man, sage, astrologer, seer".

In Astronomy, the Seven Rishis form the constellation of the Great Bear. In Hindu astronomy, the stars of the Big Dipper are named after the Saptarishis or the seven sages. Metaphorically, they stand for the seven senses or the seven vital airs of the body.

This gives more support to the theory that they might have been extra-terrestrial beings who came down to help mankind. Considering the times in which they cognised the hymns, this is a very plausible theory. That is why perhaps we know very little of their lives or their parents or lineage. We know them only through their colossal revelations called the Vedas.

Hinduism maintains that the *rishis* were superior to the gods. They existed before the gods since they came directly from the mind of Brahma, the Creator, in the trinity. The gods or *devas* were creations of their minds.

These spiritual giants lived in the Himalayas and strode across the Indo-Gangetic plains long before the dawn of historic time. They were the sublime expression of the perfect human being. They were the crown and cream of Nature's evolutionary cycle. Modern humans are only recently beginning to envisage the possibility of the existence of such superior specimens of humanity. These men were really supra-human, multi-sensory beings who had the gift of inner vision and were able to see the past, present and future as one huge canvas unrolling in front of them. They could go to the realms of the gods and demons, the demigods and the titans of mythological lore, and describe the events that went on at that time and even describe something which would take place at a future time.

The chronological age of the *rishis* is impossible to gauge. Time is divided into four *yugas* or eons in Hinduism, which are cyclical and keep repeating endlessly. These *yugas* are known as Satya Yuga, Treta Yuga, Dwapara Yuga and Kali Yuga. We are now living in the Kali Yuga. The lives of the *rishis* seem to have spanned across the first three *yugas* or eons. Thousands of years passed before the Satya Yuga gave place to the Treta Yuga and to Dwapara. However, to the *rishis*, Time was an ever continuous river which had no meaning so it mattered not to them that they lived through the Satya Yuga and entered the other *yugas* with ease effortlessly as if floating on the cloud of Time.

They were truly ancient beings who had the power to choose the hour of their arrival and departure from this world. The compassion and love they bore to this land, the land of their choice or origin is inexhaustible. They have chosen to incarnate themselves even in this Kali Yuga—the age of decadence in order to upkeep the eternal *Dharma*. It is said that some of them, like Markandeya, continue to live in the eternal snows of the Himalayas, unseen by any human eye. It is only due to the power of their *tapasya* (austerity) that the world continues to retain its integrity.

Western historians have declared that the "authors" of the Vedas were an Aryan tribe that came across the Himalayas from the plateau of Asia Minor. This is known as the "Aryan Invasion" and our own historians have blindly accepted this concept and written it down in our history books and this is what is taught to Indian children today. How they came to form such a view is difficult to understand. The obvious place to get information about the *rishis* and the Vedic way of life is from the Vedas themselves. Nobody bothered to delve into this obvious source of information, perhaps because they were incapable of understanding them. But when we look into the Vedas, we see that nowhere is there any mention of such an invasion or exodus from Asia Minor across the mountains to the subcontinent of India. It is not possible that the Vedas would have missed out mentioning such a stupendous venture. Therefore, we can safely conclude that the Aryan invasion was a myth created by people with vested interests who were anxious to prove that this amazing knowledge was an implant from outside. The truth is that the holy land of India has produced countless such amazing souls who are steeped in the divine essence and who can actually be called walking gods. They appeared in the remote past and continue to come even up to the present age.

When we go deeper into the Vedas, we will realise that the first portion called the Samhitas or the hymns were ecstatic tributes to the various *devas*. These were revelations as the *rishis* themselves declared and had no human origin. That portion was obviously cognised when these great beings were living in the holy mountain of the Himalayas. They lived in caves and derived their food from the ether and communed with the Divine and His infinite lieutenants known as *devas*. At that time it is possible that they did not have much to do with any other human beings though it is obvious that they did communicate with each other. Perhaps this type of life existed for the whole of the Satya Yuga, which is the first of the four eons of Hinduism in which everything existed in Truth alone. Perhaps at the end of this *yuga* they had gleaned as much as possible from the etheric sphere or perhaps as much as they could imbibe. They knew that the time was ripe to pass on this transcendental knowledge to the rest of humanity.

Therefore, they descended from the heights of the Himalayas and stepped into the great plain of north India which was fed by the great river known as Saraswati. Again the Western historians have proclaimed that the Saraswati was a mythical river. Now why the *rishis* should have concocted such a fable of a mythical river is a mystery to anyone who reads the Vedas with no prejudice. The Vedas clearly state all the geographical details of this river from its source to its end. Thankfully, modern satellite photos have verified that every word stated in the Vedas about the river Saraswati is true and that the river disappeared at some time in the hoary past due to seismic movements of the earth's plates.

Now to come to the *rishis,* they came down to the plain and the next two portions of the Vedas were obviously authored and not cognised by them as were the Samhitas. In these two portions they did their best to inculcate the Vedic form of life, lived according to the high doctrines of the cosmic *dharma* or law of righteousness. Thus, all along the river they established their modest *ashramas* or abodes. They married and had progeny to whom were taught the esoteric secrets of the Samhita portion. Many hamlets and soon towns and cities grew up along the banks in which this type of communal living was taught.

The next eon or *yuga* is known as Treta in which some of the *rishis* left their *ashramas* and took up residence in the palaces of the kings since they knew that it was of utmost importance that the ones in power should follow the laws of *dharma* so that the land could flourish according to the ethical rules which they themselves had laid down. Moreover, it was only the kings who had the power to conduct great *yajnas* like the Somaveda, Ashwamedha, Rajasuya, etc., which was essential to the well-being of the land. To the kings they taught all the esoteric secrets

of government, weaponry and art of ruling. Some of them were
even given the great nuclear weapon known as the "Brahmastra".
But this was an esoteric secret which was given only to those
who were morally capable of using it at the right time for the
good of the world and not for personal gratification. To the
farmers they gave the knowledge of agriculture while many
secrets of medicinal plants were imparted to the physicians. Lord
Rama was one of the great kings of the Treta Yuga. The *guru* of
his dynasty—the solar race—was the famous *rishi* Vasishta. To
Rama he not only imparted the esoteric secrets of statecraft but
also the great message of the Upanishads known as the "Yoga
Vasishta" by mastering which Rama became a truly evolved soul.
Proof of the existence of Rama is to be found in the *Ramayana*
itself. This will be dealt with later.

This *yuga* gave way to the next called Dwapara in which the
great *avatara* of Krishna took place. Here again we meet the
rishis and realise how much they must have affected and
influenced life both in the court and outside, in the world. All
the vast scientific knowledge they had amassed was passed on to
the people of the land and that is why you find that India had
such a glorious civilization while Europeans were still living like
barbarians. This must have come as a shock to the first Westerners
who came to India! So they took great pains to suppress this fact
from the whole world and declared that India had no historical
records and whatever was said in the Vedas and Puranas was
pure invention and had no basis in fact. In one fell swoop all
our glorious culture was put under the title of myth and fable!
Unfortunately, Indian historians aped all this nonsense and even
today Indian children are taught in schools to despise their
religion and scorn their gods on which our whole culture is based.
The fact is that the early western historians had vested interests

and knew that the only way to impose their religion on the Indians was to belittle their culture and cast scorn on their gods. Maybe they did this through their ignorance of the mystical and esoteric details of our scriptures. However that might be, the time has come to expose such falsehood and allow the whole world to realise their inheritance, for the *rishis* did not intend the great secrets of the Vedas to be confined to India alone but wanted everything to be shared by the whole world.

As mentioned before, the concept of Time in Hinduism is cyclical. One creation is followed by a dissolution. The Saptarishis are the seven sages who are sent by Brahma—the Creator in the Hindu trinity—in every age or *manvantara* in order to uncover the wisdom of the Vedas from the etheric spheres. The *rishis* about whom we know, belonged to the seventh *manvantara* or age, which is the present one in which the patriarch is known as Vaivasvata Manu. The work of the *rishis* is to decode and make available to the ordinary, five-sensory mortal, the great knowledge of creation which they could hear through their inner ears. The *riks* and the *samans* were the sounds which came to them through the etheric sphere and they memorised them perfectly in their minds.

Many different lists of the names of the seven sages are given. Probably this differs from age to age. The *rishis* of the first *manvantara* are supposed to be Marichi, Atri, Angiras, Pulaha, Kratu, Pulastya and Vasishta. There are other lists in the other Manvantaras or eons. But most lists include Vasishta, Atri, Gautama, Bharadwaja, Viswamitra, Jamadagni, Kashyapa and Agastya. These Saptarishis are of course all Brahmarishis.

A Brahmarishi is one who is constantly in communion with the Brahman, that is to say, he is always in a state of cosmic consciousness in which he is immediately in touch with everything in the cosmos. They can be called the highest class of *rishis*. They had attained the divine knowledge called *brahmajnana* or unity with the Brahman. The source of a *Brahmarishi's* power is the Brahman, or Supreme Godhead. This knowledge of the Supreme is attained after years of *tapasya*, meditation, study and selfless service to the Supreme, resulting in total self-purification. It is a combination of physical, mental and spiritual exertion. In the Vedas, a *rishi* is strictly defined as one to whom the Vedic hymns were originally revealed. They are the ones who have *mantra-drashta* or the ability to see the *mantras*. Other sages can never be called *rishis, maharshis* or *Brahmarishis,* whatever be their merits. Since the order was created divinely by Lord Brahma, it is impossible for Hindu priests and scholars, or contemporary saints to anoint *rishis, maharshis* or *Brahmarishis,* although many persons use such epithets for themselves or for their *gurus.*

Actually the Vedic term for the Saptarishis was *Braahmanas* since they were the ones who were created by Brahma and knew the Brahman. They came to be known as *Brahmarishis* later, because during the post Vedic period the term *Braahmana* came to be used for a person who was born in the Brahmin caste, which meant that they were born in the *gotra* or clan of one of these *Brahmarishis.* Thus, we find another list of Saptarishis who are also *Gotra-pravartakas,* i.e. founders of the Brahamanical clans. This second list appeared at a later period in history but they are still very ancient. It is an amazing thing that these families have existed to the present age. Hence, the present-day Brahmins or *Braahmanas* claim to have an unbroken lineage coming down from the Vedic *rishis* of more than ten thousand years ago. To this very day all Brahmins claim to have been born in the *gotra* of one of these incredibly ancient sages—like Vasishta, or

Vishvamitra or Bhrighu or Angiras, etc. Even today marriages between couples of the same *gotra* are forbidden and the children of a Brahmin couple have to take the *gotra* of their father in order to ensure the purity of the line. This is another unique feature of Hindu culture. No other culture can claim to have people who can trace their lineage to such antiquity.

Let us take a peep into the life of these great beings. The *Saptarishis* or seven sages certainly must have had this experience of living in the Brahman. Hence, they were all known as Brahmarishis. Nature itself was only a backdrop for their mind. Everything that happens, happens within the mind. There are times known as *sandhyas* which are conducive for meditation. These *sandhyas* are points of time when the sun's rays have the greatest power to evoke thoughts of the Supreme in the minds of mortals. They occur thrice during the day—in the early morning when night meets day, at 12 noon when the sun is at its zenith, and in the evening when day meets night. At these points of time, the human mind is completely attuned to nature. But of course it is a fact that the minds of the *Brahmarishis* who were always attuned to nature, could hardly be compared with the modern human mind since they could perceive things which were not visible or apparent to us who are five-sensory human beings. Even so they chose these times to meditate on that Brahman. During the early hours of the morning and when the sun was at its zenith and again when it set in the western sky, the *rishis* would sit for meditation. Early morning at 3 a.m. was the time known as *Brahma-muhurtam*. This was the time that they could most clearly cognise the divine hymns. They felt the hymns as vibrations in their hearts.

Even at other times, when they walked around they were in the superconscious state known as *samadhi*. They did not have

to work for their living since they needed nothing and were
dependent on nothing. They gleaned their sustenance from the
ether. They looked at everything but saw only the Brahman.
Nothing existed except the Brahman. THAT alone pervaded
everything. They were one with THAT and therefore they did
not exist as separate personalities. Only THAT-ONE existed.
There was no two. That Supreme Truth which manifests itself
all the time in everything is an eternal, infinite and absolute
self-existence, self-awareness and self-delight—*sat-chid-ananda*.
It supports and pervades all things. It is present in the human
being as the *atman*. It is not only the Absolute but also the
omnipresent reality in which all that is relative exists as ITS
forms and movements. (See chapter on Brahman).

What exactly is science? Science is something that tries to
discover the different laws of nature. Our ancient *rishis* who
were the custodians of our culture were the greatest scientists
ever known to man. They were a special type of scientists. They
can be called spiritual scientists. They realised that the foundation
of the universe as well as of the human being is spiritual not
material. All the gross objects, which we see in the world, actually
have their source in the subtle and not vice versa as science will
have us believe. The *rishis* also looked at the world and like
every scientist wanted to find out the basic constituent of
everything but unlike the Western scientist they realised that
they would never find the meaning of anything in the world if
they did not know the laws governing the functioning of their
minds. So, psychology which is such a baby science in the West
was the first one that the *rishis* explored. They realised that the
world existed because of the human mind and unless they learnt
to control the mind, they would never be able to find the
meaning of anything in the universe, far less control it.

Thus, the *rishis* were spiritual scientists who opened our eyes to a world of mystery and beauty and not one of arid facts. If we could only behave in the way that they have taught us, we would certainly have made a heaven on earth. However, the *rishis* were aware of human limitations and sought methods to surmount them. The intellect is the most powerful and versatile instrument known to us. Scientists make use of it to price open the mysteries of the universe. It has led us to split the atom and reach the moon but when it comes to discovering the truth of our innermost self, the intellect is confounded. It is capable of analysing any object. It is a highly efficient instrument for objective study but the *rishis* realised that it is sadly inadequate when it comes to subjective analysis. When the Self itself becomes the object of study, the intellect is unable to surmount its inherent weakness and analyse itself. The Self is the torch which lights up the intellect so how can it see itself? In other fields of investigation, the investigator is different from the object of investigation but here the investigator is being investigated by himself! Sugar can never know the taste of tea. It can only dissolve in it and become one with it. The *rishis* devised a means by which the intellect could become so subtle that it could be dissolved. They found that in the state of deep meditation the intellect becomes so subtle that it dissolves like sugar into the object of investigation which is the Self itself. Thus, the intellect's search for the Self ends in a glorious experience of the Divine rather than a comprehension of it.

All forms in the physical world are created by the Supreme Consciousness through the shaping of light and the *rishis* who lived immersed in the pure consciousness of the Brahman were quite capable of conjuring up any form they chose through the medium of light. This was a natural thing for them. But even though they could materialise anything they wished, they did not seek to carve in stone or wood or make effigies or temples or in any way try to immortalise themselves in this world even though they were perfectly competent to do so if they wished. These beings had submerged themselves in the ocean of existence, consciousness and bliss and they had no trace of ego even though they existed in the human body. They can be known only through their words in the Vedas. They have left nothing else. They left no chronicle of their achievements, or images that might have survived the course of time. They knew that this world was only as real as the morning mist and would melt with the rising of the sun. The sun of their consciousness was at its zenith and they did not desire the trifles of the world. They have taught us the truth that we will not gain universality unless we are prepared to lose our individuality.

There was nothing that they didn't know about Nature. She did not hide any of her abstruse wisdom from them. The *rishis* had extraordinary powers or *siddhis*. They could control the elements, travel with ease in the astral worlds, cover vast distances rapidly through the sky without any aircraft, catch sound and light waves in their minds and discern what was happening miles away as if on a TV screen. Their look could penetrate rocks and drill holes in metals and they could have anything they wanted just by formulating a wish in their minds. No other civilization except the present one has reached such heights of knowledge as they had achieved but unlike this culture that craves for material wealth, they deemed that all knowledge of the external world was inferior knowledge and the highest knowledge was that of the true Self or Brahman. The Vedas show that their knowledge of science in many fields, like mathematics, geometry, astrology, astronomy and physics, was immense. Without the use of modern instrumentation, they were able to discover more things about this universe than what was discovered up to the 19th century by western scientists. The Vedas show that they knew that the earth went round the sun and that we are living in an expanding universe and that matter is only energy in motion. They calculated the distance of stars and planets and could foretell the coming of the different comets. They even wrote predictions about the horoscopes of people who would come after them. They could conjure up cities and palaces and wondrous meals and aerial vehicles even though they did not choose to live in any of them.

However, their main task was to impart the knowledge of Reality to others but since IT can only be known by direct experience, they tried many types of methods called *yogas* in order to share this truth with the masses. Having understood the nature of that Brahman, they felt a compulsion to share their experience and exhort people to gain this direct experience for themselves. The experience of Brahman reveals the unity of life which underlies all living things. From this is born a tremendous love for all creatures and a deep desire to see human beings free themselves from the illusions and limitations of the lower worlds in which they are involved. Love always wants to share what it gets and thus the *rishis* did everything in their power to unfold this Reality to the rest of human kind. Thus the Vedas and Upanishads are full of the experiences and exhortations of those who have experienced this Ultimate Reality and felt a deep desire to share it with others.

These *rishis* had no desires. They were quite happy with the forms which existed in the world, which had been fashioned by that Supreme Consciousness. They were content with whatever nature provided, they did not yearn to possess more and more for the simple reason that they possessed the wish-fulfilling cow of plenty in their own minds which was capable of granting every desire they had. Having found the secret of all existence, they continued to live only with the one desire, *Lokasamgraham*— "the good of the world." They were the embodiments of compassion.

They chose to live their life in little hermitages or *ashramas* situated in the middle of jungles, where wild animals roamed unafraid. Every day was a new day. They never stored or hoarded for the next day. The only thing they tended very carefully was fire or *agni*. Into that fire they poured their oblations to the gods. They kept a few cows which supplied the butter and ghee necessary for these oblations. They cultivated the land only to the extent that they needed. They were the very embodiments of simplicity and contentment. They desired nothing from the world, for they had found the source of all happiness within themselves. Therefore, they could not be tempted by the baubles of a world which they knew to be ephemeral.

They needed no commandments to keep them to the right path, for they were the very embodiments of *dharma* or the cosmic order. They are the ones who have given to humanity the idea of what *dharma* or cosmic law means, through the example of their own lives. They did not wish to conquer or control, even though they had the power to control the whole world if necessary. They were conscious of their inner power and so they were unafraid of anyone or anything. Actually all of us possess this inner power but we do not know it and thus we think we have to depend on external powers to protect us. We are riddled with fears and we try to protect ourselves by maintaining police forces and accumulating weapons and armies.

Their amazing experience could not be communicated in ordinary language so they were taught to their disciples in the form of questions and answers and this is what is known as the Upanishads, which come at the end of every Veda. The Upanishads use terse and concise language to point out Reality.

However, unlike the world of science which is open only to a few intellectuals, the magic world of the *rishis* has benefited even the uneducated and the children. The *rishis* opened our eyes to a world of mystery and beauty and not one of arid facts. They have shown us that if heaven exists, it has to be made on this very earth.

> In the beginning was the golden womb (Hiranyagarbha),
> The seed of elemental existence,
> The only Lord of all that was born,
> He upheld the heaven and earth together,
> To what God other than Him, should we dedicate our life?
>
> *Atharva Veda 4.2.7*

> I am "rta", the Truth. I was born in the beginning of creation before the birth of the gods. The rishis call me "amrita".
>
> *Sama Veda 594*

> I am "Satya", the Truth. I manifest myself in the great epic. I appear as the Truth through the "jataveda" fire. None is above me. I am the Ultimate.
>
> *Atharva Veda 11.5*

Loka Samasthath Sukhino Bhavantu!

ॐ

Vishvakarmaaya Namaha!

CHAPTER III

The Vedas

In the great teaching of the Vedas, there is no touch of
sectarianism. It is of all ages, climes and nationalities, and is
the royal road for the attainment of the Great Knowledge.

Thoreau

India was the motherland of our race and Sanskrit the mother
of Europe's languages. India was the mother of our philosophy
and much of our mathematics, of the ideals embodied in
Christianity, of self government and democracy. In many ways
Mother India is the mother of us all.

Will Durant (American Historian 1885–1981)

Sanskrit is the mother of all the European languages. It is the
most suitable language for computer software.

Reported by the Forbes Magazine—July 1987

The two primary factors that distinguish the individual
uniqueness of the great world religious traditions are (a) the
scriptural authority upon which the tradition is based, and (b)
the fundamental religious tenet(s) that it espouses. If we ask the

question what is a Jew for example, the answer is someone who accepts the Torah as his scriptural guide and believes in the monotheistic concept of God espoused in these scriptures. Who is a Christian? A person who accepts the Gospels as his scriptural guide and believes that Jesus is the only son of God who incarnated himself in order to save humankind from its sins. Who is a Muslim? Someone who accepts the Quran as his scriptural guide, and believes that there is no God but Allah and that Mohammed is his only prophet. In general, what determines whether a person is a follower of any particular religion is whether or not he accepts, and attempts to live by, the scriptural authority of that religion. This is no less true of Hinduism than it is of any other religion on earth. Thus, the question of what is a Hindu is very easily answered. By definition, a Hindu is an individual who accepts the Vedas as the authoritative guide to his religion, and who strives to live in accordance with *Dharma*, God's divine laws as revealed in the Vedas and explained in easy language in the Puranas. In keeping with this standard definition, the great exponents of the six traditional schools of Hindu philosophy (*Shad-darshanas*) insisted on the acceptance of the scriptural authority (*shabda-pramana*) of the Vedas as the primary criterion for distinguishing a Hindu from a non-Hindu, as well as distinguishing Hindu philosophical positions from non-Hindu ones. It has been the historically accepted standard that if you accept the Vedas (meaning the complete *shruti* and *smriti* canon of the Vedic scriptures, such as the four Vedas, Upanishads, *Mahabharata, Ramayana, Bhagavad-Gita* and Puranas, etc.) as your scriptural authority, and live your life in accordance with the dharmic principles as embedded in these scriptures, you are a Hindu. Thus, any Indian who rejects the authority of the Veda is obviously not a Hindu—regardless of their birth.

On the other hand, an American, Canadian, Russian, Brazilian, Indonesian or Indian who accepts the authority of the Veda obviously is a Hindu. They are Hindus, not by race, but by commitment.

The Vedas are the sacred heritage not only of India but of all humanity. Till recently, translations and interpretations of these sacred books have been made by Western historians and scholars who had little or no concept of such lofty ideals and ideas. Our own Indian historians blindly copied what was said by the Westerners and therefore our great heritage has been denied not only to the world but also to the Indians who are the true inheritors of this divine knowledge.

The way in which the Vedas came down to us is unique. They were first heard by some great *rishis* who imparted it orally to their disciples. It was handed down in this manner through the ages. Much later, the knowledge was scribed using letters. This is the way in which this ancient teaching has come down to us in the present time.

Before going into the Vedas, let us know a bit more of the great soul who has scribed the Vedas for us. He is known as Veda Vyasa. He is Hinduism's first *guru*. He was born on the Purnima (full moon) day of the month of Ashad (June/July). As we have seen from the chapter on the Vedas, Vyasa was the one who simplified and compiled the Vedas and divided them into four. This is why he is known as Veda Vyasa. He also composed the seventeen Puranas and wrote the great epic, the *Mahabharata*. Lord Ganesha is supposed to have written down this epic as he dictated the words. Later on, he wrote many other works, most famous of which are the Brahma Sutras. After composing all these Puranas, he still did not get peace. When he told this to the Sage Narada, the latter replied, "Though you have written

यदा यदा हि धर्मस्य ग्लानिर्भवति भारत ।
अभ्युत्थानमधर्मस्य तदाऽऽत्मानं सृजाम्यहम् ॥

Veda Vyasa

extensively on *dharma, artha* and *kama*, you have not dealt with *moksha* or liberation of the self. This is not possible without knowing the Lord in his manifest form. Today he manifests as Krishna. Therefore, you should compose a sacred text narrating Krishna's glory which will inspire devotion in the hearts of all devotees. This is the only work left for you to do. Only then will you attain peace."

It is said that Vyasa then composed the eighteenth Mahapurana known as the *Sreemad Bhagavatha Purana,* which is the Veda of the Vaishnavites. Only then did he experience peace of mind. He has given exact and accurate measurements for the beginning of the Kali Yuga and from this we can infer that the *Sreemad Bhagavatha* was composed prior to 3082 BCE. Hence, the dates given by Western scholars for this work is completely wrong.

In terms of time, the Vedas are known as *anadi* or without beginning. They have existed from the dawn of time as we know it. We also say that they are *apaurusheya* or not the work of man! The modern mind hemmed with notions of time and space can hardly accept such statements. So the Western scholars say that the *rishis* or sages wrote these hymns. However, the *rishis* would be the first to deny this statement. The *rishis* called themselves *mantra drishtas* or the seers of the *mantras,* which meant that the *rishis* did not create or compose them. When we say that Newton discovered the law of gravity, it does not mean that he actually created it but that he brought an existing fact to the notice of the world. Likewise, the *rishis* cognised the *mantras* already in existence in etheric space and made them known to us. These *mantras,* like the laws of nature, have always existed. The names of the *rishis* are associated with them since they were the ones who brought the already existing *mantra*s to our conscious knowledge. We always bow to their memory when repeating the *mantras*.

All other religions have been able to fix a date for their sacred books. The teachings of the Buddha can be dated to 2,500 BC when the Buddha lived. There is no argument about the date of the New Testament which was 2000 years ago. Everyone agrees that the *Koran* was composed 1200 years ago. But so far no one has been able to fix the age of the Vedas.

It is a fundamental belief of the Sanatana Dharma that the Vedas are *sanatana* (eternal) and *apaurusheya* (not composed by any human being). Most westerners and Western educated Indians cannot accept the fact that the Vedas are without beginning. Much time and money have been spent on research on this subject and people have fixed the time at 6000 BC since certain planetary positions have been mentioned in the Vedas which took place at that time.

It would be easy to fix dates by planetary positions for cultures which have existed only for a few centuries but for cultures that have existed for millennia this will not be possible, for the same type of planetary position could have existed many times within the course of millennia. The Vedas reckon time as existing before the time of our current universe so how can we fix their age by our current time limits? The same disposition of stars could have taken place not just once but many times in the past. Therefore, such calculations cannot be used to calculate the age of the Vedas which were given to us by the *rishis* who could see beyond the confines of Time and Space.

Another method used in confirming the age of the Vedas is through the language used. All the scripts which are used in India today owe their origin to the Braahmi script. Of course in the case of edicts engraved by kings on metal and stone, this would be a great help to confirm their age but as far as the Vedas are concerned, they were never at any time engraved on metal or stone so how could their age be determined by the script?

Still another method of determining age is by the style of talking. The Vedas are not easily understandable as other languages which are in daily use. Vedic language is not a spoken language even though the Vedas are chanted every day in all parts of India. Even spoken languages have changed tremendously. The original Anglo-Saxon language which is less than 1000 years old cannot be easily understood by the modern Englishman. So this method cannot be used with the Vedas since they are still being chanted as they were from the dawn of time. The *rishis* took great pains to see that the sounds would not suffer any mutations as words in everyday use. The reason why the Vedic sounds have been maintained in their pristine purity is because only by the correct intonation of the *mantras* would the desired effect be produced.

Modern Western researchers in their thirst for dating everything declare the *Rig Veda* to be the oldest, whereas our *Shastras* say that they are all without beginning. All four were available to the world from the dawn of creation. The *Rig Veda* itself contains references to *Yajur* and *Sama Vedas*. The Purusha Sukta which comes in the ninetieth hymn of the tenth *mandala* of the *Rig Veda*, refers to the other Vedas. So how can some be labelled as earlier and some later.

At the beginning of every cosmic cycle, the Paramatma (the Absolute) breathes the divine words into the mind of Brahma. Later, different *rishis* through divine grace heard these divine words known as *shruti*. The vast amount of knowledge in the Vedas was compiled into the four books known as *Rig Veda*,

Yajur Veda, Sama Veda and *Atharva Veda* by the great sage Vyasa. Because of the invaluable work he did, he has been called Veda Vyasa. The four Vedas form the very core of the Hindu religion. They are the supreme authority and known as *Pramaana*. They contain the divine, infallible knowledge revealed to the *rishis* who were the crown and glory of the human race and thus were fit to receive and impart to humanity the words of the Supreme. The purpose of this revelation was to enlighten and spread this knowledge so that human beings might live happily in this world and become aware of their innate divinity. Vedic literature provides us with more original and ancient teachings than what we have from the rest of the world put together. At the end of every Brahma's cosmic period, the Vedic knowledge in its gross form disappears only to reappear in Brahma's next cycle of creation. In reality it is eternal and thus according to the Hindu tradition, the question of dating hardly arises. Hence, all the dates and periods attributed by Western scholars are an attempt to ridicule the sacred and eternal heritage of India. Even the meanings given by Western scholars are warped. Without the guidance of a qualified *guru,* the Vedas cannot be learnt or their meanings understood!

If the *rishis* were not the authors of the Vedas, can we then conclude that God created them? This is also not true because in Hinduism, we do not believe that God created the world one fine day. Creation is supposed to be cyclical and not linear as in western theology. One creation or *shrishti* is followed by a *laya* or dissolution, after which another creation or *shrishti* takes place. This is an endless process. The one eternal and non-changing Being is known as Brahman or the impersonal God who has existed always. IT is the time continuum from which the universe of matter appears and disappears from time to time. Getting back to the Vedas, let us take the question as to whether the Brahman created them? If this were true, it would mean that they were created one fine day and thus cannot be termed *anadi* or without beginning. The Veda itself clears this confusion and says that they are the very breath of the Paramatma (Brahman) or the Supreme Self. Our breath is an essential part of us and thus the Vedas are an essential part of the Brahman and has existed from all time since the Brahman has existed from all time. So they have co-existed with IT and thus they are *anadi*.

Modern science defines sound as vibration. Different objects have vibrations of different frequencies and thus appear different to the human eye. Due to their *tapas* or austerity, the *rishis* became aware of the cosmic breath in the form of vibrations, which resulted in the creation of the world. Just as electromagnetic waves are converted into sonic waves, which can be captured and heard by us, by using a radio or TV, the cosmic vibrations became audible to the *rishis* who used only their internal apparatus. These were decoded by them and were given to all humanity in the form of the Vedic *mantras*.

Another important fact is that the Vedas are known as *shruti*, or that which is heard. The Vedic sounds were heard by the *rishis* who were properly attuned to receive them through their *tapasya*. The Vedas were passed from generation to generation in the ancient method of learning by listening, in the master-disciple tradition. Why was the Veda not written down? The first reason is that writing was unknown at the time when the Vedas were coded and arranged by Veda Vyasa. Another equally and perhaps more important reason is that some sounds do not lend themselves to be accurately reproduced phonetically. The science of phonetics, which is such a recent one in the West, was highly advanced in Vedic times. There are many sounds in the Veda which fall in between two syllables. These can only be transmitted orally. Moreover, the Vedic *mantras* have to be recited in a certain specified rhythm to produce the correct vibrations. Some sounds have to be in a high chromatic scale, some in the medium and others on a low scale. However much we try to aid the pronunciation by remarks in asterisks, errors, etc., it would still lead to improper accent, intonation and pronunciation. This would lead to a lessening of the intended effect or even produce an opposite effect. It is easy to imagine the consequence on us of a sound produced in a high or low pitch and of another in the same pattern. Our emotional response and even the cosmic forces which regulate the orderliness of nature would change with the differences in intonation.

To get a desired station on the TV or radio, perfect tuning is necessary. So it is with the Vedic *mantras*. The *swara* or pitch and amplitude of sound should be perfect. Just as a small change in wavelength brings us to a different TV station, so also any change in the chanting of the Vedic *mantra* produces a different effect. It is because of this that it has been stipulated that the Vedas should only be learnt by ear from a competent *guru*.

Most of the research done on the Vedas has been by the westerners who have taken the trouble to unearth much of our ancient wisdom and have been struck by their greatness. In fact, we owe a lot to these westerners who have actually taken the trouble to find out some of our ancient scripts and preserve them. However, they did not realise that the essential purpose of the Vedas was to ensure the well-being of the whole universe, not just of human beings, by spreading the sound of the Vedic *mantras* and encouraging the performance of the Vedic rites. The Veda, which is a living force intended for the betterment of the universe, has been decoded and incarcerated into voluminous tomes to lie idle on library shelves!

The Vedas taught worship of the gods of nature, such as the sun, sky, wind, and fire but they emphasized the fact that behind the façade of these many gods, there is but one Supreme God. In fact, the concept of one universal God was originally expressed in the *Rig Veda* itself:

Ekam sat vipra bahudha vadanti.
(Only One exists; sages call it by various names.)

The hymns of the Vedas invoke the Supreme Being who is the sole master of creation. This Supreme Reality is not merely an abstract philosophical concept, but a dynamic reality which we have to invoke every minute for our personal fulfilment. Vedic theism is a vibrant concept. Even though we might not know the Supreme, even though we might deny Him, the fact is that He is with us every moment. He is intimately connected with us at every moment. We might forget Him, we might ignore Him but He will not neglect us. That Supreme, though unmanifest, is manifested through His divine manifestations. He is the effulgence of the sun; He is the mighty force behind nature; He is the light of all lights, terror of all terrors, and sweetness of everything that is sweet, and the actor behind every activity. The Vedas try to contact Him through His creation. In Vedic poetry this tiny self and the Supreme Self are described as two birds that are mutual friends and companions and who live on the same branch of a tree. The *jivatma* or the embodied soul tastes the fruits of the tree (of life). When they are sweet, the *jivatma* rejoices, when they are sour or bitter, it feels despondent and sad. The Paramatma or Supreme Lord (the other bird on the same tree) watches the joys and sorrows of its companion with compassion but will not interfere until it is replete with all the sense pleasures offered by the world. Once replete it loses its taste for sensual pleasures and turns towards the other bird, which has been its constant companion and realises that in Him lies joy without sorrow and love without any expectation of return.

The hymns of the Vedas are grouped into worship offered to the different *devas* like Agni, Indra, Varuna, Soma, Rudra, etc. These *devas* represent God's various powers and attributes. The Vedas have definitely stated that these *devas* are only aspects of the ONE Supreme. The importance given to these *devas* can be understood only when one sees the same Supreme Divinity behind the spleandour of all His manifestations in Nature.

The Vedic hymns can be grouped into six sections—hymns on creation, devotional hymns, hymns on revelation, hymns for certain types of action, hymns on the spleandour of the Lord, and hymns on the positive sciences.

Knowing the Vedas to be of supreme importance and a perfect treasure-house of inexhaustible and infallible wisdom, the *rishis* took infinite pains to ensure that the purity and perfection of the sound and vibrations was preserved for posterity. In order to do this, they created a caste called the Brahmins (knowers of the Brahman), whose only duty was to memorise and pass on this knowledge to the future generations. The modern-day Brahmins can actually trace their lineage to the *gotra rishi* or the *rishi* to whose line they belonged. They were the custodians of this supreme wisdom and the kings had the responsibility of seeing to their welfare. This had both a good and bad side as everything. It certainly ensured the purity of the knowledge and even today the Vedas are recited exactly as they were recited ten thousand years ago, which is a remarkable phenomenon and would never have taken place had the Brahmin caste not been created. Even the Jews have kept aside the rabbis only for the purpose of learning their scriptures. In Israel, the rabbis and those who take to a religious life are exempt from military duty and other governmental duties like were the ancient Brahmins. However, the creation of a special caste had the disadvantage that the Veda was not easily available to the common people.

Just as some type of life-giving serums are preserved with greatest care in laboratories so the *rishis* took infinite pains to see that the Veda *mantras,* which are for universal benefit, were preserved without resort to writing. The Vedanga called *siksha* is the place where guidance for perfect pronunciation is given. The *rishis* were masters of the science of phonetics and modern researchers are quite incompetent to judge them.

We have discussed how the Vedas are *anadi* or without a beginning. Now we will take up their claim that they are endless. How can such a claim be made. Actually the Vedas are a vast ocean of endless knowledge since "Knowledge" is endless. What has come to us is only a portion which was revealed to the *rishis.* As has been already mentioned, the Vedas are the breath of the Brahman or Paramatma. The vibrations caused by that breath always exist in space in spite of all the destructive deluges which have taken place from time to time in the universe. Those vibrations have no decay or death and are always available to those who are attuned to them.

Another important aspect of the Vedas is that the sound of the *mantras* when chanted with the correct intonation activates our nerve centres and also affects the atmosphere, resulting in individual as well as collective well-being. Collective does not refer only to humanity. No other religious text emphasises the well-being of the animal and plant world as much as the Vedas. *"Sham no astu dwipade sham chaturpade"*—Let four-legged and two-legged creatures prosper. The same verse goes on to pray for the well-being of shrubs, trees, mountains and rivers—in fact the whole of creation.

Modern research has demonstrated the effect of music on the growth of plants—how the yield is increased, etc. The Vedic seers being experts in phonetics as has been said, knew that the Vedic *mantras* had such extraordinary powers. Thus, the outstanding feature of the Vedas lies in the fact that apart from the actual meaning of the words, the sound of the *mantras* has great effect so just listening to them, will give us great benefit even if we do not understand the meaning.

The Vedas give instructions for ensuring the well-being of the individual from birth to death and beyond to other worlds. It gives instructions for society and for its leaders. Every Veda has three portions called Samhita, Brahmana, and Aranyaka. This again is only a classification. Generally, when we speak of mastering the Vedas, we mean only the mastering of the Samhita portion. This is because the Samhitas are the foundation or life-breath of each Shaakha or branch and these are the hymns which were seen or heard by the *rishis*. It is the Samhita portion which is known as *anadi* or eternal.

The most important of the Vedic rituals is known as *yajna*. *Yajna* involves the performance of certain prescribed rituals with the aid of Fire or Agni to the accompaniment of the Veda *mantras*. *Yajna* is derived from the root word *yaj*, which means to worship or to sacrifice. Apart from small and big *yajnas* which are described in the Vedas which can be done by human beings, there is also reference to the cosmic *yajna* which goes on incessantly in Nature, producing sunshine, clouds, rainfall, vegetation and the different natural cycles. To perform any rite or ritual with a feeling of devotion as an offering to the Supreme can be termed as a *yajna* and this is the meaning given in the

Bhagavad-Gita. Lord Krishna says that any activity of the human being which is intended to contribute something to the society with a selfless intention can be called a *yajna*.

The entire 18th chapter of the *Yajur Veda* deals with this type of *yajna*, contributing to the general human good. This *yajna* is not a fire ritual. It refers to the human being's dynamic activity to explore and utilise Nature's resources for the common good. Any coordinated, well-planned effort for the common good can be called a *yajna*. This is a sacred act and hence is known as a sacrifice or a selfless act. The fire *yajnas* were conducted in huge open air enclosures known as *yajna shalaas,* and they were really the very first scientific laboratories. Here the sages examined the flora and fauna of the land, surveyed organic and inorganic resources and laid the foundations of a welfare state. The domestication of animals, the science and craft of agriculture and the utilization of all types of resources for food, clothing and housing were some of the earliest undertakings of the Vedic age. They wooed Nature, the universal mother— the earth with lovely hymns. They did not defile or desecrate her or try to rob her of her resources.

> Rightly I am the son of the Earth. The Earth is my mother.
> May the earth goddess who bears her treasure stored in many
> places, gold, gems, and riches, give opulence, grant great
> happiness to us bestowing them with love.

In a *yajna* many things are offered to Agni or the god of Fire, to the accompaniment of *mantras*. This is known as *homa*. Offerings to many gods are made through Agni, who is the mediator. Even though many divinities are mentioned, it would be wrong to label the Vedas as postulating polytheism. The Vedas emphatically proclaim that there is only one God and That has manifested itself as the different deities. The Veda talks of that Paramatma or Supreme Soul as manifesting itself through the various divinities. Vedic theism is pure and simple and is a most natural monotheism invoking ONE God, the Supreme Lord, the mighty force behind all forces and the divine light behind all effulgences. Just as the presence of the *atma* or soul is recognised by the activity of the body, similarly the existence of the Supreme Reality in the cosmos can be realised by the purposeful dynamism of the Lord's creation. Hence, the Vedic verses worship the Lord by invoking Nature's bounties known as *devas*. The Vedas refer us directly to the glory of God and his creation and ask us to establish a personal link with Him in the innermost core of our heart, where you can feel His throb. Man-based religions came at a much later date. Man's natural religion is eternally with him, for it is the Sanatana Dharma (the eternal law of cosmic righteousness).

The immortal soul assumes a human form for benevolent purposes. Man is not an individual. He is a social organism. God loves those who serve other beings whether they be human beings, cattle or plants. His glory lies in being a member of a big family. Though he has his personal blood relationships yet he is linked with every individual whether near or far. The human being thus lives, works and dies for society. He is expected to develop his craft, sciences and technology and lead society from poverty to prosperity. Through a series of such lives, the human being is expected to attain his fullness. This is his liberation. In that state we shall revert to our self-effulgent form and enjoy divine bliss. Every breath we take is part of the universal breath and every breath we give out is our contribution to universal life. This *prana*, this life force, is the same in everything and everyone and is spread everywhere simultaneously. Our lives can only become perfect if we participate in this great interchange with the universe. As the *Bhagavad-Gita* tells us in Chapter Three, *Sahayajna praja sristwa purovacha prajapati.*—The creator created all of us and instilled the idea of *yajna* or selfless action in us. No man is an island and no one can live without any sort of dependence on others and on nature. There is no me and mine as we think but all things are connected in an amazing way to the energy field. "*Mamta* and *ahamta*" (me and mine) have always been considered to be the two knots which alienate us from God. In this unified field there is no place for me and mine.

Now let us look at some of the facts discovered by the quantum physicists. They observed that subatomic particles had no meaning by themselves in isolation but only in relationship with everything else. At its elemental level, which is the quantum level, matter could not be chopped up into intelligible units but was completely indivisible. If we want to understand the universe, we will have to see it as a dynamic web of interconnectedness.

As Lynne Mactaggart says in her book, *The Field,*

> Human beings are a coalescence of energy in a field of energy which is connected to every other thing in this universe. This energy field is the central engine of our being. We can never be estranged from the other aspects of this universe since we are all bound fundamentally to this field!

This was indeed the teaching of the Vedas which they endeavoured to establish in a practical way into the life of the individual through their *yajnas* and rituals.

When a *mantra* for a certain deity is chanted, it calls forth that particular *deva* or deity. Spiritually evolved persons can actually see the deity when the *mantras* are chanted. Even if they cannot actually see them, they feel their presence. This is something like using an Ouija board for manifesting spirits. The mediums can actually see the spirits. Hinduism is unique in this respect that our rituals can actually contact the divine forces. These *devas* are the subtle divine forces which exist in nature, which help humans to conduct their lives in the proper way and also fulfil their desires. By worshipping them and offering libations to them, the Vedas teach that they will be more inclined to help us. Thus, Lord Krishna says in the *Bhagavad-Gita*,

> Do thou worship the *devas* through *yajnas* and let them bring you prosperity by giving rains and such things. Thus helping each other, you will both prosper.

RIG VEDA

The whole of the *Rig Veda Samhita* is in the form of *riks* or 'hymns of praise' to the various deities. Each *rik* is a *mantra*. The Samhita portion of the *Rig Veda* contains an astonishing stock of 35,000 words in 10,170 verses or *riks* which have the intrinsic potentiality for coining new words. The most astonishing thing about this is that these verses were chanted by the *rishis* at a time when language, as we know it, did not exist. Since the *Rig Veda* talks of Agni both at the beginning and at the end, it has been mistakenly said to advocate only the worship of Agni. Actually Agni or fire should be taken to mean the light of the soul or consciousness (*atma chaitanya*)—the glow of the soul's awakening. The final *sukta* of the *Rig Veda* says,

> Let all meet and think as with one mind. Let all hearts unite in love. Let the goal be common. May all live in happiness with a common purpose!

YAJUR VEDA

The word *yajus* is derived from the root *yaj*, which means worship. The word *yajna* as we have seen is also derived from it. The chief purpose of the *Yajur Veda* is to show us how to use the *mantras* in the *Rig Veda* in a practical way in the *yajnas*. Almost all the *mantras* in the *Rig Veda* in the form of hymns, are also to be found in the *Yajur Veda*. In addition, it describes in prose the details for the performance of the different *yajnas*. *Sama Veda* teaches us how to chant the hymns in a poetic way and *Yajur Veda* teaches us the actual performance of the *yajnas* using these hymns and *mantras*. There are two branches of the *Yajur Veda* known as *shukla* (white) and *krishna* (black).

If we want to perform any of the great *yajnas* of the Vedas, we have to go the *Yajur Veda*. Somayaga, Vaajapeya, Rajasuya, Ashwamedha and many other great *yagnas* are to be found only in this Veda. These are to be found in the *Taitareeya Samhita* of the *Krishna Yajur Veda*. This Veda also contains some *mantras* and hymns which are not to be found in the *Rig Veda*. The most famous of these is the Sri Rudram or the hymn in praise of Lord Shiva.

SAMA VEDA

"Sama" means *shanti* or peace. In the *Sama Veda*, many of the hymns of the *Rig Veda* are set to music. Sama Gaana or the music of the *Sama Veda* can be said to be the basis and source of the seven notes which are fundamental to all music. It is also the source from which both the Hindustani music of the north and the Carnatic music of the south derived its inspiration. By singing the Sama hymns it is said that all the gods can be propitiated. In all *yajnas* one of the priests has to chant the *Sama Veda* in order to keep the gods happy. This is the speciality of the *Sama Veda* and thus in the *Bhagavad-Gita*, Lord Krishna proclaims that amongst the Vedas, he is *Sama Veda*. Even in the *Lalita Sahasranaama* or the thousand and one names to Lalita, the divine mother is said to be *Saamagaana Priya*—one who loves the music of the *Sama Veda*.

ATHARVA VEDA

Atharva was the name of a great *rishi*, who was the one to bring the hymns of the *Atharva Veda* to our knowledge. The Atharva *mantras* are in prose as well as in verse. In this Veda many esoteric secrets as well as cures for various ailments are revealed. The *mantras* are meant to ward off evil, bestow perfect health, destroy enemies, etc. It also has hymns to some *devas* that are not mentioned in the other three Vedas. It has a famous hymn to Nature called "The Prithvi Suktam." Three of the ten major Upanishads are taken from this Veda—*Prasna*, *Mundaka* and *Mandukya*. It is said that one who wants to attain liberation has to make a thorough study of the *Mandukya Upanishad*, which is from this Veda.

Unfortunately, this Veda which was once prevalent in north India seems to have vanished from these parts. Even in south India there are no pure AtharvaVedins left. A few families of Atharva Vedins can still be found in Gujarat, Saurashtra and Nepal. But from the few *mantras* and hymns of this Veda, which are available to us now, we can understand that this Veda is a veritable storehouse of scientific information. Unfortunately we do not have anyone in this modern world with the enormous spiritual and intellectual capacity that is capable of capturing any of these vibrations from the sphere.

Book 11 of this Veda has a full hymn devoted to every little thing concerning the human body, starting from the outer covering to the innermost complex. Many sciences are found in this Veda which the modern world found out many centuries later. Physics, chemistry, geology, medicine, astronomy, astrology, etc. are all discussed here. It has a lot of information on filtration, solution, crystallization, distillation and sublimation, all of which was used for medical purposes. Everything concerning what is now known as oxides of copper, iron, zinc and sulphates of iron, copper, gold amalgam, white lead, how to make dyes with a variety of vegetable products were fully dealt with. What is most important about these scientific facts given in all the Vedas is that science was not simply a mere theoretical subject found only in laboratories but it was a living, throbbing study which found its utility in all aspects of human life, leading to a fuller and happier life for both humans, animals and plants.

Chemistry was used to help find medical remedies. Astrology also had a definite bearing on chemistry and as such in medicine since the planets—Sun, Moon, Saturn, Jupiter, Mars, Venus and Mercury—were associated with different metals like gold, silver, lead, tin, iron, copper and mercury and these metals were used in gem therapy. Many references to this are given in this Veda.

Vedic mathematics is now seen to be of a superior quality. Consecutivity of numbers from 1 to 10 is found in the 11th book of the *Atharva Veda* and addition of numbers with multiples of 10 in the 5th book and multiplication by 11 in the 19th book. Notation by decimal value was well known in India even from those ancient times.

Although the four Vedas may appear to be different in some aspects like the method of recitation, all of them have a common goal—to ensure the well-being of the universe and to help everyone towards spiritual progress. Another singular feature of all the Vedas is that none of them say, "This is the only way", and "this is the only God." They all say that any path followed with faith and devotion to any *deva* (god) will lead to the same goal since the goal is one. No other holy book in any other religion advocates the pursuit of different paths. Every religion insists that its own doctrine alone will lead to salvation. The Vedas alone have such a breadth of vision that all four of them say that the same truth can be realised in many ways, since Truth is One and the same for all!

All Vedas have four portions. As mentioned before, the Samhitas or the *mantras* or hymns are the most important in as much as these are the ones seen by the *rishis* and which are said to have existed in the etheric sphere for all time. So far we have been talking only about the Samhitas. Two of the other portions are known as Braahmanas and Aranyakas. The Braahmanas explain how the Vedic rituals or *yajnas* are to be performed. They act as a guide to explain how each of the *mantras* has to be understood.

Aranyaka is derived from the word *aaranya* or forest. *Yajnas* and other rituals are prescribed for those who live in homes and lead the life of a householder. But it must be understood that Vedic rituals are intended not only for material benefits but also for mental purity. It is only those who have attained mental purity who should take to the solitude of the forests for further concentration and meditation. All other practices are only a preparation for the ultimate goal of life, which is to meditate and find out the true nature of the Self.

According to the Aranyakas, it is important to understand the reasons why *yajnas* are required to be performed. These two portions of the Veda—the Braahmanas and the Aranyakas— contain a vast amount of scientific knowledge which has only been discovered in very recent times by the modern world. As has been mentioned, chemistry, physics, geometry, mathematics, astronomy, astrology, botany, geology, anatomy and medicine are fully dealt with in these two portions of the Vedas. All the arts were touched upon as well as agriculture, architecture and transportation. All the things which would lead to a full and happy life were dealt with in each of all the four Vedas. The *Atharva Veda* is actually a storehouse of esoteric secrets on health but as mentioned before, only very little of this is available to us now. Countless hymns are found in this Veda about medicines and cures for a number of diseases which are still to be found. Of these, only a few hymns are given as samples from each of the Vedas. Ample advice is given in these portions to enable the human being to live a long, healthy and happy life, profitable both to him and to the world.

Of course the last portion of each Veda is known as the Upanishads which will be dealt with in a different chapter.

The Veda thus recognises the existence of two worlds and gives methods by which both can be satisfied. The difference between modern science and Vedic science is that modern science totally ignores the existence of another world in which the dualities of this world do not exist. The Vedas on the other hand always understood this and gave the first portion called *karma kanda,* which gives instructions for leading a good and dharmic life which was a preparation for the second portion, which deals with the transcendental reality. Thus, the first portion of the Vedas actually points to the second.

However, with the dawn of this quantum age, scientists have begun to think that there may be something called a life current flowing through the universe which some religions have called the divine consciousness or God or Brahman or whatever. They are trying to give proof for what mankind has had faith in, but no solid evidence, from the dawn of time. Thus science has put an end to dualism in the final sense. Scientists have proved in the laboratory that the dualistic world which we think we can see is a myth, a shadow cast on the wall. The only reality is that higher collective consciousness which exists for all time and in all places. You may call it God or whatever else you choose to call it. The Vedas called it Brahman as we have seen.

Another important point to be discussed about the Vedas is the language in which they were written. Just as Hinduism is the oldest of all religions, Sanskrit is the oldest living language in the world. No one knows how it came into being and who made it. Right from the first verse of the *Rig Veda*, the language has not changed even by a hair's breath. There has been no sound shift, no addition, no inspiration, and no change in import. The word "Sanskrit" means "perfect" and it was perfect from the time it came into being. It has not evolved from some initial imperfection. It exists now as it did before the dawn of history. It has mathematical precision and therefore zero deviation. The question about its origin cannot be answered since its beginning is shrouded in mystery as the Vedas are. The scriptures say that it came from the primary sound called *pranava* or *Aum* through which the divine descended in order to create the world of the seen and the heard. Brahma is the name given to that part of the Supreme that personifies the creative aspect. The Vedas as we have seen are *anadi* or without beginning, which means that Sanskrit is also *anadi* or without beginning. The primary concern of other languages is communication through the *vaikhari* (spoken) medium. This is considered to be an inferior mode of communication in the Sanskrit-Vedic tradition. Sanskrit sounds are not merely meant for verbal communication but for removing the gross wrapping of materialism and exposing us to the vibrations of the divinity underlying all creation. It is most lyrical and poetic and awakens the divine chords within us and helps us to align ourselves to the positive vibrations of nature.

All languages have their origin in time and space and keep changing with the changing times and places in which they are spoken. For example, English is spoken quite differently in the United States than in England. But Sanskrit hasn't changed since the time it was first uttered in Vedic times. Every other language has a human source since they were man-made and people keep changing and adding to the vocabulary. But Sanskrit, like the Vedas, does not have a human source and therefore has never changed. Like the Vedas it is eternal and everlasting.

In other languages, words are not properly defined and therefore ambiguous. They are not natural since they are human based and therefore they can never be used for scientific purposes. Sanskrit however is considered to be the language which is most suited for computers since it is so precise. All artificial intelligence which is used in machines like computers makes use of binary language 0-1 and the various combinations and permutations spun round them. Sanskrit is totally free of all ambiguity and therefore most suited for computers.

It is the most phonetic language in the world. The meaning of many Sanskrit words can be known through the sound they produce. It is based on a creation of innumerable words with the help of seed sounds called *dhatus* and thus is capable of producing more and more words. The Sanskrit language represents the thoughts, traditions and cultural heritage of the whole of India. It is not the language of a community or a special region but has been the golden thread which has connected the whole of India into one single unit. As such the government has a duty to see that it is kept alive and taught in all schools. Scholars abroad have discovered how the learning of Sanskrit has helped in the growth of memory in children and there are many schools in the UK which teach Sanskrit to their students.

Beyond all senses, mind and intellect and ego, is the essence of existence, the ultimate cause. One who realises that endless entity is relieved from the cycle of birth and death.

The unborn Supreme Self is beyond all descriptions. Scriptures and speculation give us no clue. The right path alone can take us to the wisdom that reveals its undeniable presence in all mortal beings.

Kathopanishad

Loka Samasthath Sukhino Bhavantu!

ॐ

Aprameyaaya Namaha!

CHAPTER IV

Brahman and Atman

If there is one place on this earth where all the dreams of
living men have found a home from the very earliest days
when man began the dream of existence, it is India.

Romain Rolland. French philosopher. 1886–1944

By getting to smaller and smaller units, we do not come to
fundamental units, or indivisible units, but we come to a
point where division has no meaning.

Werner Heisenberg

Before we go into the actual teaching of this chapter, it would
be good to get rid of the confusions arising from the word
"Brahman." There are quite a few words which sound and are
spelt very much like this so let us try to differentiate between
them. Brahma is the creator in the Hindu trinity consisting of
Brahma, Vishnu and Shiva.

Brahman is the Ultimate Advaitic (non-dual) Reality of
Hinduism. It is the immutable, self-existence on which the rest
of the creation that moves and evolves is founded.

Braahmanas constitute the second portion of every Veda and give details about how *yajnas* and other fire rituals are to be conducted. Along with the Aranyakas, they constitute the *karma kanda* (portion dealing with action) of the Vedas.

A Brahmin or a *Braahmana* belongs to the highest, priest class of the ancient Vedic caste system. They were so called because they were the custodians of the Vedas and thus had to be highly enlightened souls who were actually knowers of the Brahman.

More and more intelligent people in the world with spiritual leanings are turning away from the orthodox ideas of most religions and trying to find that Ultimate Reality which is hidden within the heart of every human being and is the goal of all spiritual endeavour and self-discipline. "What is the nature of this Reality and how can it be realised", is the question which is most interesting to all people with a spiritual bent of mind. This Reality can no doubt be known only by direct experience. The Vedas and other scriptures of the Hindu religion have been given by those great sages who had direct personal experience of this Reality and were in a position to advise others and it is to these that we should go in order to be enlightened.

Before we go into the chapter on the Upanishads, we have to know the meaning of the word Brahman. The highest doctrine of the Sanatana Dharma as given in the Advaita Vedanta school of Hinduism declares that the Ultimate Reality is Non-dual (*Advaita*) and is that which supports both the manifest and unmanifest states of creation. The *Kathopanishad* says, "All the Vedas together talk of a single Being." What is that Being? The Vedas declare that that Being is that which is represented symbolically by the sound "Aum" ॐ.

This Reality is an integrated state which is changeless, indivisible and beyond human comprehension, beyond space and time. However, it can be known by direct experience by transcending all the levels of the mind, thus enabling consciousness to experience its real underlying nature in the realm of the unmanifest. This Ultimate Reality is called the Brahman in Hinduism. Its counterpart or reflection in the human being is known as the *atman.*

Brahman is the supra-cosmic force that sustains the cosmos of living and non-living beings. IT is the Cosmic Self that upholds everything as well as the Self or *atma* in each individual. The Brahman alone is, and because IT exists, everything else exists, for everything is in its essential nature nothing but the Brahman. Thus the first attribute of the Brahman is that IT is Pure Existence. In truth Brahman alone exists. Everything else is a superimposition on IT. The manifest universe is constantly changing and temporary whereas the Brahman is imperishable, changeless, steadfast and eternal. It is the only Reality. Everything else is unreal in as much as everything else is transitory, ephemeral and elusive. By this classification, the world is unreal since it is transitory. Many centuries before Einstein, our *rishis* pointed out that the universe of forms is relative. Einstein said "Everything is relative, nothing is absolute." The Advaita Vedanta of Hinduism says, "Only the Absolute is real, everything else is relative!" Even in this modern age many people cannot understand this. It is only the *rishis* and the scientists who can appreciate such a statement.

Thus, immutability is a criterion of Reality and thus a condition of Brahman. Any changeable entity is bound to have a beginning and an end and is bound to decay and die. Therefore, the Brahman has neither beginning nor end. It is *anadi* (without beginning) and *ananta* (without end).

The Brahman is not only Sat or Existence, it is also pure consciousness—that consciousness that knows itself in all that exists. *Chit* or *chaitanya* or consciousness is not a product of anything. It is the nature of the Supreme Reality and the primary substratum of everything. Consciousness is not an attribute of the Brahman since IT has no attributes. Vedanta says that Brahman is an undifferentiated, homogeneous whole of consciousness—*prajnaaghanam* (filled with consciousness.) Before the manifestation of the world, there was no matter and no energy. The world did not come out of nothing. That positive entity that ever exists and existed before the cosmic manifestation is not insentient. There is a grand design in the cosmic anatomy and physiology. For the maintenance of the cosmic processes, intelligent co-ordination, control and execution are unavoidable. Thus, Hinduism says that Brahman is that Super Consciousness by which everything is kept under control.

As has been pointed out, Brahman is not a product of anything so IT is changeless and can never be modified. It is formless and therefore does not occupy space. Anything that maintains form and position expends energy. Anything which has qualities has some action and action cannot be accomplished without expenditure of energy. Anything that spends energy undergoes modification. The Brahman being immutable and eternal has got no form, no qualities and no functions. Being changeless IT does not undergo decay and being imperishable IT does not grow. Growth, decay and death imply change. IT is non-relational so there is no question of anyone perceiving it or IT perceiving anything else.

Now the question may be asked, if the Brahman is the only Reality, how can IT be said to pervade everything? What does everything imply? Here we have to differentiate between three types of realities. The Brahman is known as the Absolute Reality, which cannot be contradicted under any circumstances. Since IT is Absolute Existence, the universe has relative or empirical reality and of course there is something called illusory reality such as a mirage in the desert.

The existence of the world is dependent on the Brahman and even this is never stable and always changing so the universe has only a relative reality. The mirage of course is an illusory reality. So when we say that the Brahman pervades everything, we mean that the whole empirical universe is pervaded by the Brahman.

The waves, ripples and surf on the ocean are only names which we give to the water in the ocean. They really have no separate existence. They exist only because the ocean exists. So also the world exists because of the substratum of the Brahman.

However, the Brahman is not involved in the creation of the universe. There is no change in the rope which was mistaken for the snake. Gold changes into different types of ornaments but in itself it is not changed. In the process of change it gets different names (*nama*) and forms (*rupa*). Thus there is no change in the Brahman. It is only *maya* that gives the appearance of change. One of the similes given in the Vedas to make us understand this is the allegory of the spider. The whole beautiful web has come out of the spider but having made it, she doesn't go away but sits in the middle of the web. This analogy is taken one step further and Hinduism says that at the end of this cycle of creation, the Brahman will draw the web of the universe completely back into Itself.

The Brahman has no cause and is not the cause of anything else. It is not the agent or the material or efficient cause of anything. It is *avyakta*—not perceptible by the five senses and *achintya*—that which cannot be thought of in the mind. Vedanta gives a very precise psychological and physical account of the process of any type of perception by any of the five senses. The sense organ receives the external stimuli and transmits it to the specific centre in the brain. The brain gets a certain feeling, which depends on the particular centre which is stimulated and that is our sensation. What happens in the brain centre is not known by us. The sense organ, the conducting nerves and the brain matter itself are all insentient. Despite this we get knowledge through this method. Vedanta says that knowledge is possible only due to the reflection of Consciousness on the insentient organs. Because of the presence of this Consciousness of the Brahman, the eye is able to see, the ear is able to hear, the nose is able to smell, the tongue to taste, the skin to touch and the mind to think. This being the case, the senses by themselves are not able to cognise the Brahman. The person that sees is the origin or cause of the thing that is seen. The cause of the whole world is the pure knowledge which is inside us. Without the light of pure consciousness our sense organs are like clods of earth. Thus the purport of all the Vedas is to make us realise by our own experience what that Brahman is and thus live in a state of bliss.

The Brahman is self-effulgent, self-luminous (*swayam-jyoti*). It illumines the whole universe and is not illumined by anything else. The sun, moon, stars and other effulgent things like lightning are all illumined by the light of the Brahman. Thus the *Bhagavad-Gita* says about the state of the Brahman—"There nothing shines—no sun, no moon, etc." The effulgence of the Brahman is such that even a thousand suns will not appear to be shining in ITS presence just as thousands of electric bulbs cannot be said to be effulgent in broad daylight!

Brahman is the inner soul of all. It is Consciousness in conscious beings and Consciousness in inconscient things. It is Time and timelessness, Space and all that is in space, Causality as well as cause and effect, the Thinker and the thought, the Warrior and his courage and his cowardice. At the same time it is not bound by Time, Space or Causality. Any non-changing entity, ever free from modifications is bound to be eternal. Therefore the Brahman is eternal and beyond the three periods of time—past, present and future. It is the uncaused cause of everything.

The scriptures made many attempts at describing the Brahman by using contradictions.

The *Yajur Veda* says:

It moves, it moves not.
It is far and it is near,
It is within all this,
And it is outside all this.

The *Kena Upanishad* says,

The Brahman is known to him who thinks he does not know it. He who thinks it is known to him does not know it. It is not understood by those who say they understand it. It is understood by those who do not understand it!

By such conundrums did the Upanishads try to describe IT.

They also used the method of negation, by saying, *neti, neti*—not this, not this.

All this only goes to show the inability of describing the Brahman.

The Brahman is beyond words and therefore beyond description and is something which cannot be classified. We cannot use any language for the Brahman since it is not an object. It is One without a second and is non-relational. Hence language cannot describe IT. Though we use the word "the Brahman", the fact is that it does not help us to conceptualise IT. But the human mind cannot comprehend that which is totally without attributes so the *rishis* have described IT as *Sat-chit-ananda*— existence, consciousness and bliss. IT alone exists. Everything else is a superimposition on IT.

We have already seen that it is both *sat*—existence—and *chit*—consciousness. The third classification of the Brahman is that it is *ananda*, the secret bliss of existence which is the ether of our being and without which none can breathe or live. It is because everything contains all these attributes of the Brahman that the world appears to exist and has consciousness and holds bliss. Even someone who is suffering terribly clings to life because of this element of bliss. *Ananda* has no opposite since it is a self-contained state of deep contentment, uncontaminated by opposites. What happens in the empirical world is witnessed by that Pure Consciousness of the Brahman. The Brahman is the only witness (*sakshi*) of the world play. After the dissolution of the universe, the relative existence disappears and only the Brahman (Absolute Existence) remains as the solitary witness of the void.

Thus, the scriptures all declare that the Brahman cannot be known through logic but even so the scriptures all ask us to know the Brahman. How to know something which is unknowable? Actually this is not as difficult as it appears. At the end of all acts and rituals, we repeat the words *Aum Tat Sat*. This is to emphasise the truth that the Supreme alone exists and IT alone is the truth. *Tat* means "That" or the Supreme and Sat means "truth". By referring to IT as "That", it does not mean that IT is far away. The Brahman you are referring to as "That" which implies distance, is actually closer than the closest.

The *mahavakyas* or great *mantras* of the Upanishads give us the method of knowing this proximity. The Self or the *atman* in each of us is nothing but the Brahman. *Tat twam asi* means "That thou art". Here the word *tat* "that" stands for the Brahman and *twam* stands for "thou" or the personal self. This *mantra* can well be changed into "Thou, thou art"—"you are you". When one removes the idea of the world and the body and concentrates on one's identity with the Brahman, one will get the immediate realisation that you are nothing but the Brahman. Hence the next *mahavakya—aham brahmasmi*—I am Brahman. You also realise that your own Self is the Brahman. Hence, the third *mahavakya—ayam atma cha brahma cha*—I am the *atma* which is also the Brahman. Then the great cosmic awareness dawns on the person and he says, *atmaivedam sarvam*—all this is indeed the *atma* (self), *brahmaivedam sarvam*—all this is indeed the Brahman. After this realisation, the difference between subject and object disappears, there is nothing like you and I, seer and object. The knower, the knowable and knowledge all melt into one pure Consciousness alone. Nothing else remains—*sarvam khalvidam Brahma*—everything is the Brahman. All differences and dualities disappear into the great melting pot of the Brahman. This state of consciousness is of course very rare and is known as Cosmic Consciousness but in order to live in the world, our ordinary consciousness has to re-assert itself or else the personality will no longer be able to live in the physical world.

Thus *Atma Sakshatkara* is the same as *Brahma Sakshatkara.* "Knowledge of the Self" is the same as "Knowledge of the Brahman." So when you see the world as Brahman, you are actually projecting your own Self into the world and seeing the world as your own Self! Just think of what this implies. We all know that all our petty love boils down to the love of the Self in us. As the great sage Yajnavalkya told his wife Maitreyi,

> The husband loves his wife for the sake of the Self, the wife loves the husband for the sake of the Self, and the mother loves her child for the sake of her own Self.

So the love of the Self is the supreme love and there is nothing higher than this so when we project our Self into the world and see the whole world as nothing but a projection of our own beloved Self, it follows that we will love the whole world as our own Self. This is why the enlightened souls have no difficulty in loving the whole of creation and dying for the sake of another if called upon to do so.

So the question is asked. What about the majority of human beings to whom the world appears so real and so solid? Has it no reality? Advaita Vedanta postulates that the world is a world of shadows (modern science has used the same words). It has as much reality as the dancing patterns which pass off as the drama of life on the unchanging TV screen. Without that immutable, colourless, unshaken screen behind, the show which is being projected would have no meaning. The show consists only of changing patterns of light. (Again this is what physics postulates.) Let it be noted that the idea of a shadow world, which modern science came to know only in the 20th century, was the very foundation of the Vedanta philosophy formulated centuries ago. The knowledge of the formless, immutable Brahman is the foundation of all Hindu thought since it comes from the Vedas which are the cornerstones of Hinduism.

However, to give them their due, the quantum physicist did discover something novel which the ancient physicist could not accept—that the only thing which can be called real in this shadow world is the consciousness of the spectator or the experimenter. Without that consciousness even this shadow world would not exist. Everything is centred round the experimenter. This was a great breakthrough. Till now the experimenter's job was always to get out of the way of the experiment and not interfere with the purely mechanical process involved in the experiment. Now it was proved by the scientist that the individual consciousness has everything to do with the final outcome of the experiment. This consciousness stems from a phenomenon known as super-radiance, which is a state of perfect coherence.

The *rishis* of old knew that this is a shadow world—a world of *maya*. But as we have seen, they asked the million dollar question: "If this is a shadow world then what is the Being that casts the shadow? A shadow obviously cannot exist on its own. What is it that holds all these things together? All our scriptures have given the answer. This shadow world is a becoming but there is a Being which is the cause of these shadows. This exists because THAT exists. If THAT were not to be, then "This" will cease to be". Krishna declares, "All things exist in Me but mark my mystery, I do not exist in them." What he means to say is that God is not a sum total of all creation. Even though they are in Him, He is not in them and that is why no amount of enquiry into the shadow world can give us the truth of Absolute Consciousness. The fish exist in the water but the water does not exist in the fish or because of the fish. Fish cannot exist without water but water can and does exist without fish!

In another simile Krishna says, "Everything is strung on me as pearls on a string." The necklace has a shape and value only due to the string which holds them together. If the string is broken, the necklace will no longer exist. The pearls will roll around in a random fashion like negative particles.

Since the Brahman is that Reality which enfolds us from birth to death and beyond, it follows that It should be available in this life itself. The aim of the Vedas and Puranas is to help us to gain *moksha* (liberation) whilst living in this world itself. This is the greatness of Hinduism. All other faiths talk of liberation only after death. No one has come back to give us an account of the state after death. Therefore, the Sanatana Dharma insists that this state can and must be attained while in this very world. The *Bhagavad-Gita* says, *Ihaiva thairgita sarge*. "Liberation must be attained here and now." "What use is a liberation for us after death," asks Lord Krishna. If we apply ourselves to the dictates of the Vedas and the Puranas of which the *Bhagavad-Gita* is a classic example, we will attain this state in this very life itself. Whereas other paths only give temporary solace and hope of a better state after death (which is most dubious), Hinduism goes to the very root of bondage which is existence itself and helps the individual destroy the sense of separation from the Supreme and thus provides a permanent release instead of a temporary cure. Western religions like Western medicine give only symptomatic cures while the Vedic religion gives eternal bliss.

This path of approach through intellect and intuition is known as the *jnana marga* or the path of knowledge but Hinduism offers many paths to God. In fact, the picture which Hinduism projects to the outside world consists of numerous gods. What about them is the question? How do they fit into this picture of the immutable Brahman and the illusory world?"

What is the necessity for the formless to take on forms? This question will be dealt with in the next chapter on "Bhakti Yoga."

In the Sanatana Dharma, the Supreme head is the Brahman as has been said, and He is reflected in our own hearts as the Self or *atman*. So eventually our own consciousness has to be followed. We may refer to our *guru* or spiritual preceptor for guidance but these *gurus* are chosen by our own selves so even here the reference is to our own inner guide that will prompt us to choose. *Gurus* have to be enlightened souls who instinctively know who their disciples should be. When the great Indologist, Paul Brunton went to Sri Chandrashekharendra Saraswati, the saint of Kanchipuram, the sage told him to go to Thiruvannamalai where he would find his *guru*. He went there and met the great sage, Sri Ramana Maharishi who later became his *guru*. The *guru* knows the disciple's mentality and state of evolution, and will give him that sort of spiritual guidance which is right for him. The *guru* may not give the same teachings to all his disciples. There are no hard and fast rules in spirituality which can be followed by everyone indiscriminately without reference to his or her own needs and development. Hence, the *guru parampara* (lineage) is not an authoritarian command. Even after having chosen our *guru*, it is said that we should not follow blindly everything he says. We should bring the light of our own reason to bear on all things, including scriptural injunctions. But once we have tested and found our *guru* to be the one for us, we should follow his advice with faith and trust since the *guru* knows our own abilities and nature better than we do. But even here it should be understood that the *guru* only points out the way. He is not expected to carry us on his back so to speak. The whole responsibility of following his words and of choosing or rejecting the advice falls on us. Of course this imposes a strain on the individual. It is easy to blindly follow someone else's instructions as to how we should behave but more difficult when the whole responsibility is put on ourselves.

The *rishis* realised that the world as it appeared to the common man was totally different from what it appeared to the realised soul. For us the world is real because we are five sensory beings and we take as absolute truth whatever the five senses tell us. The enlightened soul however lives in what is known as a state of Cosmic Consciousness in which the whole world is experienced as pure Consciousness.

Therefore, they reiterated that these two were separate worlds and should not be confused with each other. The rules that apply to one need not necessarily apply to the other. Nowadays enlightenment has become a hackneyed word. Many novices who have read a little about the Upanishads and about the state of the Brahman which is actually something like the quantum state but much deeper and meaningful, try to mix up the two and whenever they get defeated in any argument they fall back on what it called the "Vedantic shuffle". They get out of a difficult position by saying that in any case everything is *maya* so why bother? Neither the Vedas nor the Vedanta supports this type of statement.

The teacher or *guru* of the Upanishads insisted that the rules of the inner world should not be applied to the outer until one has reached a state of Cosmic Consciousness and that students should be wary of mixing up the two.

A funny story is often told to prove the point. The teacher had been telling the students that everything was the Brahman, whatever you could see or touch or hear or smell and even beyond the senses. The students set out for a walk and saw a mad elephant rushing towards them. The elephant man sitting on top kept shouting to people to get off the road. All the students except one took to their heels. The poor bewildered one stood in the middle of the road and said "The elephant is Brahman and I am also Brahman. He will not hurt me." Of course the elephant did not know he was the Brahman so he came and took the poor boy in his trunk and tossed him like a straw to the side of the road. Luckily, the boy survived and when he returned to his *guru,* he complained bitterly, "You told me that everything was Brahman so why did the elephant harm me."

The *guru* said, "I have told you not to mix up the laws of one world with the other. Even if you did so, why did you not respect the advice of the elephant man who was also Brahman and who told you to keep off the path of the maddened elephant?"

I bow to that Para Brahman which is pure consciousness,
Unsullied, indestructible, desireless, formless, beyond the three gunas,
Not perceivable, One alone, ever in the turiya state of consciousness,
This can only be gauged through the *mantra* "*Aum*".

Rig Veda

Who knows what the truth is,
Or who may here declare it?
What is the proper path?
That leads to the place of divine forces?
Only their inferior abiding places are perceived,
Not those which are situated,
In superior mysterious locations.

Rig Veda

Loka Samasthath Sukhino Bhavantu!

ॐ

Shantidaaya Namaha!

CHAPTER V

The Upanishads

Still there are moments when one feels free from one's own identification with human limitations and inadequacies. At such moments, one imagines that one stands on some spot of a small planet, gazing with astonishment at the cold yet profoundly moving beauty of the eternal, the unfathomable. Life and death flow into one and there is neither evolution nor destiny, only Being.

Albert Einstein

In India I found a race of mortals living on the earth, but not adhering to it. Inhabiting cities but not being fixed to them. Possessing everything but possessed by nothing.

Apollonius Tyaneus. Greek traveller of the 1st century AD

Whence arises all the order and beauty we see in the World.

Isaac Newton

The Upanishads are the fourth portion of the Vedas and come at the end of the Aranyakas. The main theme of the Upanishads is a philosophical enquiry into the nature of Truth and the methods of controlling the mind by which this Truth can be realised. Though Truth is a matter of direct realisation by one's own individual efforts, the *rishis* have gifted us the Vedas, which give us a vast and priceless literature giving the experiences and exhortations of those who have gained direct realisation of this Truth.

The Upanishads constitute what is called the *jnana kanda* or portion dealing with the path of wisdom (*jnana marga*), while the Brahmanas and Aranyakas are known as *karma kanda* or the portion dealing with action. The *jnana kanda* is much smaller and is written in a concise form. Foreign scholars who have read the Upanishads as a purely intellectual exercise, have not even been able to touch the fringes of that transcendental Truth as explained in the Upanishads. However, most of them have been struck by the profound wisdom embedded in them. The special characteristic of the Upanishads is that they contain *mantras* which transmute their import through vibrations into actual experiences.

The word Upanishad can be broken up into *upa-ni-shad*, which means "to sit by the side". Literally, the disciple sat by the side of the teacher during the discourse. It can also mean "that which takes you to the side of the Brahman." The teachings of the Upanishads were esoteric teachings given only to those who were fit to receive them. They are such an important part of the Vedas that they are sometimes referred as *shruti siras* or the head of the Vedas.

The *karma kanda* of the Vedas prescribe a way of life which would make it possible for the realisation of its philosophy just by following the precepts given therein. Such a person who has followed the lifestyle prescribed in the *karma kanda* is ready to retire and meditate and thus attain the summit of all philosophical experience—that the Soul and the Supreme Being (*jivatma* and *Paramatma*) are one and the same.

"From the words of the poet men take what meanings please them, but their last meaning always points to Thee," said the great poet Tagore. Similar is the case with the Upanishads. They are filled with exquisite poems but whatever their apparent meaning, the fact is that they always point to that Absolute Reality which is both within and without.

The second part of the Vedas gives us methods by which we can make use of Nature to live a good life. All the sciences come in this part. This is known as *apara vidya* or that knowledge which is verifiable through experiments. But as has been pointed out, all the time the inner essence of the Vedas direct us towards the unity of life, the discovery of which is the goal of life. That was called *para vidya* or Supreme Knowledge, which is verifiable only through personal experience. Thus, the last portion of the Vedas, known as Vedanta or the Upanishads, gives us that Supreme Knowledge by knowing which everything else is automatically known. The Braahmanas or the second part of the Vedas deals with the world as seen by classical physics whereas the Upanishads deal with the quantum world. When the latter becomes a matter of actual experience, the so-called real world experienced by the majority of humanity is seen to be an illusion as the modern-day quantum physicists have found to their astonishment.

Sometimes it might seem to us that the *karma kanda* (Braahmanas) and the *jnana kanda* (Upanishads) of the Vedas are at variance with each other. In order to understand this apparent discrepancy, we have to understand what life is about. The Braahmanas gives us a lot of scientific knowledge—technical knowledge on how to live a happy and contented life in the world outside. Even though the *rishis* realised that the goal of life was to discover the Self within and establish oneself in that unity, they also realised that for most people duality alone was real and unity just a dream. The Vedas do say *Brahma Satyam, jagat mithya*—the Brahman alone is real and the world an illusion—yet they were fully conscious of the fact that for the majority of humans the reverse is true. In their compassion they did not want to reject the majority and thus the second part of the Vedas give us, as we have seen all the rituals by following which one can have a good and auspicious life in the world. However, they did not do this at the cost of defiling nature and plundering her resources and leaving her barren as we are doing now. Their method was quite different. They wooed the *devas* or the subtle forces of Nature, who are the ones who help us in our normal activities. They did not desecrate Nature as we are doing now. Therefore, they maintained the balance of Nature and brought about prosperity to humankind as well as to animals and plants. As long as we think the world to be real, we have to propitiate these *devas* so that we can continue to live in comfort and prosperity. Modern science also gives us many techniques and devices by which we can live in comfort and affluence but it considers the human being, Nature and God to be totally disconnected.

Therefore, many of the modern innovations and contraptions which we are using do not take into consideration the fact that Nature is actually a living entity, throbbing with life and think nothing of wresting from her whatever we want. This is what has led to the unhappiness that modern man suffers despite the fact that we have more gadgets and so-called materialistic comforts than any other generation preceding us.

Even though the Braahmanas (second portion of the Vedas) help us in material life, eventually it is the Upanishads which actually give us advice on how to get liberation.

Many Upanishads must have existed but only one hundred and eight are available to us now. Among these, ten have been depicted as most important since Adi Shankaracharya, the founder of the Vedantic school of philosophy, has written commentaries on them. These ten are *Mundaka, Eesha, Kena, Katha, Aitareya, Taitareeya, Chandogya, Prashna, Svetashvatara,* and *Brihadaranyaka.*

The Upanishads are given in the form of a *guru*-disciple discourse. The disciples would sit close to the *guru* and ask him questions. The later would answer them and then ask questions of his own which were very often abstruse. The questions were always meant to make the student delve within himself and discover the answers for himself. The answers were never given on a plate. The disciple had every right to question the teacher and argue with him if necessary until he was intellectually satisfied that what the *guru* had said was right. Very often the *guru* would give contradictory advice to different students depending on their level of understanding. The famous hymn which was always chanted at the beginning of a session shows how the teacher accepted the student as an equal.

> May He protect us. May He take pleasure in us.
> May we perform great deeds together,
> May spiritual knowledge shine before us,
> May we never have occasion to disagree with each other.
> May Peace, Peace, Peace be everywhere.

The *Ishavasya Upanishad* comes at the end of the *Shukla-Yajur Veda Samhita*. It begins with the famous couplet,

Ishavasyamidam sarvam yadkim cha jagatyam jagat...

Everything that you can think of in this universe is filled with God alone. Claim nothing and enjoy. Do not covet His property.

Another oft quoted couplet from this Upanishad is,

Aum poornamada, poornamidam, poornath poornamutachyate, poornasya, poornamaadaaya, poornamevavashishyathe.

That is full. This is also full. Fullness can come only from fullness. Take away the full from the full and fullness will still remain.

They have put a stopper in the neck of the bottle. Pull it out O Lord and let out Reality. I am full of longing.

Unmoving, It moves; It is far away, yet near, within all, yet outside all.

Of a certainty, the man who can see all creatures in himself, himself in all creatures, knows no sorrow.

Kenopanishad comes in the *Sama Veda*. "Kena" means "what" or at "whose command?"

The student questions the teacher, "What has called my mind to the hunt"? What has made my life begin? What wags in my tongue? What god has opened my eye and ear?"

The teacher answers,

It lives in all that lives, hearing through the ear, thinking through the mind, speaking through the tongue, seeing through the eye.

That which makes the tongue speak, but which no tongue can explain, that which makes the mind think, but needs no mind to think, that which makes the eye see but which needs no eye to see, that which makes the ear to hear but which

needs no ear to hear, that which makes life, live, but needs no
life to live—that alone is the Spirit!

One who says he knows the *atma*, knows it not, one who
says he knows it not, knows it. One, who says he sees it, sees
it not.

It is interesting that *Kenopanishad* is the only Upanishad in
which the goddess makes an appearance. She is supposed to be
especially fond of Sama Gaana so it is befitting that she makes
her emergence in the *Sama Veda*.

The gods in their arrogance failed to find the Supreme Reality
so She makes Her appearance in this Upanishad in the form of
Divine Wisdom and imparts the Supreme Wisdom to Indra,
king of the gods. She discloses the fact that all our powers are
derived from Para Shakti or the mysterious power of the
Brahman.

The Goddess tells the gods,

All of you have attained your greatness through the Supreme
Spirit. Do thou praise the glory of that Spirit.

Austerity, self-control, meditation are the foundation of this
knowledge. The Vedas are its house, Truth, its shrine.

The *Kathopanishad* comes in the *Krishna Yajur Veda* and is
in the form of a story. "Katha" means story.

It begins with the famous *mantra* which is chanted before
starting any teaching.

*Aum Sahanavavatu, sahanabhunaktu, saha veeryam
karavavahai,
Tejasvinaamateetamastu, ma vidwishavahai
Aum Shanti! Shanti! Shanti!*

May He protect us. May He be pleased with us.
May we perform great deeds together,

May spiritual knowledge shine in us,
May we never have occasion to disagree with each other.
May Peace, Peace, Peace be everywhere.

In the form of a dialogue between Yama, the God of Death and the boy Nachiketas, son of a king, the Upanishad expounds many great truths. The idea of the *jivanmukta* or the soul that is liberated even while living in the body is also found here. The boy Nachiketas asks for three boons from Yama, the God of Death. Of these, the third one is the most interesting.

He asks, "Some say that when a man dies he continues to exist, others that he does not. Explain and that shall be my third gift."

Who else but the God of Death would be the most competent person to tell us about the nature of death? Yama tries his best to avoid this question but the boy is adamant and thus Yama tells him:

The senses are made to turn outward and therefore man looks outward, not into himself. Now and again a daring soul, desiring immortality has looked inwards and found himself. The ignorant man, running after pleasure, sinks into the entanglements of death, but the wise man seeking the undying, does not run after things that die. He, through whom we see, taste, smell, feel, hear, enjoy and knows everything, He is that Self.

That boundless Power, source of every power, manifesting itself as life, entering every heart, living there among the elements, that is the Self.

When that Person in the heart, no bigger than a thumb, is known as maker of past and future, what more is there to fear? That is the Self.

The death of an organism does not destroy the essence of life in it. In fact, Hinduism postulates that even when *pralaya* or annihilation of the world occurs, which modern science calls nuclear fusion, the essence of life would return to the original galactic storehouse for another cycle of life and death. Similarly, the consciousness that leaves the body at the time of death continues to keep the light of life burning somewhere else. Our children do not perish when we die. They carry on the torch of consciousness to future generations.

"Death may put out some lamps but the light of life is kept burning eternally."

The motto, "Utthishtata! Jagrita! Arise, awake! Learn at the feet of the Masters. It is a hard path, the sharp edge of the razor!" which Vivekananda quoted was from this Upanishad.

Many of the examples given by Lord Krishna in the *Sreemad Bhagavad-Gita* are found in this Upanishad.

> The Self knows all. It is not born, does not die, is not the effect of any cause. It is eternal, self- existent, imperishable, ancient. How can the killing of the body, kill It? He who thinks that he kills and he who thinks that he is killed is ignorant. He does not kill nor is he killed.

The analogy of the upturned peepul tree found in the *Bhagavad-Gita* is also from this Upanishad.

> Eternal creation is a tree, with roots above, branches on the ground, pure eternal Spirit, living in all things and beyond which none can go—that is the Self.

The imagery of the body as the chariot is also found here.

> The Self rides in the chariot of the body, the intellect is the firm-footed charioteer, the discursive mind, the reins, the senses are the horses and the objects of desire, the path.

The three Upanishads—*Prasna, Mundaka* and *Mandukya*—come in the *Atharva Veda.*

Prasna means enquiry. The six sages went to the Sage Pippalada and asked six questions to which he gave answers.

"Who created everything?"

The sage answered, "God created the world and he who recognises him as such gets whatever he wants from the world."

"What power made the body? What gave it life?" "Which is the greatest?"

"May life, Master of the three worlds, protect us as a mother protects her children. Grant us wisdom, grant us luck."

"When does life begin? How does it get into the body? How does it get out of the body?"

"Life falls from the Self as shadow falls from man, Life and Self are interwoven. Life comes into the body so that desires of the mind may be satisfied."

"He who knows the source and power of life, how it enters, where it lives, how it divides itself into five, how it is related to the Self, attains immortality."

"Who is the waker, sleeper, dreamer and enjoyer in man's body? On whom do they depend?"

"As the rays of the setting sun gather themselves up into his orb to come out again at sunrise, the senses gather themselves into the mind and the man is said to be asleep. When they come out again, he is said to be awake. When the mind is lost in the light of the Self, it dreams no more. It is lost in happiness. My son, all things fly to the Self as birds fly to the tree for rest."

"Lord, where does the man go after death, if he meditates on 'Aum' all his life?"

"*Aum* is the conditioned and unconditioned Spirit. The wise man with its help alone attains the one or the other."

"He who meditates on the three syllables, A, U, M as upon God, is joined to the light of the sun. Peeling his negativity off as the snake peels off its skin, he goes through that light to the Kingdom of Heaven, to the God who is greater than the greatest of all creatures though living in our body."

Mundaka means shaven head and this Upanishad is followed mainly by *sannyasins* or renunciates who have shaven heads.

The following famous *shloka* comes from this Upanishad:

May our ears hear only good, may our eyes see only good, and May we serve Him with the whole strength of our body. Throughout our life, may we carry out His will. May peace, peace, peace, prevail on earth.

As the web springs from the spider and is again withdrawn, as the plant springs from the soil, hairs from the body of man, so springs the world from the Eternal.

He looks at all things; knows all things. All things, their nourishment, their names, their forms are from His will. All that He has willed is right.

The sparks, though of one nature with the fire, leap from it; uncounted beings leap from the Everlasting, but these my son, merge into it again.
The Everlasting is shapeless, birthless and breathless, without a mind, above everything, outside everything, inside everything.

The famous allegory of the arrow of the mind being shot at the target of the Brahman so that it becomes totally dissolved in it, is found in this Upanishad.

Take the bow of our sacred knowledge, lay against it the arrow of devotion, pull the string of concentration, and strike the target. *Aum* is the bow, the personal self (*jivatma*), the arrow, impersonal Self (*Paramatma*), the target. Aim accurately, sink therein.

In a beautiful golden scabbard hides, the stainless, indivisible, luminous Spirit. Neither sun, moon, star, neither fire nor lightning lights Him. When He shines, everything begins to shine; everything in the world reflects His light.

Spirit is everywhere upon the right upon the left, above, below, behind, in front. What is the world but the Spirit?

The beautiful allegory of the two birds sitting on one tree with one eating the fruits and the other looking on unperturbed is in this Upanishad.

Two birds, bound to one another in friendship, have made their homes on the same tree. One sits still while the other pecks at the fruit.

The two birds are the *jivatma* (embodied soul) and the *Paramatma* (supreme soul). Both have their abode in the tree of the body. The *jivatma* pecks at all the fruits, enjoys some and is disappointed with some. The *Paramatma* just watches the antics of the other bird.

The one who desires one thing after another, brooding over them, is born where his desires can be satisfied.

He who has found Him seeks no more, the riddle is solved, desire gone, he is at peace. Having approached from everywhere that which is everywhere, whole, he passes into that Whole.

This verse is chanted when one goes to meet a saint. "As rivers lose name and shape in the sea, wise men lose name and shape in God, glittering beyond all distances."

The motto of our country, *satyameva jayate, naanrutam*— "Truth alone triumphs, not falsehood", is also from this Upanishad.

Next comes the *Mandukya Upanishad*. This is the smallest of all the Upanishads and contains only twelve *mantras*. But it is one of the most famous and most effective. *Mandukam* means "frog." Quite a few conjectures are given as to why it should have been called "The Frog Upanishad." Varuna was the *rishi* to whom this was revealed and it is said that he had taken on the form of a frog at one time. Another and perhaps more plausible reason is that this Upanishad tells us how to leap like a frog from the first to the fourth step of consciousness without difficulty. Only a frog can skip a couple of steps and reach the last. The three stages of consciousness are *jagrita*, the waking state, *swapna*, dream state, *sushupti*, deep sleep and finally *turiya* or the fourth state which is the underlying state of awareness of the Supreme. The Upanishad says that it is possible to reach this state in one leap like a frog by meditation on *Aum*.

The *mantra* "*Aum*" is also known as the *pranava mantra*. This Upanishad declares that one can experience the identity of the *jivatma* and *Paramatma* by meditating on the *pranava mantra*. That *turiya* state of non-duality is beautifully described here as *Shivam/Advaitam*—auspicious and non-dual. This is the state into which all creation melts at the end of a certain period of time.

> The Self is the Lord of all, inhabitant of the hearts of all. He is the source of all; creator and dissolver of all beings. There is nothing that He does not know.

The only proof of his existence is union with Him. The world disappears in Him. This is the 4th state of consciousness, the most worthy of all.

This Self though beyond words is that supreme word "*Aum.*" Though indivisible, it can be divided into three letters, corresponding to the three conditions of the Self. The word "A" corresponds to the waking state, the second letter "U" corresponds to the dreaming state and the letter "M" is the deep sleep. The fourth state of the Self corresponds to *Aum* as the one indivisible word. Thus *Aum* is nothing but the Self. He who understands this with the help of his *jivatma* merges himself into the *Paramatma*.

All the *mantras* which are used in rituals are found in the *Taittiriya Upanishad*. It has three parts of which the first is called Shikshavali. All aspects of imparting education are given in this portion. Precepts like *Satyam vacha, Dharmam chara*—"Speak the truth, follow *dharma*", are found in this portion.

Give with faith; if you lack faith, give nothing. Give in proportion to your means. Give with courtesy. Give to the deserving. Give as the lovers of God give.

Mother, father, teacher and guest should be treated like divinities,

is another popularly quoted *mantra* from this portion.

God lives in the hollow of the heart, filling it with immortality, light, intelligence. Where the skull divides and where it is customary to divide the hair, like the hollow where the gate of God swings like the uvula within the palate.

If liberation from this mortal existence is the goal of life, why should one marry is the question? The answer given by the Upanishad is that it is our duty to pass on the torch of the noble teachings of the Veda to posterity.

The next portion is known as Anandavalli and dissects the personality into different parts. The body is known as the *annamaya kosha* or the sheath of food since the body thrives on physical nourishment. Inside this is the *pranamaya kosha* or the sheath of breath or life. Next comes the *manomaya kosha* or the mental sheath. The *vijnanamaya kosha* is the intellectual sheath which gives us the power of reasoning. The *anandamaya kosha* is the sheath of bliss which is at the core of all the rest. The Upanishad says that this is the natural state of the *atman*—the state of bliss or *ananda*. Like all the Upanishads, we are given advice on how to attain this state which is actually our natural state.

> He who denies the Spirit, denies himself, he who affirms it, affirms himself. This blissful Self is the soul of the knowing Self.
>
> Everything is self-created. He is that essence. Drinking that essence, man rejoices. If man did not lose himself in that joy, he would not be able to breathe, He could not live. Self is the sole giver of joy.
>
> He who knows that spiritual joy that mind cannot grasp, or tongue speak, fears nothing. Should he do wrong, or leave good undone, he knows no remorse. What he does, what he does not, is sanctified; what he does not, what he does, is sanctified.

The third portion of this Upanishad is called Brighuvalli since this portion was taught by Varuna to his son Brighu. The father tells the boy to plunge into deep meditation and actually experience what he has been taught. Brighu does deep penance and comes up first with the idea that the *annamaya kosha* or the body is the ultimate truth. Continuing his penance, he progressively discards the other two sheaths—*pranamaya* and *vijnanamaya,* and finally arrives at the state of bliss—*anandamaya kosha,* beyond which he cannot go and thus concludes that this is the ultimate truth.

> Bhrigu meditated and found that bliss is Spirit. From bliss all things are born, in bliss they live, toward bliss they move, into bliss they return. This is what Brighu, son of Varuna, found in the hollow of his heart.

> He who knows this stands on a rock; commands everything; enjoys everything; brings up a family; gathers flocks and herds; grows famous through the light of the Spirit; is a noble man.

The Upanishad does not scorn a worldly life but insists that it is only by leading a dharmic life (righteous life) that we can reach the final stage. It actually gives us advice on how important food is to us.

> Respect food. Life is food; body lives on food; body is life, life is body; they are food to one another.

> Bow down to Spirit as the sole object of desire, and thus become the goal of all desire; worship Spirit as the master of all and thus become the master of all!

The *Aitareya Upanishad* comes at the end of the *Aitareya Aranyaka.* The rishi Aitareya was the one who gave it to us. It tells us how the various elements take their places in the body.

> Fire is the characteristic of speech and entered the mouth, air in the character of scent entered the nose, sun in the character of sight entered the eyes, the four quarters in the character of hearing entered the ears; vegetation in the character of hair entered the skin, moon in the character of mind entered the heart, death in the character of *apana* (downward breath)

entered the navel, water in the character of seed, entered the loins.

The Spirit thought, how should I enter the body?" He opened the suture of the skull, entered through the gate which is called the gate of joy (Brahmarandram). He found three places where he could live, three conditions where he could move— waking, dreaming, sleeping.

He entered the body, named its various parts and wondered if there could be anything there which was not Spirit and rejoiced to find there was nothing but Himself.

This Upanishad gives us many interesting facts as to how a *jiva* (embodied soul) takes birth in a particular woman's womb from the father and is born into the world and takes birth again and again in various wombs and worlds depending on its sins and merits (*papa* and *punya*). Liberation from this can only come with the realisation of the Supreme.

First he becomes the seed of a man, which is gathered from all the limbs of the body. Man nourishes himself within himself as seed. When he ejects the seed into a woman, he himself is born. That is his first incarnation.

The seed merges in the woman's body. Because it becomes her body, it does not harm her. She nourishes the self of the man within herself.

Protect her, for she is protecting the seed. Before and after the birth of the child, man blesses the child, thus blessing himself. Man lives in his child. This is his second incarnation.

The son being the father over again, carries the traditions of the family and the father having completed his fate, exhausted his years, dies and is born again. This is his third incarnation.

It gives the interesting story of the sage called Vamadeva who came to know about all his various births while still in his mother's womb. As soon as he was born, he flew like a hawk into the void and refused to enter into another cycle of birth and death.

> When lying in the womb I understood how the gods worked.
> They put me into that iron-gated, hundred-gated, prison.
> But I fled quickly like a hawk.

Vamadeva thought to himself, "On whom should I meditate?"

> He is Spirit, Creator, God, all gods, earth, air, water, wind, fire, constituents of life, all greater and lesser combinations; seminal, egg-born, womb-born, sweat-born, soil-born, horses, cows, men, elephants, birds, everything that breathes, movable, immovable, all founded upon, all moved by that one Intelligence. Intelligence is Spirit.

With this knowledge, Sage Vamadeva did all that he desired, left this world for the higher regions became immortal... yea became immortal.

The last two Upanishads—the *Chandogya* and the *Brihadaranyaka*—are the largest and together they are as big as the rest of the eight. *Chandoga* means one who sings the Sama hymns. Of course this Upanishad comes in the *Sama Veda*. Just as the allegories used in the *Kathopanishad* are largely used in the *Bhagavad-Gita*, so also the Chandogya *mantras* are used in the Brahma Sutras of Vyasa.

Chandogya Upanishad contains many interesting stories. The Brahmin boy Swetaketu, son of Uddalaka Aruni, was swelling with pride at his birth and knowledge.

His father humbled him by various tests. "I shall teach you that by knowing which you will have known everything."

"How is that possible?" asked the son.

By knowing one nugget of gold you will know all things made of gold. They differ only in name and form. Their reality is gold alone.

Remember, my son! The body bereft of Self dies. The Self does not die.

That Being is the seed, all else but His expression. He is Truth, He is the Self.

O Swetaketu! Thou art that! Tat Twam asi!

Uddalaka now asked his son to fetch a banyan fruit and break it and take one small seed. He then asked him to break that seed and see what was inside that.

"I see nothing, Lord!" said the boy.

Uddalaka said, "My son! This great banyan tree has sprung up from a seed so small that you cannot see it. That Being is the seed; all else are but His expressions. He is Truth. He is the Self.

Thou art That O Swetaketu! (Tat Twam Asi)!"

Uddalaka said, "Put this salt into water and see me tomorrow morning."

Next morning he asked Swetaketu to bring the salt he had put into the water.

Uddalaka looked but could not find the salt. The father now asked him to taste the water from the top, the middle and the bottom and he found that everything was salty.

Uddalaka said, "My son though you do not see that Being in the world, He is here. That Being is the seed, all else is but His expression. He is Truth, He is the Self. Thou art That O Swetaketu! Tat Twam asi!"

Tat Twam Asi is one of the Mahavakyas, as will be explained below.

This Upanishad also contains many interesting stories. Satyakama was born into a low caste family but longed to receive instruction from a great *guru*. In those days only Brahmins were given instruction in the Vedas but since he did not hide the fact of his lowly birth, his Guru accepted him. Only a true Brahmin, he said, would tell the truth, even though this might disqualify him for discipleship.

The story of the Sage Narada is also told here. Even though he knew all the Shastras (scriptures) he had not understood the truth of the *atma*. The secret is taught to him by the Sage Sanatkumara. The sage tells him to start from *ahara shuddhi* or purity of food which would lead to purity of mind and intellect, which would eventually lead him to union with the Supreme.

> Pure food creates pure intellect. Pure intellect creates strong memory. Strong memory cuts all the knots of the heart. Sanatkumara's description of the Brahman.
>
> He is below, above, behind, in front, on the right, on the left, He is everything. If I put the word "I" instead of He, I can say, I am below, I am above, I am behind, I am in front, I am on the right, I am on the left, I am everything. If I put the word "Self" instead of He, I can say, The Self is below, above, behind, in front, to the right, to the left. The Self is everything. The personal Self is the same as the impersonal Self. (*Atma* and Brahman are equal).
>
> He, who knows this cares nothing for death, cares nothing for disease, cares nothing for misery, and looks at everything with the eye of the Self, gets everything, goes everywhere, yet remains one, though multiplied threefold, fivefold, sevenfold, elevenfold, hundredfold!

The description of the Self as the space in the heart is given here.

> In this body, in this town of the Spirit, there is a little house shaped like a lotus and in that house there is a little space. One should know what is there.

> What lies in that space, does not decay when the body decays, nor does it fall when the body falls. That space is the home of the Spirit. The Self is there, beyond decay and death, sin and sorrow, hunger and thirst. His aim is truth, His will is truth. Man can live in the body as long as he obeys the law, as a man may live in a farm or a town or province, if he obeys the law.

> This body is under sentence of death. Nevertheless it is the house of the immortal, the un-embodied. As long as He is in the body, He likes and dislikes. As long as He is in the body there is no escape. When He has cast off the body, likes and dislikes do not touch Him.

Briha means "large" and *Brihadaranyaka Upanishad* is the largest of all the Upanishads. Normally, all Upanishads with the exception of the *Ishavasya* come at the end of the Aranyaka portion of the Vedas. That is one reason why they are called Vedanta, or the end of the Vedas. However, the *Brihadaranyaka* replaces the whole Aranyaka portion of the *Shukla Yajur Veda*.

It starts with the famous *mantra*, "*asato ma sad gamaya, tamaso ma jyotir gamaya, mrityor ma amrutam gamaya*"—"Lead me from the unreal to the real, from darkness to light and from death to immortality."

This Upanishad contains six chapters. The first two chapters are known as "Madhu Kanda." Madhu means honey and it refers to the sweet juicy stage of bliss. The one who has experienced the *atman* will feel the whole world to be sweet like honey. The world also will find that such people are sweet to them.

> The Self entered into everything even the tips of the fingernails. He is hidden like the razor in its case. Though He lives in the world and maintains it, the ignorant cannot see Him.

> When He is breathing, they name Him breath; when speaking, they name Him speech; when seeing, they name Him eye, when hearing, they name Him ear, when thinking, they name Him mind. But He is not wholly there. All these names are the names of His actions.

> The Self is dearer than all else; dearer than son, dearer than wealth, dearer than anything. Self is God; therefore one should worship the Self as Love. Who worships Self as love, his love shall never perish.

> Even today, he who knows that he is the Spirit, becomes Spirit, becomes everything. Neither gods nor men can prevent him for he has become themselves.

This Upanishad used the method known as *neti, neti,* "not this, not this" in order to get to the truth of the *atman.* By negating all the lower worlds and the different personality sheaths, one can eventually get to the truth of the Supreme. This realisation leads to the feeling that this phenomenal world and all the creatures in it are *anandarasa* or the essence of bliss.

> They describe Spirit as, "not this not this." The first means, there is nothing except Spirit, the second means "there is nothing beyond Spirit." They call the Spirit, the Truth of all truths.

This Upanishad also gives two examples of women who were learned in debate. The woman named Gargi could discuss the nature of the Brahman on an equal footing with the *rishis* in King Janaka's council.

The Sage Yajnavalkya had two wives, Kartyayani and Maitreyi. The former was an ordinary woman but the latter demanded from her husband that she be taught the truth of the Brahman and thus he agreed to teach her.

The teaching is put beautifully in the nature of a story as is found in many of the Upanishads. Yajnavalkya divides his wealth between his two wives and is all set to leave the house and go to the forest and is stopped by Maitreyi who begs him to tell her the nature of that happiness which is forcing him to leave the comfort of his house and family and take to the life of a recluse.

Maitreyi asks him, "Lord if I were to get the wealth of the whole world, would it make me immortal?"

Yajnavalkya answers, "No! Your life will be like the life of the wealthy. There is no hope of immortality through wealth."

Maitreyi says, "What can I do with that which cannot make me immortal? Tell me what you know of immortality."

He stays back and teaches her how to differentiate between love and attachment.

> The love that a woman bears to her husband and to her children, and the husband likewise to his wife and children does not rise from anything inherent in the object but from the feeling of satisfaction it gives to the person. This is because the very nature of the self or *atman* is love. Love towards any object is always mixed with hate or indifference or disgust. Some objects arouse a feeling of love and others of hate or disgust. However, when the Self or *atman* is realised, all things become equally dear.
>
> It is certain that the wife does not love her husband for himself but loves him for herself only. The husband does not love his

wife for herself but loves her for himself only. The father does not love his sons for themselves but loves them for himself only.

Maitreyi, a man does not love anything for itself, but loves it for himself only. This Self O Maitreyi deserves to be known. If the Self is known everything else is known.

The Self is nearer than all else, dearer than son, dearer than wealth, dearer than anything else. The Self is God. Therefore one should worship the Self as Love. Who worships the Self as Love, his love can never perish.

This earth is the honey of all beings; all beings are the honey of this earth. The bright eternal Self that lives in this body and the bright eternal Self that is in the earth are one and the same. That is immortality. That is Spirit. That is all.

O Maitreyi! He is the one who knows everything. So how can the knower be known?

Later on, Yajnavalkya went to the court of King Janaka and was questioned by various people including the female ascetic Gargi as well as the king himself.

When questioned about the state of the person at the end of his life, he gives many interesting examples.

As a caterpillar having reached the end of a blade of grass, takes hold of another blade, then draws its body from the first, so the Self having reached the end of his body, takes hold of another body, then draws itself from the first.

How should the person get freed from this circle of birth and death?

When all the desires of the heart are gone, mortal becomes immortal; man becomes Spirit, even in this life. As the skin of a snake is peeled off and lies dead on an ant-hill, so this body falls and lies on the ground but the Self is bodiless, immortal, full of light, he is of the Spirit so becomes the Spirit. If a man knows that he is He, why should he hunger for a body?

One of the stories related in the last portion of this Upanishad shows us how the same advice can be interpreted by people according to their relative state of consciousness. Once the gods, humans and demons approached the creator Brahma and asked for advice. He merely gave the syllable, "da" to all of them and left them to make what they would out of this cryptic advice. The gods who were noted for their lack of self-control took it as an advice to practice *da-ma* or self-restraint. The humans whose nature is always to accumulate property decided that the grandsire's advice to them was to give *da-na* or charity and the demons whose nature is noted for its cruelty thought that Brahma had exhorted them to show *da-ya* or compassion.

Another rather strange *mantra* in this Upanishad tells us to take any pain as part of the penance extracted from us by Nature. In ancient times people used to perform many types of *tapas* or penance in order to get rid of their negative *karmas* but in modern times, none of us is capable of performing these great sacrifices. So Nature in her kindness makes us get diseases and thus reduces our karmic bonds. Negative *karma* acquired in this life can be paid for through bodily illness and discomfort. Thus, injury and disease should be regarded as a type of *tapas*, which is not self-imposed but given by a compassionate Nature to help us reduce our karmic balance. When we begin to practise this mentality, we will develop the capacity to bear illness with fortitude.

The last chapter of the Upanishad gives the knowledge of the Panchagni Vidya and the duties of householders who desire to beget noble children.

Many of the great statements and ideas which have become popular amongst ordinary people are to be found in the Upanishads. Of these, the most important *mantras* are known as the *mahavakyas* or important truths which describe the non-duality of the *atma* and the Brahman. Of these, four are considered to be especially important and are to be found, one in each of the Vedas. Normally these are only given to those who take up *sannyasa* or a life of renunciation.

The *mahavakya* from the *Taitareeya Upanishad* of the *Rig Veda* is, *prajnanam Brahma*—"Brahman is pure, divine consciousness."

The next *mahavakya* comes from the *Brihadaranyaka Upanishad* of the *Shukla Yajur Veda* and states, *Aham Brahmasmi*—"I am Brahman."

The third *mahavakya* comes from the *Chandogya Upanishad* of the *Sama Veda* and is *tat twam asi*—"That thou art."

The fourth *mahavakya* comes from the *Mandukya Upanishad* of the *Atharva Veda* and says, *Ayam atma cha Brahma*—"the *atma* and the Brahman are one." Thus, it will be seen that the Upanishads contain the ultimate message and purpose of the Vedas. They are therefore known as Vedanta—firstly because they are placed at the end of the Vedas, coming after the Aranyakas, and secondly because they are the goal or end to which the Veda points.

Scientific development of the modern age has not posed any threat to the metaphysical doctrines of the Upanishads. On the contrary, modern science is approaching nearer and nearer to Advaitic thought thus allowing the modern mind to grasp its gist easily. Previously, it could only be understood through a study of the Vedas.

In the beginning science was of the opinion that all substances on earth were different from each other. Then these substances boiled down to seventy-two elements which presented the myriad objects. The combinations of these were said to be the cause of the differences. Then came the atomic age in which the scientists discovered that the origin of all these seventy-two elements is the same—pure energy, which is known as *Shakti* in Hinduism. As the Divine Mother told the saints in the *Kenopanishad*, *Shakti* is pure consciousness which includes all knowledge and is the basis of all animate and inanimate creation.

This universal energy which atomic science has discovered is a universal consciousness about which all the Upanishads have been talking thousands of years ago. It is known as Advaita or that which is non-dual. It is beyond the reach of the physicist as well as the philosopher. It manifests in this plurality of objects, which is our normal day-to-day experience. This is what is known as *dwaita* or duality. If duality was the absolute truth, there would be no need for us to consult the Vedas or the Upanishads. We need their help only because they point to and establish the fact that the individual soul (*jivatma*) merges with the cosmic soul (*Paramatma*) and becomes the Advaitic non-dual "Brahman." In this way the Upanishads are way ahead of modern scientific research, which is still trying to find a universal basis for everything.

"Look at God's poem, It neither decays nor dies", says the Veda. Our thoughts only touch the fringes of this divine poem which connects the entire universe and runs through all human beings like a thread which binds a necklace of beads. Now and again one bead might come in contact with that thread and recognise its divinity and the fact that it is joined to all the beads in the universe.

When one is united with the beloved, all physical and mental boundaries disappear. Likewise, in self-realisation, we forget our separateness and merge with the Supreme Self.

Brihadaranyaka Upanishad

Neils Bohr said, "Anyone who is not shocked by the quantum theory has not understood it."

Einstein said,

It seems hard to look into God's cards. But I cannot for a moment believe that he plays dice, and makes use of telepathic means, as the current quantum theory alleges he does!

The divine melody, with uniform light,
Spreads over the whole world,
It disseminates the wisdom that inspires the brave,
And with this melody the pious devotees expand
Their field of knowledge.

Rig Veda

Loka Samasthath Sukhino Bhavantu!

ॐ

Paramatmaaya Namaha!

CHAPTER VI

The Puranas

The one Supreme Reality has been styled,
By various names by the learned seers,
They call One by many names.
They speak of Him as Indra, the Lord resplendent,
Mitra, the surveyor, Varuna, the virtuous,
Agni, the adorable.
Garutatman, the celestial and well-sung,
Yama, the ordainer, Mararishvan, the cosmic breath.

Rig Veda

India conquered and dominated China culturally for twenty
centuries without ever having to send a single soldier across
her border.

Hu Shih, Former ambassador of China to USA

The Vedas and Upanishads were not freely available to the
common people. Even when they were available, they were
incomprehensible to most since the language was obscure. After
the Vedic age of Hinduism, we get the Puranic age where the
great sage Vyasa wrote all the great Puranas in which were given

the stories of the gods in which the truths of the Vedas were interwoven. The sage of the Puranas did this with such skill that people did not realise that they were actually living a Vedic life when they followed the exhortations of the Puranas. The Puranic sages like Vyasa and Valmiki were as great as the Vedic *rishis*. It is only due to their compassion that we are able to comprehend the esoteric meaning of the Vedas. The one God has become the many and we worship all the gods, not necessarily knowing the important fact that all these gods are only aspects of the One God. The concept of the one Absolute cannot easily be grasped by the mind of the human being because of the dichotomy created in the mind between man and the world and the world and God. Hence, Vyasa gave us the Puranas. They actually magnify and simplify the pithy statements of the Vedas and Upanishads. The Puranas elaborated on these statements in the form of stories and anecdotes. The Vedic injunctions like restraint, patience, compassion, chastity and other *dharmas* were illustrated in the Puranas through the lives of the great and noble men and women. As a result of listening to these stories, people developed a desire to shape their own lives according to the *dharmas* which they portrayed.

The Puranas also give the idea to the common man that they are in reality the Supreme Spirit as reiterated in the Vedas. The stories created by the Puranic *rishis* were a device to circumvent the opposition of their listeners to the simple yet shocking truth of who they were in reality. It is common to oppose a truth but impossible to resist a story. As we have seen, Vyasa was the greatest of the Puranic *rishis* and he dramatised these revelations of the Upanishads and wove stories around them which could become familiar and understandable even to the poorest intellect. In fact, even children could appreciate them. Vyasa declared that if you listen carefully to a story, you would never be the same again. The story would weave its way into your heart and break down the barriers you have erected between yourself and the divine. Stories have a way of slipping through our defences and tearing open the fences we have formed round our hearts.

The forms of the gods are actually filled with great spiritual and scientific wisdom. The Vedas speak of the supernal ether or *akasa* as the abode of *vac* or sound. This is the storehouse of all sounds and is the permanent place of the light of all lights. It is the cause of all causes. From this mass of formless light emerge the rays which fashion all forms during the course of evolution. *Deva* means "the shining one" and the gods or *devas* are emanations from this light. That formless light emits rays which weave into the forms and features of the various gods. India's spiritual vision has evolved through these forms. Western educated people are unable to understand the great truths underlying these forms and consider them to be the result of a puerile imagination. They condemn them to the sea of meaningless figments of superstition coming from primitive minds. Who could believe in gods with several heads and hands and even animal heads? This Western misconception can be compared to the ignorance that uneducated people have about the significance of mathematical symbols, taking them to be mere scribblings of an immature pen.

According to Puranic perception, a deity is a facet of the Brahman, the Supreme Reality, which has a potential for infinite expressions. The human being is one of these expressions and is placed in an evolutionary stage that can take a leap forward and embrace this supreme unconditioned reality of the Brahman. This dive into the Supreme needs some springboards and the forms of the gods are the aids by which the human mind can escape from the conditioning patterns of its own thoughts and evolve to higher levels. The divine forms of the gods are a kind of symbolic language like algebraic symbols, devised by the *rishis* to help and guide us in our evolutionary journey. The divinity enshrined in the form of the deity expands the consciousness of the earnest seeker to its maximum—to the unconditioned level of the Supreme which transcends all forms!

The Itihasas or epics known as the *Mahabharata* and the *Ramayana* are integral parts of the Hindu religion as are the Vedas and the Upanishads. The *Ramayana* is the first poem to be written in the world. It is the story of Sri Rama who was an *avatara* or incarnation of Vishnu. It is a book that has influenced the life of every Indian from north to south and has even spread all over South East Asia. The *Vayu Purana* declares that we cannot appreciate the Vedas if we have not read the Puranas. The actual meaning of *itihasa* is "thus must we live". The Itihasa has to explain the four goals of life which in Hinduism are *dharma*, or virtue and righteousness, *artha* or the acquisition of wealth, *kama* or pleasure and *moksha* or liberation from this mortal life. It will be seen that *artha* and *kama*, the two materialistic goals are hemmed by the higher goals of *dharma* and *moksha*. Thus, if we follow *dharma* in our pursuit of both wealth and pleasure, it will lead us to *moksha* automatically. The need to follow *dharma* or the cosmic law is what is stressed in both the Puranas and the epics. These two great sages, Vyasa and Valmiki, presented the truth of the Vedas in a more palatable and understandable language, in the form of stories which the layman could understand. In this way they sought to preserve the truths of the Vedas and popularise them.

The Itihasa or epic called the the *Ramayana* was written by Valmiki who is known as the first of all poets. Religion as presented in the *Ramayana* and the Puranas is what is followed by countless Hindus today. Most of them have no idea of the great glories contained in the Vedas. But since the Vedic truths were embedded in the Puranas, the Hindus still strictly adhere to certain rites and rituals by following which they can progress on the scale of evolution even without having a complete knowledge of the Vedas.

It is generally believed that India has no recorded history. But our Itihasas or epics—the *Ramayana* and the *Mahabharata* give a faithful account of the history of the India of those times. Valmiki was a contemporary of Sri Rama so it is actually a first-hand account of the history of that age. Vyasa was a contemporary of the Pandavas and of Lord Krishna so he is also giving a first-hand description of the historical events which took place during his time. Western history contains nothing to match the stories of the Itihasas and Puranas which not only appeal to everyone but help us to mould our characters accordingly. Scientists and even Western-oriented philosophers are only just beginning to understand and appreciate the deep psychological and metaphysical wisdom preserved and transmitted in the form of Puranic lore and legend. In these Puranas are found the life and teachings of the great *avataras* or incarnations of God. They indeed are the word (*Aum*) become flesh whenever virtue declines, as Lord Krishna declared in the *Bhagavad-Gita*. They are the life force flowing through humanity's collective body; the true homes of our consciousness which are capable of taking us to that impersonal Absolute which our untutored minds cannot comprehend.

Rama and Krishna are the best loved of the divine incarnations of Vishnu. Krishna can be regarded as the perfect expression of the Infinite and thus he is completely identified with Vishnu so that the two can be regarded as one. These two are the most famous of the Hindu gods who are worshipped to this day.

When the Western missionaries first came to India, they were appalled to find that if history as given in the Itihasas was true, then a glorious civilization existed in India at the time when Europeans were barbarians running around brandishing crude weapons. They realised that the only way they could enforce their religion on the country would be to cast scorn at the two great gods of Hinduism—Rama and Krishna. So they took pains to prove that they were purely mythical characters materialised by the fertile brains of Valmiki and Vyasa. Unfortunately, the Hindu elite believed them since they were also inculcated with the false belief that all civilizations started with the Greeks.

Indian history as recorded by Valmiki in the *Ramayana* clearly states all the details of Rama's lineage. He belonged to the Surya Vamsa and was the 64th ruler of the Ikshwaku dynasty. The names of his predecessors are also given. What more proof is needed to establish his reality? Yet, the Western historians were bent on proving him to be a myth. There are twenty-three places in India which have memorials to commemorate the events in his life. The whole of Hindu India as well as many parts of South East Asia believe in the historicity of Rama and Krishna. Most of the festivals in India revolve round the events in the lives of these great incarnations. This is the heritage of every Indian regardless of creed or religion since both of them belonged to a period when the world had never heard of Mohammed or Christ.

Thanks to modern techniques, today we can scientifically guage the data found in the *Ramayana*, and it has been proved that there did indeed exist a divine personality called Rama, who ruled India more than ten thousand years ago. Thanks to Valmiki's extraordinary astronomical observations, it is possible today to pinpoint the exact dates given in the *Ramayana*. Valmiki was not only the first poet, he was also the first Indian astronomer and thus the first world astronomer. His study of planetary configurations has stood the test of time. Latest computer software has corroborated his calculations. Valmiki gives Dasaratha's zodiac sign as Pisces and his star as Revathi. Rama left for his exile at one of the conjuctions of these stars. Modern calculations have shown that this configuration took place on Jan. 5th, 5089 BC. Valmiki says that Rama was twenty-five years old at that time. He also mentions the solar eclipse which took place at the time of Rama's fight with the *asuras,* Khara and Dhushana. He said that it was *amavasya* (new moon) and Mars was in the middle flanked by Venus on one side and Mercury on the other. When this data was fed into the software, it came out with the date Oct. 7th, 5077 BC.

By following other planetary configurations as mentioned by Valmiki in other places, we can see that Ravana was killed on Dec. 4th, 5076 BC. Rama completed his exile on Jan. 2nd, 5075 in the bright phase (*shukla paksha*) of the month of Chaitra, the month of his birth and returned to Ayodhya at the age of thirty-nine.

Now let us take a look at the life of Krishna, the next great god of Hinduism. Most Hindus swallowed what was told to them by the western historians and believed that he was only a myth. Luckily, this century, which is famous for its thirst for investigations, has unearthed many astonishing facts. These investigations prove, for those who need proof that our scriptures were absolutely correct in their description of the fabulous city of Dwaraka, which was built by Krishna as the stronghold of the Yadavas. They also prove that Krishna was indeed the superman or supreme incarnation of God as our scriptures declare.

The modern city of Dwaraka is in Saurashtra and is a great pilgrim destination since our scriptures declare it to be the seat of the Yadava clan and Lord Krishna's capital. However, according to the stories mentioned in many of the Puranas, like the *Mahabharata, Harivamsa, Vishnu Purana*, and so on, the fabled city of Dwaraka was washed away into the sea soon after the Lord left his mortal body as he himself had predicted.

In 1983, some excavations were done outside the modern city of Dwaraka, which revealed the existence of a glorious city of ancient times. The most interesting discovery was that of a set of seven temples built one on top of the other at different periods of time. The bottom-most one was the most interesting since it showed many pottery shards and seals that clearly pointed to the existence of a fantastic city at about the time mentioned in the *Mahabharata*. These findings encouraged the marine archaeology centre of the National Institute of Oceanography to take up serious excavating work along the coast of the island known as Bet Dwaraka.

The strongest archaeological support for the existence of the legendary city of Dwaraka comes from the structures discovered in the late 1980s under the seabed off the coast of modern Dwaraka in Gujarat by a team of archaeologists and divers led by Dr S.R. Rao, one of India's most respected archaeologists.

Conducting twelve expeditions from 1983–90, Rao identified two underwater settlements, one near the present-day Dwaraka and the other off the nearby island of Bet Dwaraka. This tallies with the two Dwarakas mentioned in the epic.

Another important find by the divers was a conch seal that established the submerged township's connection with the Dwaraka of the *Mahabharata*. The seal corroborates the reference made in the ancient text, the *Harivamsa*, that every citizen of Dwaraka had to carry such a seal for purposes of identification. Krishna had declared that only one who carried such a seal could enter the city. A similar seal has been found onshore.

From 1998–2001, many underwater explorations revealed the existence of a highly civilized city that existed at that site with great maritime connections with many other countries, which must have been washed away by a tsunami or something similar. In fact, the *Mahabharata* gives an eye-witness account of the disappearance of Dwaraka under the horrified eyes of Arjuna. Modern excavations show that Dwaraka was a large, well-fortified city with an excellent drainage system, massive gates, and a wall stretching about one hundred eighty miles. It was a sprawling city with gardens, orchards, and bastions and a population of about ten thousand people. Many clues also indicate that it must have been a bustling port. Ancient anchor stones give ample evidence of this.

All these findings have suddenly roused a lot of interest among Hindus both in India and abroad since it is solid proof of the existence of one of the favourite gods in the Hindu pantheon, namely Lord Krishna.

Around the same time, archaeologists from other countries were also busy. Along the coast of the Bay of Cambay and off the coast of modern Dwaraka, they found evidence of a settlement deep under the sea. In seventy feet of water, archaeologists discovered sandstone walls and cobbled streets. Looking up the descriptions of the city of Dwaraka as found in the ancient Hindu scriptures, they realized that this must be the remains of the legendary city of Dwaraka ruled by the great God King, Krishna. Wood and pottery shards were found that can be dated back 32,000 years, again proving that the time spans given in ancient Hindu scriptures are true even though most Westerners dismissed them as being absurd. The city had existed from 32,000–9000 BCE. This discovery proves that the life of Krishna is not mere mythology but it is a true, historical record of a towering personality who had lived on this holy land of India. For many years now, Western Indologists have deliberately shut their eyes to the glory that was ancient India, but hopefully these findings should help them to believe, if they want to believe!

Dr. Narhari Achar, professor of physics at the University of Memphis, Tennessee, has dated the Mahabharata war using astronomy and regular planetarium software. According to his research conducted in 2004–05, the titanic clash between the Pandavas and the Kauravas took place in 3067 BCE. Using the same software, Achar places the year of Krishna's birth at 3112 BCE. Actually, our Puranas set it at a far earlier date.

As has been said, the *Mahabharata* was written by Vyasa. It contains one lakh of couplets. Not content with this Vyasa went on to compose four more lakhs of *shlokas* and these constitute the eighteen Maha Puranas. The *Mahabharata* has been called the fifth Veda, which contains the essence of all the scriptures. It is really an authority on the history of Indian culture and religion. In it is found a part of the life of the great *avatara*— Lord Krishna. Vyasa was his contemporary. The great advice of Lord Krishna to Arjuna, known as the *Sreemad Bhagavad-Gita,* is found in the middle of this enormous book and contains the essence of the Upanishads.

Worship of divine forms is part of the practical aspect of Hindu spirituality. The Upanishads open us to the path of knowledge (*jnana marga*) and the Puranas lead us to the path of devotion (*bhakti marga*). Both these paths lead to the same goal—the liberation of the mind from its social and biological conditioning and its expansion to unlimited freedom. Many of the Puranas depict the war between the negative and positive aspects of the mind in its relentless struggle to expand to the unlimited freedom of the divine. These dual aspects are known as the *asuras* and the *devas.*

The picture of God implies unconditioned freedom. He has the freedom to assume any form He chooses. To limit Him to only one form is a failing of the human mind. The universe of innumerable forms is an expression of God's freedom to take on any form He chooses. The word paintings of Vyasa have given us graphic details of the forms of the various gods which have provided us with a fund of spiritual wealth from which countless Hindus have derived unfailing inspiration. Our mind has to learn to focus on some form that inspires us, before proceeding to the formless. This is the experience of every sincere seeker. It is based on a great psychological truth. Conditioned as we are to so many forms in the world, the mind of the human being is incapable of concentrating on that which is formless. Thus, even worship and ritual in Hinduism are scientifically based. Hence it is that Lord Krishna tells Arjuna in the *Bhagavad-Gita* that worship of God with form is better than worship of the formless simply because it is easier to practice.

The Puranas are studded with stories of an amazing variety of gods and goddesses who are dynamic expressions of the Truth as presented in the Vedas. These stories are not mere fairy-tales but the revelations of the Puranic *rishis*. Vyasa saw the totality of Nature—both her outer, physical phenomena as well as her inner, invisible psyche. These forms were evolved in Vyasa's mind while in a superconscious state in an attempt to give the common human being a glimpse into the Truth which was ever blazing in his heart. The symbols of the various gods like Ganesha and Hanuman are the visible signs for expressing the invisible. One who meditates on these symbols will be able to penetrate the subtle psychic presence in them and come to a comprehensive view of the totality from which they are derived. This is the truth underlying all the idols and often bizarre forms of the gods with many arms and heads and so on. They translate the Infinite in terms of the finite and the spiritual in terms of the material. By fostering our faith in the symbols and form of the deities, we can establish a rapport between the deity and us which will help to draw us closer to the Supreme at which they are pointing. There is a beautiful posture of Shiva as the divine archer where he kneels on the ground holding his bow and pointing his arrow to the heavens as if exhorting us to look above. In fact we find that all the gods are at one time or other meditating on the Supreme, thus showing us the important fact that they are only emanations from that Brahman and have to get their power from That alone.

Professor Eliade declares,

> Images, symbols and myths are not irresponsible creatures of the psyche. They resound to a need and fulfil the function of bringing to light the most hidden modalities of our being.

Thus, many Puranas were written and the Truth was photographed from different angles and from various standpoints so that it could be appreciated from diverse intellectual levels. In this unique way, Vyasa succeeded in getting the incomprehensible Supreme reflected in the liquid poetry of his Puranic literature and created myriad forms for worship which would be suitable for different personalities.

Unfortunately, the numerous forms of the gods found in Hinduism have always been a stumbling block to those who had a genuine interest in learning about the religion. Vedanta establishes the Supreme Truth as the formless Brahman. Then what is the necessity for so many gods? The formless has taken on forms only to cater to the weakness of the human mind, which is incapable of meditating or even thinking of something which is nameless and formless. The mind is bound by what is known as *nama* (name) and *rupa* (form). It is powerless to think of something which is beyond name and form. However, the human being longs to have some contact with its Maker and thus it is that Hinduism says that the formless "One" of the Vedas is capable of taking on innumerable forms. In fact, it would be a sacrilege to confine that Infinite to just one form, limited to one space and time. IT is beyond time and space and can and will take on as many forms as the human being wants. All of us are created in different models with different likes and dislikes. Hinduism gives infinite freedom to the individual to choose the type of form that he or she likes to worship. The divine is capable of many roles and all roles at the same time. He can be many things and all things simultaneously and separately to all human kind. Such is the glory of this Being, the nature of which is beyond the grasp of the mind. To limit Him to just one or other of the roles which everyday religion thrusts upon Him is to do Him an injustice and betrays our total ignorance of His mighty powers.

Our sages knew how important it was to create ideals of perfection for a society to help it to evolve. Vyasa was a great psychologist. The process of lifting ourselves to our ideal is accomplished by unflinching devotion to that ideal embodied in Rama or Krishna or any of the great *avataras* or gods. The fact that human beings are created in different models with different personalities was well known to the Puranic *rishis*. It is totally unscientific to accept all of us to follow one single path and gain liberation. Thus, we find many paths to liberation advocated in Hinduism to suit every type of personality quite unlike the Semitic religions that advocate only one path and one way for every single person regardless of his or her personality. The insistent message underlying all of Vyasa's forms was that all these forms would lead to the same formless Absolute! Thus, we see how very scientific Hinduism is and how consistent in its insistence on finding the supreme goal. Due to their great love for mankind, the Puranic sages devised infinite ways in which to reach the same high goal of union with the Absolute. The *devas* or gods are naturally much higher on the evolutionary scale than the ordinary human being. But it is also a fact that they can help themselves by helping human beings. They thrive on our love and give us more energy and protection in return for the love that we give them.

Lord Krishna says in the *Bhagavad-Gita*, "Whatever form my devotee worships with faith, I enter into that form and make his faith firm!" What a catholic statement this is—filled with compassion and wisdom.

We often think that Advaita Vedanta only advocates meditation on the formless using the great *mahavakyas* from the Upanishads. But this is not quite correct. Adi Shankara, who was the great protagonist of Advaita Vedanta, established temples to many of the great gods of Hinduism in different parts of India. He has also written many hymns eulogising these gods, all filled with devotion and love. The fact is that Advaita Vedanta does indeed recognise the existence of a creator, preserver, ruler and controller of this phenomenal universe. How could it not? It is so obvious that this grand phenomenon of the cosmos must have some cause. The perfect order, attention to minute details, breathtaking beauty, unique design and intricate workmanship presupposes a cosmic intelligence which we cannot even imagine. Advaita calls this intelligence Iswara or God. This universe emanated out of That, is maintained for a certain period of time and then re-absorbed into That. These three duties of creation, maintenance and destruction are given to the three main gods of Hinduism. Hinduism has a genius for clothing the Infinite in infinite forms and the creator in the Hindu trinity is known as Brahma (not to be mistaken for the Brahman or

Absolute). The trinity consists of Brahma, the creator, Vishnu or Narayana, the principle of harmony and Shiva, the Lord of destruction. Numerous incidents and stories are woven to interest the devotees of these gods and make them understand scientific facts in an easy way.

In the transcendental world, it is Brahma who captures the vibrations of the Supreme at the beginning of every creation and manifests all creation. On this planet, the *rishis* were the ones who captured these vibrations and imprinted them on their memories. Later on, all this was codified by Vyasa and hence he got the name Veda Vyasa. It was he who divided the hymns into four books, which are collectively known as the Veda. Each of these divisions were given to one of his disciples to memorise since with the passage of time people's memories started to become less and there was no one who was capable of memorising all the four Vedas. Thus, each of the Vedas has come down to us through these disciples.

Science has proved that when certain sound vibrations are made near plants, they induce faster growth and higher yield. Some other vibrations retard growth. This shows that sound vibrations are capable of creation, preservation and destruction. Thus, Brahma was able to create the whole universe with the Vedic sounds by his *tapas* or austerity. Since Brahma is a manifestation from the Brahman solely for the purpose of creation, he has total mastery of the Vedas.

In Hinduism, creation is not linear as we find in the West. *Shrishti, sthiti* and *samhara*—creation, maintenance and destruction—follow each other in order in a cyclical manner.

Each creation has its own Brahma and when he takes on a form, all the Vedic sounds are born in his heart. These show him the path of creation. Out of the infinite numbers of *mantras* in the Veda, only a few were revealed to the *rishis*. The *Yoga Shastra* says that the microcosm is only a mirror of the macrocosm and if the space which exists in the cosmos and the space which exists in our mind are unified, we will be able to hear the sounds in space. Only those who feel united with everything in the universe will be able to hear this.

Vishnu or Narayana is the sustainer or preserver in the Hindu Trinity. Vishnu embodies the source of beauty and order in creation. His body is the dark blue of limitless space and the galaxies hang from his neck like innumerable strands of jewels. His four arms show that he holds sway over the four quarters of the universe. His qualities draw forth love, forgiveness, beauty and compassion for all creatures. His image is found in temples all over India. Usually he is represented as a handsome man of divine radiance who holds in four hands the symbols of power and beauty. One hand holds the conch, which emits the divine call to all people to awake to the divinity within. The *chakra* or wheel is the wheel of Time, which is the only annihilator of all creatures. Another hand holds the *gada* or mace to punish wrong-doers and make them return to the right path. The fourth hand holds a beautiful lotus, the symbol of purity. The lotus has its origin in the dirt and muck of the pond but frees itself from all this and lifts up its face to the light of the sun. So also the human being even though filled with animal passions is capable of shaking these off and rising to the divinity within. A necklace of precious gems adorns Vishnu's neck and stands for the different galaxies. His vehicle is the cosmic eagle, Garuda. He rests upon the serpent of Infinity called Ananta, floating on the cosmic waters, which is the field of all possibilities, in perfect peace, dreaming the dream of the world. He is universally kind, approachable, understanding and serene. He is the protector who rescues us in time of need and supports and strengthens us from within when external resources fail. Though perfect and untouched by any pollution, yet due to his love for his creation he allows himself to be born as a human being and undergoes all the problems that a human being would have to face in order to help his devotees. Vishnu has taken on many *avataras* or incarnations since He is the one who has to save the world when any danger threatens. Ten *avataras* are commonly mentioned but the *Bhagavad Purana* says that He has taken an infinite number of *avataras*. Every time one of his devotees needs Him and calls out to Him, He takes on an incarnation since the love He bears for this creation is unfathomable.

These ten *avataras* have a scientific basis. They are supposed to tell the story of evolution from aquatic creatures to amphibian and human and so on. Hence, the first *avatara* is that of the fish (*matsya*), then comes the tortoise (*kurma*), then the boar (*varaha*), then the man-lion (*narasimha*), then the dwarf man (*vamana*), the axe man (*parashurama*), the perfect man (Sri Rama), the strong man (Balarama), the totally evolved man (Sri Krishna), and finally the epitome of destruction (Kalki), who is yet to come or perhaps has already come.

From this we see that Vyasa had a very good idea of the theory of evolution, which is such a modern concept. The *Bhagavad Purana* gives the stories of all the great *avataras* of Vishnu and also the less well-known ones. It is the greatest of the Puranas and inculcates devotion in the hearts of the listeners.

Hinduism lays great stress on the repetition of the names of God which is known as *japa*. The name of God is itself God since sound and form have a definite connection according to the science of phonetics. The epic *Mahabharata* gives us the many names of Vishnu which is a very famous hymn chanted daily in thousands of Hindu homes. The vibrations have the power to keep away all negativity from the environment. This was given to the great Prince Yudhisthira by his grandsire, Bhishma who was a great sage, to a question put to him by Yudhisthira. "How can I find a joy which will never leave me and satisfy my deepest desires?"

It is in answer to this that Bhishma gives him the *Vishnu Sahasra Nama* or the thousand and one names of Vishnu, which has a purifying and transforming influence and fills the heart with joy. Anger will turn to compassion, greed to generosity and lust to love. Each of these names carries a deep significance and a continuous repetition of the names will fill the heart of both the chanter and the listener with joy.

Next we come to Shiva—the destructive aspect of creation. There can be no creation without a corresponding destruction. The universe keeps constructing and destroying itself. Every cell in our body has to die and be replaced by a new one if life is to go on. The same applies to the universe. Even the planets have a span of life; our sun also will burn itself out one day. So we see that destruction is an important and inevitable part of creation. The character of Shiva thus shows the great knowledge the *rishis* had about the nature of the universe. The characters of the gods are all based on scientific facts.

Shiva is the most enigmatic and most compassionate of all the gods. His form invokes fear and sometimes disgust since he is covered in ashes taken from the burning ghats (where bodies are cremated), has reptiles crawling over him, and has unkempt hair and strange-looking clothes made of animal skins. His followers are a set of fierce and odd-looking creatures, like ghouls, ghosts, dwarfs, misshapen creatures, the poor, the lowly, the despised and the shunned. This is why he is called the most compassionate. All the creatures that others shun and despise, all the creatures that people fear and run away in terror, all those that arouse revulsion and loathing in people, these are the ones which are loved by the Mahadeva (the Great Lord). There is none so poor or hateful that is shunned by Shiva. He loves all indiscriminately since they are all creations of the Supreme.

Though he is always seen with the ugly and the dirty, yet He is described as *satyam, shivam, sundaram*—the source of all truth, auspiciousness and beauty. This contradiction found in his form is part of his nature and a part of all nature in which beauty and ugliness are found side by side. However, when we see His true nature and open ourselves to this source of glory, it pours into our life. In order to do this, we have to remove the negativities within ourselves—anger, greed, lust and ego. The figure of the dancing Shiva or Nataraja is closely connected with the theories of modern quantum physics.

The pioneers of modern physics were astonished when they started going into the heart of matter. At its most elemental stage, matter could not be chopped up into self-contained units or atoms. The more they delved into the core of matter, the more they were fascinated by the strange, bizarre dance of the energy particles which were totally unpredictable. Now let us look at the famous dance of Shiva Nataraja, with his whirling locks and flaying arms. Modern photographic techniques have been able to project the lines emanating from Shiva's dancing figure and have shown that this dance actually shows the extraordinary ballet of the elementary particles as seen by the physicist.

The lives of Shiva's devotees are equally unique. They abounded in south India in the 12th century. Never can one see such devotion which cared nothing for public opinion but only knew how to love God (Shiva) with the utmost devotion. Nothing or nobody was allowed to come in the way of their love for their favourite deity. They allowed allegiance to none except Shiva. He in turn tested them to the utmost but of course always saved them from all peril.

The worship of Shiva is closely connected with the worship of Shakti or the divine mother. She is given many forms in the Puranas and thus represents the female energy of the universe. Shiva and Parvati signify the opposite poles of creation which are absolutely necessary for all creation. This is pictorially represented in the famous form of Ardhanareeswara in which Shiva is the left side of the figure and Parvati the right side. Each of the gods has his own Shakti or power. Parvati is the one who is connected with Shiva as his consort. They are supposed to be eternal lovers and are very often depicted in temple sculptures bound together in a passionate embrace. Unlike Semitic religions, Hinduism never suppressed sense pleasures because the body was always considered as the temple of the soul. The method of overcoming the lower nature is not through suppression but through sublimation. The analogy of the union between male and female is given as an example of the divine experience of bliss. The Upanishad says,

> As a man when in the embrace of a beloved wife, knows nothing within or without, so the person in the embrace of the Spirit knows nothing within or without.

In Shaivism, Shiva stands for the Supreme Brahman and Parvati for Shakti or the creative force of Brahman. Shakti or energy is the force that emanates spontaneously from the Supreme. Pure energy in any form is dangerous when not controlled. In Shaivism, it is Shiva that controls and conditions Shakti. He is the male aspect of the Brahman. He is depicted as having three eyes. *Maya* is his Shakti and contains the essence of duality, which is space, time and causality. Shiva's two eyes like ours can only see duality and when he keeps them open, the world of *maya* continues to exist. However, his third eye can only experience unity, so when he opens his third eye, the cosmos which can exist only in duality along with its creator—*maya*—will return to the plenum from which it was projected. As long as Shiva's third eye is open, nothing can exist. There is only *pralaya* or the undifferentiated consciousness of Absolute Reality. When he closes his third eye, Shiva comes under the sway of duality and his Shakti or *maya* comes to the forefront and the cosmos rises up. The sound of *Aum* is said to be the initiating sound that causes the universe of forms.

Shiva's eldest son is known as Ganesha and he has an elephant's head. This has an esoteric meaning. The Sanskrit letter *Aum* resembles the head of an elephant with an upraised trunk. Thus, Ganesha is *pranava swaroopa* (form of *Aum*). In the alphabet of forms devised by the *rishis*, Ganesha comes first. He represents the foremost initiating power of the Supreme at every stage of evolution. He is kept at the *muladhara chakra*, at the bottom of the spine and personifies the force of gravity.

Their second son is Kartikeya who is variously known as Subramania, Muruga, and so on. The story of Kartikeya is again the story of creation. He was born from the seed of Shiva which was ejected into the etheric sphere and carried by Vayu or the wind to Agni or fire, who dropped it into the water who took it and deposited it into the earth. Thus, the five elements of ether, air, fire, water and earth combined to nurture this child of Shiva—the Supreme. Similarly, each one of our gods hides great scientific truths behind their extraordinary appearances. Ganesha with his elephant head exemplifies the enlightened person who can discriminate truth from falsehood, ultimate truth from unreality. His big head is only a pictorial representation of this. His trunk is capable of lifting up big logs but it can also pick up a small pin from the ground. His position at the *muladhara chakra* or base of our spine denotes the power of gravity which holds us down to the earth.

The two great forces in nature are gravity and electromagnetism. If Ganesha represents the force of gravity, Kartikeya represents electromagnetism. His *vel* or spear works deeply within us like the powerful force that binds electrons and neutrons together. This power emanates from his spear-like energy expanding through the universe in the form of radio and light waves. We experience the dualities of light and dark, positive and negative which are the electromagnetic forces that issue from Karitkeya's *vel* (spear). His *vel* is an integral part of his form and is a most powerful weapon which glints when turned here and there and sends out these currents and magnetic waves. The worshipper of Kartikeya is capable of controlling these waves. These masters could actually decode these waves and see the pictures or hear the sounds without the necessity of using a TV screen or recorder.

Ganesha and Kartikeya are the most famous sons of Shiva and are worshipped all over India. Dharma Shasta or Ayyappa is a less well-known son who is mainly worshipped in the state of Kerala.

Though the Puranas are not really myths yet the subject of myths should be discussed in this chapter since they contain many stories which are found in other cultures and religions.

Ancient traditions the world over, not merely those from the realm of religion but also history, metaphysics, cosmology, medicines and sciences, are largely myths, sometimes quite strange and unbelievable, events with no apparent cause-and-effect or reciprocity, and beings beyond human conception. Opinions differ as to what exactly the term 'myth' means. A myth is a broad truth in regard to an event or a set of beings, men, animals or others, the factual dimensions of which have either been blurred or weeded out by time as irrelevant, and which survives in people's minds, texts, memory or traditions. In its essence it is truth's timeless pith, a mystique or philosophy, and the fiction amassing around its mere body. A strange dilemma, a myth is a truth but the term 'myth' actually means not 'truth'.

Many mythical traditions, Hindu, Christian, Islamic have myths like the Great Deluge submerging the earth and enveloping the entire cosmos under impenetrable darkness. They speak of a single human couple—progenitors of the race of man, and a Great Fish along with a boat alone surviving. The myth that explores the evolution of the earth and human race in many early civilizations, have many parallels and a strange unity in their themes. They all have similar interwoven events, mystic dimensions and a bizarre look. They cannot be termed as mere fiction or creations of fancy. Such worldwide unanimity of these traditions suggests that the event which the myth portrays, or at least its core context might have been once a reality, which being strange and rare, gathered around it a certain amount of divinity and mysticism, and was thus mythicised and re-defined or rather re-cycled in terms of a prevalent theology for promoting its dogmatic ends, or a human value.

> The mind is spontaneously liberated when its bondage with the visible world, its object, event and thoughts are terminated. It enters the realm of pure awareness free from the memory of the past and unconcerned about the uncertainties of the future.
>
> *Yogavasishta*

> The divine poet,
> Holding the sweet melodious flute,
> Reposing on the raging waves of the sea,
> Swiftly glides over the endless canopy of the sky.
>
> *Sama Veda*

Loka Samasthath Sukhino Bhavantu!

ॐ

Purushottamaaya Namaha!

CHAPTER VII

Bhakti

By contemplation on the *ananda* (bliss) aspect of the Supreme as in the case of a devotee, the *yogi* becomes aware of the bliss which pervades the manifested worlds.

Shiva Sutra

The mind is nothing but a derivative and differentiated form of centralised pure consciousness and essentially of the same nature as that consciousness.

The human being is not only a head but also a heart which yearns for loving fulfilment. The path of devotion called *bhakti marga* is given to satisfy this craving of the heart. Love always asks for a reciprocal approach and even in devotion, which is love for God, we ask for some response from God. How can the unattached and immovable Brahman supply this? Vyasa wrote the Puranas in order to supply this basic need in the human being. We have already touched upon the main gods in the previous chapter but we still have to find out why so many gods were given in the Puranas. This is a point which has baffled all Western seekers of Hinduism. But it must be understood that even though Hinduism depicts many gods, all of them point and postulate the one Supreme Brahman or Paramatma—the Supreme Soul.

In the *Ramayana,* the question is asked, "Who is the *Veda Vedya* or the one who has to be known through a study of the Vedas?" The question was answered, "When the Supreme Being, who has to be known through the Vedas, took birth in this world, He came in the form of Rama, the son of Dasaratha." In the *Bhagavad-Gita*, Lord Krishna says, *Vedaischa sarvai ahameva vedyaha.* "In all the Vedas I am the only one to be known."

Thus, all the great incarnations identified themselves with the Supreme Being and claimed no separate existence for themselves. This can be said of all the great gods of the Hindu faith. They all point to the Supreme. There is a very beautiful picture of Lord Shiva, the divine archer who points his arrow at the Absolute, thus pointing out to everyone what they should aim for. Thus, we find that whenever any of the gods are extolled in the Puranas, most of the adjectives used for them can also be applied to the Brahman. The Vedas labelled That Supreme as *sat-chit-ananda*—existence-consciousness-bliss. Its aspect as bliss is emphasised when IT takes on a form. When any person whether Hindu or otherwise clings to one form alone and does not realise that it is only a pointer to the Supreme, he is like a person who clings to the signpost thinking that he has reached his destination.

In the twelfth chapter of the *Sreemad Bhagavad-Gita*, Arjuna asks a pertinent question as to which of the two is preferable, "Worship of God with form or worship of the formless, immutable Brahman?"

Lord Krishna gives a very appropriate answer. He replies that both are equally good and will lead to the same goal of

liberation but of the two, worship of God with form is better
for the human being for the very reasons which are given above—
that we are incapable of conceiving of anything which is nameless
and formless. Actually, the supreme vision is that which sees the
same God in both the manifest and in the unmanifest. But such
a vision is very rare, so to make it easier for the common man to
approach the divinity, Hinduism gives many gods out of which
any one can be chosen depending on our personality and
delectation. Hinduism postulates thirty-three crores of gods. It
is believed that human beings have as many different types of
temperaments so every type can choose a god suitable to his or
her particular nature. Krishna says in the *Bhagavad-Gita*,

> In howsoever a way a person approaches me, I will go to him
> in that very same form, for people approach me in many
> ways O Arjuna!

What a truly noble statement to make. Whether you
approach him as Christ, Allah or Jehovah or Krishna, it matters
not, for the same force is in all and that force or energy or spirit
will approach you in that very form which appeals to you most
and fulfil your desires, because in the end there is only one form!
However, this should not be taken to mean that Hinduism
considers all religions to be the same. If the devotee does not
realise that the form of Christ or Allah is not confined to that
particular form but actually points to the Supreme Brahman,
then his or her devotion would lead to fundamentalism which
is what is taking place now. Hence, Hinduism always insists
that knowledge should precede devotion. One should understand
the nature of the Supreme in its essence before starting the
worship of the form.

The feeble instrument of the human mind lodged in this frail body finds it impossible to comprehend the loftiness of God's impersonality. We are proud of our personalities and no stretch of imagination can tell us the meaning of utter impersonality so the devotees of the impersonal Brahman impose a rigid rein on their inherent natures and by a method of constant suffering and repression, they reach their goal. The impersonal Brahman neither accepts nor rejects their overtures nor offers any assistance to those that clamber up to Him in this painful manner. But it should not be misunderstood that just because it is a more difficult path, it it a better path. Hence, Krishna tells Arjuna that worship of the Purushottama or Iswara is easier for embodied beings like us. The devotee of God with form can always approach Him at whatever time or place and be assured of an instant answer.

In the *Bhagavad-Gita*, when Krishna refers to himself in the first person singular it is not only to the transcendent Brahman to which he refers but to that which is both transcendent and immanent. He is at the same time, the Purushottama, Parameswara and Paramatma—the Supreme Person, Supreme Lord and the Supreme Soul all at once. It is to this godhead in the unity of all His aspects that our devotion should be directed in a constant *yoga*. The divine is capable of many roles and all roles at the same time since the only reason He has taken on a form is to bless His devotee in whatever role the devotee wishes to have Him enact. This is the sweetness of the *bhakti yoga*. The devotee who clings to the Lord as her sole and only support in all aspects of her life, spiritual, material, mental and intellectual has perforce to be helped by Him in all aspects, for she has no other recourse. This type of complete surrender is the easier path since the entire responsibility of our lives is left in the capable hands of the divine. The scriptures define the two paths of *bhakti* and *jnana* in this way. The path of the *jnani* is said to be the "monkey path" while the path of the *bhakta* is called the "kitten path." The baby monkey like the *jnani* has to cling on to his mother for dear life while she jumps from branch to branch. The moment he loosens his hold, he will fall to the hard ground below. The kitten on the other hand, like the devotee, is carried by the mother cat from place to place without any exertion on his own part. Thus, the devotee believes that a total surrender of the ego is all that the Lord asks. If that is there, He will carry the devotee without the least difficulty as easily as the mother cat carries its young!

However, the path of devotion also has its pitfalls. It is not as easy as it appears. It is very easy to fall into the misconception that the form which we worship is the best one if not the only one! Such a type of devotion easily leads to fanaticism as has been mentioned. Hence Hinduism insists on a true knowledge of the essence of that which we are offering worship to. The idol is only a symbol which appeals to us. It points to that Infinite, formless One of the Upanishads. The signpost on the road only points to the place where we want to reach. Some people mistake the signpost for the goal and start worshipping it and this is what leads to all the trouble. Only after gaining knowledge of the Supreme can we have the freedom to worship whatever form that appeals to us and then we will be on the right path. The Puranas say,

Akaashath patitam toyam yada gachati sagaraath, sarva deva namaskaram keshavam pratigachati.

Just as all the water that falls from the heavens reaches the ocean so worship of any God reaches the Supreme.

Just imagine the height of this knowledge and compassion which encompasses everything in its infinitely loving arms. This is why Hinduism never tried to convert anyone since it considered that all paths would eventually reach the same goal. The truth is that there is only one goal even though the seekers of different faiths do not realise this.

The path of devotion has its own difficulties for it demands nothing less than a complete submerging of our ego into the hands of our favourite deity along with a constant communion every second of the day. Most of us, being highly egoistic, will find this very difficult to do. This path is said to be easier only because we can continuously call for help. We have a hotline to Him and the *mantra* is the number. Every time we fall we can cry to Him and He will come running to help us. One child learns to walk the hard way, running and falling many times, the other constantly clutches its mother's hand for support and both reach the same goal. The option is ours. The devotee who casts on God the entire responsibility of her life is bound to be helped by God at every moment of her life.

Many methods are given for promoting devotion in us and one of the easiest is *japa* or the repetition of our favourite God's name as many times as possible. *Japa yoga* actually has a scientific basis. It is based on the science of phonetics. Names of gods are *mantras* which have the propensity to conjure up the form of the deity. This is because the *mantra* is a sound which contains the form of the deity; something like the sound "dog" contains within it a picture of a dog! Thus, the mind which has been attuned to the form of its favourite deity keeps invoking Him through a constant repetition and the sound inflames the mind with thought of the deity and it becomes his constant companion. According to Lord Krishna, as given in the

Bhagavad-Gita, this is one of the easiest and best methods of keeping in touch with our *ishta deva* (favourite deity). Even a purely mechanical repetition has the power to wipe off the dross of material negativity from our minds and thus allow the form to become clearer and clearer in our hearts. The *mantra* is a spiritually charged word and when we plug our mind to it, we receive the divine current directly even without our knowledge. If even a mechanical repetition has this power, think of the power generated by someone who uses it consciously and lovingly, repeating it at all times whatever the task she is engaged in. *Bhakti yoga* is indeed the *yoga* of love and it becomes perfect only when we begin to see God in everything around us in the world. This is when *bhakti* joins hands with *jnana.*

The devotee allows the divine will to run through her without blocking it by her personal ego. All her actions are done by the divine and she becomes a mere instrument in His hands. This ensures that her every action is swift and sure and perfect. Combinations and calculations which are far too complicated for the normal human mind are foreseen by the divine so no hitch occurs in any action. Every detail is looked into by her divine lover and all her wishes are forseen. Such is the tenderness and care which is bestowed on her that it would be impossible to describe this state to one who has never experienced it. Our personal God is also the perfect lover, perfect father and perfect mother all rolled into one. If we only have the courage to jump unhesitatingly into His arms, He will cradle us and carry us through the crocodile-infested waters of the world. Another reason for her great feeling of security is that her beloved is not staying apart from her but is always seated within her heart. Neither time nor space separates her from her beloved. He is ever present, ever loving, ever exciting, never boring—ever the perfect lover.

When the heart overflows with love for the divine, there is no place in it for love of the world. This is the secret of *bhakti yoga*. You might think that this is easier said than done. But ask any lover and he will say that he has no difficulty in keeping his mind on his beloved. Love for someone generates thoughts about that person easily and automatically. If this is so even in the mundane world, how much more will it be for the divine. Once our minds start flowing towards God, we will find that the whole of life takes on a golden hue. The true lover has no problem in walking in the sun or rain or hail or frost so long as his beloved is with him. So also any problem of the mundane world becomes easily conquerable when one has the divine beloved by her side. This is the glory of the path of devotion.

Vyasa painted glorious word pictures in the Puranas in order to give ample scope for the devotee to soak herself in the stories of the Divine Beloved, in whatever form her heart depicts Him. It is said that even after writing the *Mahabharata* and so many Puranas, Vyasa was still sunk in gloom and could find no peace of mind. The Sage Narada came to him and told him that the reason for his restlessness was due to the fact that he had not written the glorious tales of the great *avataras* of Vishnu, especially of his *avatara* as Krishna. It was then that he wrote the *Sreemad Bhagavad Purana,* which describes all the incarnations of Vishnu culminating in his famous role as Krishna. This is a book which ignites devotion in the heart of even the stone-hearted and after writing this, Vyasa also found peace.

O stream of consciousness divine,
These offering are presented to you with adoration.
May you acknowledge and accept our praises,
And place us under your kind care,
May we ever take your shelter,
As a traveller takes refuge under a tree.

Rig Veda

This immortal nature of the universe takes its place,
In the hearts of mortal humans,
And it also blesses them,
In all their sacred aspirations.
With its spiritual radiance,
Reflecting by intense love,
And knowing all secrets of wisdom,
It shines extensively.

Rig Veda

Loka Samasthath Sukhino Bhavantu!

ॐ

Sarvatjnaaya Namaha!

CHAPTER VIII

Karma

We owe a lot to the Indians who taught us how to count without which no worthwhile scientific discovery could have been made.

Albert Einstein

It is already becoming clearer that a chapter which has a western beginning will have to have an Indian ending if it's not to end in the self-destruction of the human race. At this supremely dangerous moment in history, the only way of salvation for mankind is the Indian way.

Dr Arnold Toynbee, British Historian

We have dealt with the two great paths or *yogas* of Hinduism— *jnana* and *bhakti*—wisdom and devotion. Now we have to take up another of the great paths known as *karma*. Hinduism is the only religion which teaches us that we are totally responsible for our lives. We cannot blame God or our parents or our friends or anyone else for our problems. We are the creators of our destinies. The law of *karma* is one of the foundation stones of the Sanatana Dharma and it declares categorically that our own actions are what shape our destinies. More than the actual actions, it is our intentions which create our future. As we desire so we shall get. The only things that we can control in our lives are our actions. However, we cannot control the results of the action since they are governed by some other law and this is called the Law of Karma in Hinduism. We have no control over it since it is a natural law. To put it simply, the person who hates others will keep receiving hate from them; the person who feels love for others will keep getting love in return. In other words, you receive from the world what you give to it.

Any action which is done with a certain desire or motive has to be fulfilled. The fruit of that desire will come bouncing back to us one day or the other. If some actions do not get their results in this life then one has to take another life in order to enjoy the benefits or be punished for our good and bad actions. Like all laws of nature, the Law of Karma cannot be diverted or bypassed. This is why the Hindus believe in reincarnation, which is actually based on this scientific law of nature.

The law of nature is pretty straight forward. We desire many things without knowing the way in which our desires will manifest. Sometimes they come to pass as we wish it but very often they result in something which we never expect. When we act, we should examine our motivation to see if it is pure or tainted with selfishness. As we think or desire so we shall get and become. This is a law of nature so it is very important that we desire the right things. Every intention, every desire leaves an imperceptible mark on our mind that slowly builds our future. So it is absurd to blame God for anything that happens to us. We have only ourselves to blame or praise for the result of our actions. "As we sow, so we shall reap." This is an implacable law of nature.

   The relationship between cause and effect which takes place between physical objects and persons reflects a natural law which is not limited to physical reality. This is what is known as the Law of Karma in Hinduism. Everybody and everything in the physical world is part of that universal law which we as limited human beings are not able to perceive. All the laws of nature have their corresponding components in the life of the human being. Hence, you find that our Law of Karma is only a spiritual interpretation of Newton's third law of motion, which states that every action has its equal and opposite reaction. This law of motion finds its subtle expression by producing the results of the actions of the human being. Every time we act with a certain desire or with a certain intention, we are instigating a cause which will have to end in an effect. This effect may or may not be what we expect. When it turns out to be what we expect, we are very proud of our prowess in having produced such an effect but when it turns out to be quite different from what we expect, we tend to blame others for the way it has turned out. We are happy to accept results if they are favourable to us but not at all happy about accepting that which is undesirable or unfavourable. We totally forget that both effects have been caused by us—by our intentions, the results of which we cannot judge or gauge. Any action, according to the third law of motion, has its equal and opposite reaction. If you throw a ball at a wall, it has to return to you with equal force. Similarly, if you harm someone (with intent to harm), that harm will have to return to you in some way or the other. The intention of the doer is thrown back at him, as it were, in an equal and opposite reaction.

   The Law of Karma is a law of nature and has nothing to do with morality. Ethics and morality are man-made and apt to change with place and time. The Law of Karma, however, is an impersonal law. The universe does not judge. It is only the human being that judges. Moral rules are man-made; breaking them is an offence and have to be punished by the laws of the land. Natural laws are also enforced by Nature but in a totally different way.

The universal law metes out non-judgemental justice. Therefore, according to Hinduism, this law actually serves us as an impersonal teacher of our responsibility. But a person who does not understand how this law works may get angry and frustrated and start blaming God, the world and others, in fact anyone except himself as to how people are treating him. By doing this the person is actually creating more negative *karmas* for himself. In order to become liberated, each person will have to balance his or her karmic debts in this life or else the imbalance will be carried on to another life like an unfinished account book in which the balance is carried on from year to year. Most accountants try to balance their books at the end of every financial year so as not to carry on these debts. Similarly, we also should make an attempt to finish off our debts in this life. This can be done only when we realise that everything that happens to us has been created by our own intentions either of the immediate past life or some previous ones. We might meet many different types of personalities during the course of our life, some supportive, some hostile, some loving, some suspicious and unlikeable. If we do not want to acquire more *karma*, we should not judge any of their actions. Any experience we have, good or bad, is only the effect of some cause we have started at some other time perhaps in some other lifetime. If we accept the experience without judgement, that particular cycle of cause and effect will be finished in this life but if we react, we will be starting another cycle, the effect of which will have to be experienced by us at some other time in this life or some other life.

Of course we will recognise negativity when we see it but we should not judge it. Judging is not our business. When we judge we create negative *karma*. Judgement is an action of the personality, never of the Self. Nature does not judge. God is an impersonal witness of the actions of the human being and will not interfere unless called upon to do so. To blame Him for our negative experiences is a waste of time. When we see a beggar you can be certain that he is experiencing the effect of a cause he has instigated in a previous life. Probably he refused charity to someone who was desperately in need of it and now a compassionate Nature is giving him a chance to be on the receiving end and thus balance his debts. Of course this does not mean that you should not help him. Your duty if you have the money and the means is to help him to your fullest capacity. It is not your duty to judge his worth or otherwise. If you refuse to help him, you will be starting another cycle of cause and effect which you will have to experience. Instead of trying to balance the pros and cons yourself, all you have to do is to help the beggar if you have the means to do it without questioning his worth or his past *karma*. That is not your problem. Your problem is to make sure that you do not intake more negative *karma* by refusing to help a person who appears to be in need. Whether or not he actually deserves to be helped, is not your problem.

Naturally, we are bound to see a selfish person as a selfish person and a murderer as a murderer but we are not the ones to judge them. We cannot see the karmic debt that is being paid off by the selfishness and the murder. This does not mean that we should not act in the way which is appropriate to the situation. We can and must call the murderer to book and hand him over to the police but that is all that we are called upon to do. The moment we start judging him from the human point of view, we become involved in the process of cause and effect. In every situation you can either look at it from the angle of your higher Self or your personality which is your lower human self.

Gandhiji was beaten several times during his life. Although on two occasions he nearly died, he refused to prosecute his attackers because he saw that they were doing what they thought was right. Even when his assassinator, Godse pointed the gun, pointblank at his heart, he must have held no grudge since all he did was to fold his palms in salutation and repeat "Ram, Ram!" Actually, even a good judge should meet out non-judgemental justice. Going purely by what the jury says, he should pass his judgement without trying to judge for himself. Non-judgemental justice allows you a great deal of freedom. Most of us go through life taking on the task of judging others and thus creating a lot of negative *karmas* for ourselves. A knowledge of the Law of Karma allows us to go our own way without judging but only doing what we are called upon to do because we know that nothing escapes this law which is all-pervasive so everyone will get his or her just deserts without our interference.

Every relationship that we have with anyone however trivial has a karmic basis. Whether we will finish off our karmic bond with them in this life will depend on whether we react or respond to the stimuli we receive from them. Like, dislike and indifference are the three types of responses we normally have to anything and anyone. All these might cause further karmic bonds if they are not called for. Even if our dislike or indifference has a cause, we should not react with a similar feeling. The only way to negate the cycle of cause and effect is to accept. We have to learn to accept the person as he or she is without trying to project our own likes or dislikes on him or her.

In Hinduism, this Law of Karma is closely related to reincarnation. The universe does not like to leave anything incomplete. Every cause has to produce an effect. Until it does so, the circle is incomplete. Sometimes it happens that this balancing of energy may not take place in this lifetime. Therefore, the embodied soul has to take on another form in order to complete the process. The effects of my actions have to be experienced by me and not by anyone else. If I die before I experience it, I will be compelled to take on another body so as to complete the process. If, in this life, I find that I'm repeatedly being cruelly treated by others, I might strike back and treat others as they have been treating me (tit for tat) you say. However, if I understand the Law of Karma I will realise that I must have treated many people cruelly in my previous life and now I'm being given an opportunity to balance the effects of my past *karma* by having many people treat me cruelly. If I understand this and accept this without hatred for those who do injustice to me, then I will have washed off that *karma* from my plate and can start my next life with a clean conscience. Thus, every experience we have in this life, whether good or bad, is actually the means employed by a compassionate universe to enable us to balance our debts and start afresh. The way we accept our lives will pave the way for our future lives. If we lash out with pain and hatred at those who revile us, we might have balanced one karmic debt but we will be starting another one. If however we accept this without rancour and without reacting, we will be nullifying the effects of that particular *karma* and will be able to end that cycle of cause and effect. The *jivatma* (embodied soul) thus takes a new birth carrying what is known as his or her *prarabdha karma*, which is actually all the actions which it has started or caused in a previous life. The effects of these have to be experienced by the *jivatma*. It cannot be wiped out. But it can stop itself from instigating new *karmas* which are the causative factors for new effects in the future. How this can be done is beautifully explained by Lord Krishna in the *Sreemad Bhagavad-Gita*. The *jivatma* takes on a physical reality in order to balance its *karmas* within the framework of the Law of Karma. We can only evolve within this framework both as individuals and groups and societies.

Therefore, in order to progress spiritually, the individual has to balance his karmic debts. He has to experience the effects that he has caused either in this life or in another. All our relationships are given to us in order to balance some debt or other. This applies to the other party also. But of course how they choose to heal themselves is their problem, whereas our problem is somehow to pay our debts as fast as possible in a way by which we will not incur more karmic debts.

If you hurt others, you are actually hurting yourself even though you may not know it. "Do to others what you would have them do to you", is a basic dictum of all religions. "As you sow so you shall reap."

Anyone who performs actions only for himself without any care or consideration for others and for the world around him will have to suffer. This is the law of nature. Any selfish act immediately isolates us from the world and from nature and many such acts eventually bring unhappiness, discontent, ill health and continuous bad luck which we blame on others and on our fate, never realizing that it is only a consequence of our own selfish actions. Here is where the Law of Karma comes into play. Our world is shaped by our own actions. In this respect we must understand that our thoughts are also actions. As Krishna says, in the human being, motivation is even more important than the actual action. A violent act may do some good to the person concerned like a surgeon cutting off a gangrenous hand in order to save the patient's life, but when the hand is cut off by a thief who wants to steal the golden bangle on it, then the same action becomes violent and violates the law of nature and thus brings its own violent consequences on the doer. This is the very basis of the Law of Karma.

Now we come to the reason for which the Vedas give so many details about behaviour and action. How can we be held responsible for our actions if we do not know how to act? Thus, the Vedas have different sections all of which give us certain patterns of behaviour which should be practised by all sections of society in order to know the Infinite Being which the Vedas point out. Let it be understood that in and through all the rituals and codes of conduct mentioned in the Vedas, one fact is reiterated and that is to know that Supreme. In order to know That, we should practise certain mental disciplines so that the thought of that Being is kept steady before us. The performances of sacrifices, of doing penance, giving charity, going to temples, social service, marriage rites and all such duties are meant only to give us mental purity (*chitta shuddhi*) and to steady the wavering mind (*chitta vritti nirodha*). The object of all the various duties and acts enjoined on us in the Vedas is to help realise that Brahman through a disciplined path.

Instead of letting the sense organs and mind drag us where they will, we should perform the prescribed Vedic and Puranic rituals by which we will be able to develop the capacity to see inwardly. The intellect is actually capable of grasping everything and can reach That by knowing which all things will become known but to do this, it has to analyse and find out and eliminate all those things which are not necessary for its progress. Attachment to the body increases by performing impure acts and leads to loss of mental peace. But the repetition of the Vedic *mantras* and observing the rituals given in the Puranas, which are designed to bring universal well-being, will lead us to spiritual maturity and allow us to gain *moksha* or liberation.

> The self-realised soul transcends time and space and abides in pure consciousness. No evil thoughts, desires or fear can ever enter his enlightened mind.
>
> *Ashtavakra Gita*

> The cosmic pair of day and night,
> Come to cherish our noble deeds,
> Like two deer in a forest,
> Like two wild cattle on fresh pastures,
> Like two swans flying in the sky.
>
> *Rig Veda*

Loka Samasthath Sukhino Bhavantu!

ॐ

Twashtaaya Namaha!

CHAPTER IX

Advaita Vedanta

Many of the advances in the sciences that we consider to have been made in Europe were in fact made in India centuries ago.

Grant Duff, British Historian of India

Adi Shankaracharya, the founder of the Advaita Vedanta school of Indian philosophy which is taken from the Upanishads, describes the cognition of the illusory world in a way which is very close to what the quantum physicist says.

Its form cannot be determined with any degree of certainty. It is apparent like a dream, water or a mirage. It is fugitive, its own form being evinced and not evinced. Therefore it has no end, no fixity, and no determinacy and never stays as a particular form, exclusive of other forms. It can never be determined conclusively.

Heisenberg's principle of indeterminacy (the uncertainty principle) repeats this in modern language. Heisenberg said that it was impossible to determine with absolute precision both the position and the momentum of a particle simultaneously. When the position of the particle is determined with accuracy, its velocity is automatically altered. Consequently, the momentum of the particle is changed. As a result the value of the momentum of the particle becomes uncertain at the time of the accurate determination of its position. The more accurate the determination of one, the greater the uncertainty of the other. We can only know approximately both the position and the momentum of the particle simultaneously. The more we know about one, the less we know about the other. When we know the one with absolute precision, we know nothing whatsoever about the other! How close is this to Shankara's assertion made more than two thousand years ago.

Of course Shankara, being a great spiritualist, went one step further in describing the nature of the illusory world. He said that the human mind very cleverly superimposes reality on the unreal. The classic example he gives of this is the rope and the snake. In the darkness of the night one might imagine a snake to be lying on the side of a room. When we bring a light it will be seen that the snake is actually a rope coiled up. Here the unreal is superimposed on the real. The snake cannot be considered as real because once knowledge is obtained with the flashing of the light, the snake disappears. It cannot be totally unreal either since for all practical purposes it did exist for the viewer for a short while, causing fear, palpitation and all the other side-effects.

He goes on to say that we have created this world of concrete objects and superimposed a false reality on them. Again and again all our scriptures say that absolute reality is beyond these three *upadhis—desha, kaala* and *nimitta* or space, time and causality. This world which we think of as real is only *maya* or an appearance. It has no permanent reality. It is only a passing show and has no permanence.

In the experiments about atomic events, we come to realise that the elementary particles themselves are not real. They merely form a world of potentialities or possibilities rather than one of actual facts. These sub-atomic particles have no objective existence. They are not like particles of dust.

Thus Heisenberg concludes,

Elementary particles are not real as objects of daily life, like stones and sticks. In spite of all our attempts in the search for the ultimate stuff of the universe, we finally have come to the conclusion that there is nothing like that!

The theory of relativity shows that we can observe only relations, while the quantum theory says that we can observe only probabilities. Together they have come to the conclusion that the mathematical equations that handle particles of wave packets in their different states do not actually represent them in actual fact. They merely indicate the different kinds of knowledge we may have about them. Therefore, modern science has given up all claims to be specific. It deals with the grounds of possible knowledge and not with the essence of a fundamental reality which is beyond their scope.

In the conscious state we experience a reality created by the processing of sensory information relayed by the nerves to the brain. Memory and emotions can modify these inputs in order to create separate aspects of the external world. But all these neural activities are of no use without some type of consciousness which integrates all these experiences into a coherent whole. Many animals also have this capacity. Despite all our abilities, without consciousness, we cannot experience existence. It is because of consciousness that our brain has meaningful experiences both of the external world as well as the internal world of feelings and emotions.

This is where religion and especially Hindu spiritualism steps in to show us that some things exist which are beyond the level of the mind.

Normally, quantum particles act in a haphazard fashion of chaos or disorder but when the individual consciousness is brought to bear on them, they lose their individuality and begin to act as a single unit. This coherence extends into the world. This coherence of consciousness represents the greatest form of order known to nature and can help to shape and create order in the world. In meditation and especially in the state of *samadhi,* our brain reaches that zero point field of the *chitta* which has perfect coherence.

This is the substructure which underlies the whole universe. It is a recording medium of everything, by which everything can communicate with everything else.

Maharishi Mahesh Yogi demonstrated that a number of individuals meditating at the same time can produce a great amount of coherence in the world outside. This was also proved by the physicists who undertook experiments which showed that the more the people who were wishing for the same thing, the more likely it was to succeed. Even machines are affected by our attitude.

Even though quantum physics has gone a long way in supporting the Advaitic view of Hindu spirituality of a shadow world of *Maya*, as well as of a human consciousness which is universal and eternal, it still has not been able to postulate or prove the existence of an Ultimate Reality which has ever existed and which will ever exist and which alone is—*Sat-chit* and

Ananda. Not only that it EXISTS but that it is pure CONSCIOUSNESS and that it is filled with BLISS. This can only be experienced by the sage, the seer and the mystic who connects himself with the source and thus draws his inspiration from it. As the *Gita* says, such a man can no longer be labelled a human being but has to be given the title of God. The future of the world lies in the production of such god men and not in the production of more nuclear weapons.

Vedanta says that this body of ours, which is made of the five elements, is perishable. BUT we are not solely these bodies. Our reality is something far greater since we are actually the *atman*—which is imperishable and eternal and untouched by the changes of the body which take place in the world of space/time.

When we read this we will no doubt be amazed to find how modern Shankara's concept was. The extreme view of the universe as given by Shankara's teacher, Gaudapada, postulates that the universe is not real—*Brahma Satyam, jagat mithya.* "The Brahman alone is real, the world is unreal." It never came into existence; it has no existence at present and will not have an existence in the future.

This extreme view of Advaita Vedanta actually fits in with the extreme view of quantum physics. However, Adi Shankara and other Vedantins recognised the empirical existence of the world. Even though all the things that we might see in a magic show are not real, yet they have a sequence and are meaningful to the spectators. In our relative and dependent existence anything that has a relative existence cannot be ignored. The universe and our lives can be considered meaningful only in this sense.

Thus, we see that Vedanta does not say that the universe is *asat* or unreal. Even that which we think of as *asat* or non-existent is actually *sat* or existent. We recognise something as existent (*sat*) when it is perceived by our senses directly or indirectly. What is not perceptible to our senses we consider it as non-existent (*asat*). Hence, existence and non-existence are relative terms based on the ability or inability of our senses to perceive them. So when we say that the universe was non-existent before creation, we mean that it was not perceivable by our senses at that time. Advaita says that the universe is always existent in a subtle form and is perceivable by the senses only when it takes on a gross form.

Avyakta (unmanifest) and *vyakta* (manifest) are the two terms used by Vedanta to describe these subtle and gross states. The manifestation of the universe from the Unmanifest is known as creation. What Vedanta means by creation is a manifestation or an emanation of something which existed in an unmanifest state. Therefore, the universe cannot be called either *sat* (existent) or *asat* (non-existent). However, for us what is manifested is *sat* (existent) and what is unmanifest is *asat*. Vedanta says that this *sat* is only a transient existence which is perceivable to us for a short while; it has no permanence; whereas what we think of as *asat* is actually something which is eternally existent but non-perceivable by our five senses.

This concept was first given in the "Nasadiya Sukta" of the *Rig Veda*. Before the universe came into being, it was neither *sat* nor *asat*. It was not *sat* since it could not be perceived by the senses and it was not *asat* since it existed in a subtle state.

Before the universe came into being, Brahman alone existed. Since the universe could not be produced out of nothing, we must conclude that it is an emanation from Brahman. Since

Brahman is actionless and ever whole, Vedanta says that *maya* which is the power of the Brahman is the material cause of the universe, and Iswara, the image of Brahman reflected in *maya*, is the efficient cause.

To understand this fully we will have to understand the concept of Brahman as given in Advaita Vedanta. Brahman is undifferentiated, homogeneous existence. It is functionless, eternal, timeless, unchangeable and non-modifiable. So how can it be the cause of the universe? It cannot be the material cause of the universe since it is changeless and does not undergo modification. It cannot be the efficient cause since it is non-active and non-functional. It does nothing. (This has been described fully in the chapter on Brahman.)

Can we then say that the universe was produced out of nothing? Vedanta does not accept this. Something cannot come out of nothing and nothing cannot become something. Vedanta does not recognise "nothingness" or void or vacuum, *shunya*. It says that everything is plenum or fullness, *poorna*.

> *Poornamidam, poornamidam, Poornath poornamudachyate*
> That is full, this is also full. Out of the full, fullness comes,
> If you take away fullness from the full, fullness alone remains.

Physics has come to the conclusion that there is no such thing as a void. Virtual particles can come into being spontaneously out of the void and vanish again into the void. The vacuum is far from being empty. It contains an unlimited number of particles which keep coming and vanishing all the time.

As Fritjof Capra says,

> The physical vacuum is not a state of mere nothingness but contains the potentiality for all forms of the particle world.

These forms in turn are not independent physical entities but merely transient manifestations of the underlying Void. The relation between the virtual particles and the vacuum is dynamic. The vacuum is truly a living Void, pulsating in endless rhythms of creation and destruction.

Thus, if the universe has come out of Brahman which is ever full, then the universe also must be ever full. In other words, the universe must also be Brahman!

However, Brahman cannot be divided into parts like the universe, so what we think of as parts or differences are actually a superimposition on the reality of the Brahman, which is the only reality. So the universe has only an empirical reality like the mirage on the desert sands and does not have an ultimate reality. Hence they called it *maya*. So we are really seeing something which actually does not exist in the form that we imagine it to be. Again this is what quantum physics says, that what we think of as solid matter (the world) is only energy in motion!

From this we understand that there is one great difference between the views of modern science regarding creation and the Vedantic view. Even though science claims that the universe was created out of a big bang, it gives no cause for the explosion or for the indefinable nature of the initial entry. They can tell us a lot about what happened millions of years after the big bang but they cannot tell us what existed before the explosion. They cannot tell us how a universe obeying all these intricate physical laws could emerge from a big explosion. Could it have been created by some God or is it a sheer coincidence? The off chance of the emergence of a universe with all the necessary parameters for creation is an impossibility.

Martin Rees, an expert on cosmology, says that all the ingredients necessary for creating this universe must have been envisaged by the initial entity that existed before the big bang. From super galaxies to the lowest form of life, everything contains matter and forces that have been created with great mathematical precision. What kind of mighty brain could have brought out the blueprint of this complex universe in which we are living? Martin Rees gives six numbers as a recipe for our universe which are so crucial that if any one of them had not been chosen correctly, nothing would have emerged as we see it today. In fact we would not even be here contemplating these possibilities! The first of these is 10 to the power of 36, which is a vital number since it shows how feeble gravity is as compared to the electrical forces that hold atoms together. If this were not so, gravity would have crushed everything else and there would have been no question of a universe. There are five other numbers which are equally vital for the building of this complex cosmos but we need not go into them now. Suffice to say that all these marvels which we see now could not have come about by mere chance.

The solution given by the Vedas is that of a superintelligent vacuum, but this is something which the scientists are loathe to accept since it is way beyond their known parameters. This leaves them with a string of coincidences, which is as irrational as accepting the grace of a superintellect. Both explanations lack experimental evidence, though the Vedic explanation of the super consciousness of the Brahman has the experiential evidence of the *rishis* which again the scientist cannot accept. Till today the mystery of the emergence of this type of an incredible creation remains unsolved in the scientific world. The latest scientific discovery apparently is of something called a Higgs-Bosun particle, which is being called the God particle in common parlance. This is such an important find that the whole scientific world is agog with it, for they think that it might be something which will solve the riddle of life once and for all. But again it is a very elusive particle which defies all attempts to pinpoint it to one place and time. It never stays for long in one place so proper experiments on it are very difficult but the scientific world still hopes that something will come of it. According to the *Aitareya Upanishad*, the creator is present in all forms of life even though we cannot see it. It is as elusive as the God particle. This intelligent energy is the very essence of our existence though it appears in varying degrees of intensity in different creatures.

The cosmogony of Advaita Vedanta is evolutionary. Brahman did not suddenly create the universe one fine day or even in seven days. Shankaracharya says that the universe evolved gradually and that things did not appear suddenly in their final shapes. However, the Advaitic concept of evolution is different from the Darwinian. Darwin's theory of evolution is species-oriented and not spiritually oriented. It has three phases: inorganic, organic and species. The evolutionary sequence given in the *Taitareeya Upanishad* also follows this pattern—inorganic, organic and species. It also goes on to describe the appearance of psyche from matter to life, life to mind, mind to intellect and intellect to bliss. The Darwinian process is not guided by any intelligence. Vedanta however says that Brahman is *chit* or pure consciousness. The power or *Shakti* of that consciousness, which is also known as *maya*, evolves due to the presence of that intelligence within it. Consciousness is eternal and timeless; *Maya* is also eternal and timeless but unconscious. The presiding spirit called Iswara who is omniscient is also eternal and timeless. The universe does not come out of nothing nor does it become nothing. *Maya, Shakti* or *Prakriti*, though insentient, is the active principle of the Brahman but remains in a dormant state until the time comes for another creation and evolution. The creation takes place under the gaze of the cosmic intelligence or Brahman. *Srishti, sthiti* and *samhara* (creation, maintenance and destruction) follow a cyclical pattern.

Advaita Vedanta accepts the big bang theory. Since the *rishis* were experts in clothing scientific truths in poetic form, this theory is brought forward under the cloak of something called the bursting of the cosmic egg. References to the cosmic egg have been given in many of the Hindu scriptures. This cosmic egg was filled with a fluid called *apah*. Many translators describe *apah* as water but this is not so. It is a fluid whose exact nature is not known to us. The creative principle of the Brahman is known as Brahma and he resided in the cosmic egg for one divine year consisting of many light years before the egg exploded and he came out and created the universe out of the primordial substance of the cosmic egg.

In Puranic literature, the bursting of the cosmic egg has been described poetically. At the beginning of creation, Lord Narayana reposes on his serpent bed on the sea of all possibilities (the zero point field of modern physics). From his navel comes the golden lotus on which Brahma, the creator, is seated. He brings forth the Hiranyagarbha or the golden egg which bursts and creates the numerous worlds. Another version of the story goes thus.

Lord Vishnu, who is in charge of maintaining the universe, is said to be sleeping on the cosmic waters. A golden lotus came out of his navel and from this the cosmic egg was developed. Brahma, the creator, was residing inside the egg. Vishnu advised Brahma to practice austerities and he would be given the knowledge of how to create. Through his deep meditation he disturbed the fluid in the egg which resulted in the bursting of the egg. The evolutionary process started with this big bang.

When the egg exploded, *prana* was let out. Now we think of *prana* as life or the vital force of both living and non-living entities. Here *prana* denotes that substance which appeared after *apah*. Nothing in the universe can function without help from *prana*. The violent explosion caused *prana* to vibrate violently. As a result, an excessive quantity of heat was produced. In that superheated state, *akasa, aditi* or space emanated from *prana*. Brahma who is the efficient cause of creation now produced energy particles and matter particles in opposite pairs from *akasa*.

Apah, prana and *akasa* are almost the same substance and differ only in their subtlety. In that superheated state after the explosion of the cosmic egg, light particles (photons) were dominant. *Akasa* kept producing particle pairs which were reconverted into *akasa*. The *Rig Veda* describes this phenomenon as Daksa born of Aditi and again Aditi born of Daksha. Aditi has been described as both the parent and the offspring since the reverse process is possible and *akasa* may be converted into *prana*. Due to her importance in creation, Aditi was revered as a goddess, the mother of all the gods or energy particles. The particles (*renu*) were dancing vigorously in the superheated condition in an extremely chaotic manner and thus there was constant collusion, annihilation and transmutation. No atoms could be formed due to the random movements of the particles. It was an energy-dominated state and there was hardly any matter except in the form of particles and anti-particles.

These three words, *apah, prana* and *akasa,* represent the three sub-states of the single state known in Quantum physics as "the Field." The subtlest state of the field is known as *apah* or primal waters. The next state is *prana,* and finally comes *akasa.* Modern science has not differentiated these three as yet and simply calls the three as "the Field". This field consisting of these three subtle states is full of activity. Particles and anti-particles are produced from it and again and again they merge back into it. The universe expands due to the expansion of the field. According to the Upanishads, gaseous matter (*vayu*) was produced from *akasa*. *Vayu* is commonly translated as "air" in the earth's atmosphere but at that time the earth had not come into being so by *vayu*, what was meant was gaseous matter. After *akasa* came *vayu* and this is the source of hydrogen which is the simplest of all gases. Due to the compression of hydrogen, heat was produced and this heat liquefied the gas. These two processes have been described in the Upanishads as *agni* (fire), being produced from *vayu* (gas) and *apah* (liquid) is produced as a result of the heating of the gaseous matter. In the course of billions of years, the exterior parts of the planetary sphere became solidified. The word used in the scriptures for this phenomenon is *prithvi*. In course of time, these words have come to have different meanings and refer to the *pancha bhutas* (five elements) which compose the material world. These words came to mean *akasa* or *vyoma* as space, from which came *vayu* or air, and then *Agni or tejas,* which is heat energy or fire, from which came *apas* or water and finally *prithvi* (earth) or solid matter.

The so-called myths of the Puranas actually contain deep scientific truths. These truths are not the facts which Western science considered as truth before the 20th century but these are truths discovered by the quantum physicists of the 20th century. They are quite incomprehensible even to the modern mind which has been slowly educated towards such truths so how much more incomprehensible would they have been to people of the Puranic age. The *rishis,* however, as we have seen were really super-human beings. They were not five-sensory beings but multi-sensory beings who were far in advance of their age. Of course they realised that these scientific facts, however true, would be quite inconceivable to the normal human being. So they clothed these facts and wove stories round them so that people would appreciate the story even if they did not understand what it was all about. Perhaps they hoped that one day there would be born a race of the Homo sapiens who would be able to decipher their mystical language and realise that they had really known everything about the quantum state and the zero point field. We are fortunate to be living in this age where we can at least have a glimpse of their mighty intellect and be able to appreciate these facts since we have already learnt about it from modern science.

Let us examine one of their tales which has been totally misinterpreted. The story goes that before the creation of human beings, Brahma the creator made himself into two—the male was Manu and the female, Shatarupa. This story continues the story of creation after the explosion. It shows how the neutron (Brahma) was split into the proton (Manu) and the electron (Shatarupa). The bigger one was the proton and the smaller was the electron. The Upanishad goes on to say that these two particles interplayed and produced the whole universe. The scientist knows that when an electron is trapped by a proton, the former revolves round the latter and an atom of hydrogen is formed. This hydrogen atom is the primary element and is the building block of further development.

The Vedas also mention how the stars and planets were formed. They clearly mention that the stars were formed out of the gas clouds and dust of space which came out of the cosmic egg. This dust has been differentiated from the dust found on the earth.

With reference to our solar system, the scriptures clearly say that our earth and all the other planets of our system have originated from the sun. The fact that the earth is round has also been mentioned long, long before Western science discovered it. In fact they said that all the stars, planets and space itself are round in shape. The Vedic seers definitely knew that the earth and other planets revolved round the sun. The hardening of the crust of the earth and its molten interior have also been mentioned in the scriptures.

We also know that they knew of the existence of galaxies and supergalaxies. *Brahamanda* is a supergalaxy. Inside this *Brahamanda* in which we live there exists fourteen *lokas* or galaxies. The *loka* or galaxy in which we are situated is known as *Bhuh*. The other *lokas* situated above us are *bhuvah, swah, mahah, jana, tapa* and *satya*. These are all mentioned in the *Gayatri Mantra*, by chanting which we get empowered with the energy of all these *lokas*. That is why the *Gayatri Mantra* is said to be the greatest of all the Vedic *mantras*. This *mantra* also extracts the force and energy of the sun, which is the centre of our *Bhuh-loka* or galaxy. The *rishis* realised that the energy of the sun not only nourishes all life in this universe but also emanates certain spiritual vibrations which can be utilised by the human being in his journey to divinity. The seven *lokas* that are below us are known as *atala, vitala, sutala, rasatala, talatala, mahatala* and *patala*.

In the *Devi Purana*, which deals with the extraordinary stories of the cosmic mother or Devi, we find that She takes the three gods of this *loka* or galaxy in her cosmic vehicle and asks them to view all the worlds that they pass. As they pass each *loka* or galaxy, the trinity find to their astonishment that each of them contains a Brahma, Vishnu and Shiva. The goddess smilingly tells them that this is only one of the supergalaxies or

Brahamandas that are contained within her. From this and other stories we can see that the *rishis* were well aware of the fact of the infinite number of galaxies and supergalaxies that exist.

They also knew of the expanding universe. The story of Vishnu in his *avatara* as Vamana or the dwarf is one of the stories that depict this. Vishnu comes as a dwarf boy and begs the king of the land for three steps of land. The king pities him for his stupidity and tells him to ask for the whole world if he wants since he is capable of giving him anything he asks for. But Vamana insists that he wants only three steps of land since he had come to put an end to the king's great ego. The king agrees and Vamana takes on his cosmic form and measures the entire galaxy with one step. In his next step, he measures the whole of this *Brahamanda* or supergalaxy. His big toe is supposed to have made a hole in this *Brahamanda* and continued to stretch further. This is a graphic picture of the expanding universe. It shows that there is no limit to the power of God and his step can exceed even this supergalaxy and go further into unlimited space!

> Utter darkness prevailed before the beginning with no existence of any kind. The primordial void created the universe from its benevolent thoughts.
>
> *Rig Veda*

> In the boundless ocean of consciousness, waves of phenomenal worlds appear and disappear. Eternal consciousness, which is the cause of all perceptions is unaffected by the rise and fall of a universe at the end of its allotted time.
>
> *Ashtavakra Gita*

Loka Samasthath Sukhino Bhavantu!

ॐ

Anaghaaya Namaha!

CHAPTER X

The World of Maya

All matter originates and exists only by virtue of a force which brings the particles of an atom to vibration and holds this minute solar system of the atom together. We must assume behind the force the existence of a conscious and intelligent mind. This mind is the matrix of all matter.

Max Planck

You are neither earth, nor air nor sky but you live happily in all these things. You are pure intelligence that creates and witnesses the drama of existence.

Ashtavakra Gita

Who knows your true reality?
You take birth, though unborn,
You destroy evil though without movement,
You are asleep though ever wakeful.

Raghuvamsa by Kalidasa

Maya is a word which is very familiar to the Western world but very few actually know what it means. *Maya* is a word which was first used in the Advaita Vedanta school of Hinduism. Now it is used glibly by everyone. This universe of changing forms is called *maya*. It is the illusory power of the Brahman which makes us believe that the external world is the true reality. *Maya* is the external garb of the universe. She is like a well-dressed, heavily made-up woman who appears beautiful and enticing. It is only when you remove her make-up that you discover her real form. Her external garb is made up of the three *gunas* or qualities of primordial matter. She is the one who projects the three conditions of duality—space, time and causation. *Maya* is not illusion but it is that which creates some sort of delusion in us which makes us think that the shapes and forms and events in which we live, are real. It is the power of confusing concepts for reality, for confusing the map with the territory! But if we realise that *maya* is only a veil which hides Reality from us—an appearance that has been produced at some point in space and time—then we are no longer under the spell of *maya*. We will understand that it is only a display of forms. *Maya* is also known as *Shakti*, which is the power or energy of the Brahman and it is she that projects this dynamic world. It is only by stripping her of her external accoutrements that we can expose that Reality which is her support. Thus, she is not an existent reality and has no existence apart from the Brahman. Hence, the *rishis* said that the world is *maya*. Even though it appears to be solid and real, it is actually not what we think it is. Thus another meaning for the word *maya* is *ya-ma*—that which doesn't exist. So if this world is *maya*, it would follow that it is something which does not exist.

The greatest thing that quantum physics did for the spiritual-minded person was to show that the world of the senses is not a solid thing as the Newtonian scientists have been telling us. These physicists went to the heart of matter and were astounded by what they saw. Matter was not solid at all as our senses tell us but merely energy in motion. In fact, matter is composed of subatomic particles that have no design or shape and do not follow any standard order. Sometimes they behave like waves and sometimes like particles and sometimes they are both at the same time. Hence, these physicists actually proved the *maya* theory in a scientific way. Our scriptures have been telling us this truth for centuries but we with our dependence and total belief in the theories of Western science were most scornful of it. But now when the Western scientists themselves say the same thing, but of course not in the same words, we are forced to believe them even though our senses belie this truth.

The *rishis* have always been telling us that reality is not what we think it is. It is a kind of play or passing show. With the dawn of the 20th century, we find that physics has started to support this view wholeheartedly. With one squiggle of his pen, Einstein exploded the deterministic, mechanical view of matter. A revolution occurred in the thought of Western scientists—a battle between accepted beliefs and empirical truth as provided by the scientist. The theory of relativity showed that we can observe only relations, while the quantum theory declared that we can see only probabilities. Together they have come up with mathematical equations that prove that particles and waves in their different states do not actually tell us what they are but merely indicate the different kinds of knowledge that we may have about them. Therefore, modern physics deals with knowledge which might be possible and not with the essence of any fundamental reality.

The original meaning of *maya* in the Veda is the magical creative power of the Brahman. It has changed its meaning over the centuries. From the might or power of the divine magician, it has also come to signify the psychological state of anybody under the spell of the magic show. When we confuse the myriad forms of the divine play with reality, without perceiving the unity of the Brahman underlying these forms, we are under the spell of *maya*. What gives form and purpose to the drama we see on the TV screen is the firm, unchanging, white screen beneath. Without that screen which in itself has no qualities and no change or movement, the moving pictures which we are watching will not have any meaning. Similarly, the drama of our life and the lives of others has meaning only because of the unchanging, steady foundation of the Pure Consciousness of the Brahman on which it is being played.

This is what Eddington says about the world.

> The world that we experience in everyday life is a convenient mirage attuned to our very limited sense—an illusion conjured by our perceptions and our mind. All that is around us (including our own bodies) which appears so substantial is ultimately nothing but ephemeral networks of particles and waves whirling round at lightning speed, colliding, rebounding, disintegrating in almost total emptiness. So called matter is mostly emptiness, proportionately as void as galactic space, void of anything except occasional dots and spots of scattered electric charges.

The quantum world sharpens into concrete reality only when an observation is made. In the absence of an observer, the atomic world is only a possibility. The particles materialise only when we look for them. When you look for the location of a particle you can find it at that particular place but you cannot gauge its speed. When you want to gauge its speed, it becomes a wave and you can see it in motion. However, you cannot fix both its location and speed at the same time. So-called reality displays itself only when there is an observer and cannot be separated from him. Quantum physics prefers the word "participator" to "observer". We cannot observe a thing without influencing it and in reality we are actually creating our world. A particle with momentum did not exist before the experimenter conducted an experiment to measure its position. Thus, the modern-day physicists say that particles have "a tendency to exist" and not that they really exist.

Thus, the quantum physicist discovered something novel which the ancient physicist could not accept—that the only thing which can be called real in this shadow world is the consciousness of the spectator or the experimenter. Without that consciousness, even this shadow world would not exist. Everything is centred round the experimenter. This was a great breakthrough. Till now the experimenter's job was always to get out of the way of the experiment and not interfere with the purely mechanical process involved in the experiment. Now it was proved by the scientist that the individual consciousness has everything to do with the final outcome of the experiment. This consciousness stems from a phenomenon known as super-radiance, which is a state of perfect coherence.

Normally quantum particles act in a haphazard fashion of chaos or disorder but when the individual consciousness is brought to bear on them, they lose their individuality and begin to act as a single unit. This coherence extends into the world. This coherence of consciousness represents the greatest form of order known to nature and can help to shape and create order in the world. In meditation and especially in the state of *samadhi*, our brain reaches that zero point field of the *chitta* which has perfect coherence.

John Wheeler says,

Is it possible that the universe in some strange sense is brought into being by the participation of those who participate?

The vital thing here is the participation. Classical theory says the observer is the man who stands safely behind a glass wall and watches what goes on without participating in anything. This is an impossibility according to quantum physics.

Thus, the quantum physicist corroborates the claim of the *rishis* that the world exists only because we, the observers, are actively participating in it. The world is a creation of the human mind. Each of us creates our own world. These words are used by both Vedanta and by the quantum physicists. The zero point field is the most fundamental state of matter and this is a heaving sea of energy—one vast quantum field. On the quantum level, all living beings including human beings are packets of quantum energy constantly exchanging information with this inexhaustible field of energy, which is known as the *chitta* in Hindu terminology. Information about all aspects of life is relayed through the interchange of information on the quantum level. Have you watched a flight of birds gliding their way across the sky and how suddenly all of them veer to a different course as if at some hidden signal? The same phenomenon can be noticed in schools of fish. Till now it was assumed that these birds and fish had a novel method of communicating with each other by some radar or some noise signal which we cannot hear but experiments on the quantum field proved that they are all in touch with this field and receive their orders simultaneously from it. This is the substructure which underlies the whole universe. It is a recording medium of everything, by which everything can communicate with everything else.

The functions of our minds like thinking, feeling, etc. draw information from the quantum field which is pulsing simultaneously through our body and brain. In fact, we resonate with the universe.

Advaita Vedanta had declared that the universe is an illusion created by the participators in this drama. The Copenhagen interpretation of Quantum Mechanics is in complete agreement with this. It says that the world which we perceive as a physical reality is actually our mental construction of it. Although this mental construction appears to be solid, the physical world itself is not. They did not take the weak stand that the physical world as we see it "may or may not" exist but declared categorically that it "does not" exist as we see it.

The question was then raised as to how the Supreme unchangeable substance turned into the changing world. Vedanta describes this unique phenomenon by postulating *maya* as the cause of the superimposition. *Maya* has two powers, one to veil and the other to project. It veils the Brahman and projects pluralities on the non-dual. How is this done? Let us take the example of light and darkness. Light exists, darkness does not. The latter is only the absence of the former. Although darkness does not exist in reality, it has empirical existence. Similarly, the world also exists empirically.

According to the relativity theory, continuous activity is the very essence of matter. Hence, in Hinduism, *maya* is described as a state of "becoming" whereas Being is only attributed to the Brahman. The Puranas describe it poetically. Shiva in his form as the Absolute is called Bhava or "Being", whereas Parvati who is the essence of *maya* is known as Bhavani or "Becoming."

There can be no change without expenditure of energy. The Sanskrit word for energy is *Shakti* and also refers to *maya* as we have seen. *Shakti* is that which has the ability to work. Hinduism with its genius for personification says that *Shakti* is a feminine principle of Brahman which is co-existent with it. Out of this feminine principle of *Shakti,* countless goddesses have been created by the prolific minds of the *rishis.* Thus, every god is given his own *Shakti*—Shiva /Parvati, Lakshmi/Narayana, Brahma and Saraswati and so on. Thus, scientific facts are neatly interwoven into the Puranic stories.

The only way to break free from this spell of the enchantress *maya* is to come to a realisation that all the phenomena we perceive with our five senses are part of the same reality. This is known as *moksha* or liberation. This means that we begin to personally experience that everything including our own self is nothing but the Brahman. This is the very essence of Hinduism.

How do we attain this realisation? Many techniques like meditation and different types of *yoga* are given in Hinduism but we should also look at what the great sage of Thiruvannamalai known as Ramana Maharishi, who lived in the 20th century, advised. He brought forward the Upanishadic view even more forcibly. He said that the essence of consciousness is embedded in the core of the human mind. The Upanishads already state that "*Atman* and Brahman are equal." The true nature of consciousness is revealed to us only when *maya* is removed from the mind through right perception. How to remove this *maya* is the next question. Ramana advocated the method known as "self-enquiry" in order to remove the veil of *maya*. "Who am I?" is the question he asked people to use. By negating all those parts of our selves which are transitory or superficial we will come to the realisation that we are nothing other than that Supreme Consciousness of the Brahman. This is indeed liberation from all the fears that haunt the mind of the human being. Fear of death, extreme attachment to people, places and objects are banished forever with this basic knowledge which must be made a part of our everyday life.

Our enquiry into our true selves should make us realise that the Supreme Self is equally present in all beings irrespective of any perceived differences. Meditation and different types of *yoga* can only give us occasional glimpses of the Supreme Self but this abiding knowledge that existence has no separateness can at one stroke remove all our mental agonies. This can be achieved only through sustained self-enquiry.

Maya plays an important part in the Hindu view of creation. According to Hinduism, creation is cyclical and not linear as in the West. Every manifestation is preceded by a period when everything is unmanifest. Before every manifestation, the universe is potentially existent in *maya*. *Maya* has three constituents known as *gunas*. These are known as *sattva, rajas* and *tamas*. In physics these three are known as harmony, kinesis and inertia. The processes of creation (*srishti*), preservation (*sthiti*) and dissolution (*pralaya*) cannot take place when the three *gunas* of *maya* are in a state of equilibrium. As long as these three are in balance, creation is at rest. When the time comes for another manifestation, a ripple appears in the still waters of *maya* transmitted by the Brahman. This vibration is in the form of a sound which is called *Aum*. This is the first sound and from this the whole universe of names and forms is manifested. The dormant, potential, unmanifest universe becomes manifest when *rajas* or the quality of kinesis comes into prominence. The preservation of the universe in its manifested state is carried on during the stage in which *sattva* is predominant. When *tamas* becomes predominant, the process of dissolution becomes operative.

Everything in the universe has these three constituents in their make-up—sometimes *sattva* predominates, sometimes *rajas* and sometimes *tamas*. One follows the other and most things are a mixture of all three. Even in our own bodies and characters these three have free play. When *sattva* predominates, we are calm and peaceful; when *rajas* predominates, we become very active; and when *tamas* rules, we become lazy or sleepy. Of course these three keep changing their roles constantly hence we get the beautiful drama of life with its changing patterns, its painful incidents, interspersed with beautiful and serene interludes.

Maya is also said to be the material cause of the universe. But *maya* is insentient like wood or gold. Wood cannot be converted into a chair or table without a carpenter. The carpenter has the skill and is called the efficient cause. When we observe the world both on the micro and the macro levels, it is intelligently designed for specific purposes. It has both design and beauty. From the world of sub-atomic particles up to the galaxies, stars and planetary systems, there appears to be a perfect plan. In the gross and subtle structures of both the living and non-living world, we again see planning and design. However, the insentient star and planetary systems are totally ignorant of this. Even the human being who is supposed to be the most intelligent animal on earth has still not been able to decipher the mystery of the universe and the amazing arrangement of the working of his own body and brain! Without his conscious effort, his own system functions purposefully and intelligently. This happens with all systems—plants, bacteria, viruses, galaxies and so on. The materialists say this is all done "naturally". What exactly is implied by the word "naturally"? Can you take a few logs of wood, throw them in the air and expect a chair? By a deep observation of the plan of the universe and of our own bodies and minds, any rational being will have to infer the existence of an invisible planner and designer, call Him what you will.

Albert Einstein says,

> Certain it is that a conviction, akin to religious feeling of the rationality or the intelligibility of the world lies behind all scientific work of a higher order. This firm belief, a belief bound up with deep feeling in a superior mind that reveals itself in the world of experience, represents my conception of God.

The position of the Western scientist is that of the *jijnasu* or enquirer on the path of truth as the *Gita* puts it. They are eager and anxious to know the Truth but somehow this ultimate Truth seems to defy all attempts at generalizations. Hence, we see that even though we live in this highly scientific age, yet there is a great belief on the part of even educated people to believe in the occult and the miraculous. There seem to be some things in the world which defy scientific investigation. This is where religion and especially Hindu spiritualism steps in to show us that some things exist which are beyond the level of the mind.

Let us go into classical physics and see what they thought of as reality. In the West, there was always an antagonism between religion and science. In India, our religion itself was so scientific that such problems never arose. Western science was sadly cribbed and confined by the church which refused to accept any scientific theory which was not supported by the Bible. For a long time, the church supported the geocentric view of the universe that the earth was the centre of the universe. It was Copernicus who first advocated the heliocentric view in 1543. Luckily for him, his book was published on his deathbed but he was severely reprimanded and excommunicated. Later, in 1608, Galileo supported his view and declared that the earth revolved round the sun. This was considered as blasphemy by the church. He was seized by the inquisition and forced to retract his view on pain of death. However, Truth can never be totally annihilated. Galileo's views slowly took over the minds of the thinking world. Western science had a long and lonely battle before the world came to accept, somewhat reluctantly, this view of the matter.

Sir Isaac Newton is said to be the father of classical physics. He was deeply impressed by the mechanistic view of the universe as given by Descartes. This view dominated all scientific thoughts from the second half of the 17th century to the end of the 19th century. Newton believed that the world was created by God who assembled all the different objects and made a huge machine. In devising the world machine, God created the material particles, the forces between them and the fundamental laws of motion. Creation took place one fine day and God breathed into this machine the first impulse so that it would run and since then the world machine keeps running on immutable laws like a gigantic clock. All natural laws are invariable and eternal. God transcends the world and rules it from above. The Newtonian world was a lonely place in which the human being had no place. The world carried on whether we were present or not. It was almost as if we are mere witnesses to a show which goes on with or without our participation. He made man into a mere cog in a machine.

Whereas Newtonian science had totally divorced man from the universe, quantum science has demonstrated that there is a purpose and unity in life and we are an important part of it. What we do and think is critical in creating our world. We are not isolated beings living our desperate lives on a lonely planet in an indifferent universe. We are always at the centre of everything. We have the power both individually and collectively to heal ourselves and improve our own lives and the lives of others around us.

The biological findings of Darwin in his theory of natural selection had asserted that might is right and only the fittest would survive. This meant that the genetic terrorist who killed indiscriminately so as to save his own skin was the highest on the evolutionary ladder. To Darwin, the height of the evolutionary cycle was the superman who could conquer those who were weaker. Life was described as a predatory existence in which only the fittest could survive. Perhaps it was these views of life that led to terrorists like Hitler and Mussolini dominating the world through brute force, and in today's age, people like Dawood Ibrahim and the other extremists who hold the world to ransom at the point of a gun.

However, there was one obvious flaw in Darwin's theory. Preservation of the species actually depends on the infant of every creature but we find that the infant of every species is very weak and unable to look after itself. It can exist and grow only due to the love of the mother. Without this overwhelming love, which is prepared to sacrifice its own life to save its young, there would be no hope for any creature. So survival does not depend on being the strongest but on a most abstract and divine emotion called Love. It is love that has made the world survive and in love lies our only hope of survival in the future and not through brute strength and cunning as Darwin would have us believe.

For instance, scientific experiments conducted on plants and animals proved that those which were given loving care by their owners responded and bloomed much more than those which were left to their own devices. To make the tests clear, they got psychotic patients to water one set of plants and found that the molecular content of the water changed dramatically with the mental attitude of the one who was watering them and of course the plants also wilted. They then did experiments on patients and healers. The healers came from various sources—Hindu, Christian, Buddhist and Native American. But the main thing was that all of them were able to produce a positive effect on the patient. What all of them had in common was that having given a positive intention, they had kept out of the way, so to speak, and allowed that great healing force which they called God by whatever name to do the rest. So actually the cure was being controlled by that fundamental energy field which was activated by the intention of the healer. So we see that the greatest thing a doctor can do for his patient is to hope with all his heart that he or she will improve.

At various ages of time, Western science has tried to fix Reality in terms of matter, or energy, field or space. None of these proved satisfactory. Once Einstein himself thought "the field" to be the only Reality. Shortly before his death, he declared that "space" was the only reality. All attempts to fix Reality on matter, energy, particles, field and space were failures. Advaita Vedanta says that all these are products of *maya* and cannot be considered as real. Brahman is the only Reality.

In science two laws are considered fundamental and inviolate. One is the law of conservation of matter and the other the law of conservation of energy. The first says matter is neither created nor destroyed; the sum total of matter in the universe is constant. There may be transformation of matter from one form to another. The second law says energy is neither created nor destroyed; the sum total of energy in the universe is constant.

There may be transformation of energy from one form to another.

The same thing is said by Lord Krishna in the *Bhagavad-Gita* ten thousand years before. "Existence cannot come out of non-existence nor can non-existence ever become existent." (Chapter 11) This is a formal law which can never be invalidated.

Modern physics can only tell us about this lower nature which we call *maya* in Hinduism. Physics has also gone as far as the *chitta* which is on the boundary between the lower and higher but till now it is unable to tell us anything of the nature of Ultimate Reality. Eddington declared that great difference between old and new physics is that, though both are dealing with shadow symbols, the new physics has been forced to accept the fact that it is indeed dealing with shadows—a set of abstract equations and not with Reality itself. All the pictures that science draws of nature which can be proved are mathematical pictures. However, it is unable to formulate the Ultimate Reality. As Hinduism says, we can only see *maya* or the power of the Brahman; we can never see the Brahman which is the underlying cause. Even though physicists are able to reduce matter to its ultimate and fundamental state and put it into mathematical equations, yet to date they have not been able to reduce God into a mathematical equation.

Living consciousness is not an isolated entity. It is not the personal property of one individual. This much has been discovered in the quantum field. We think that each of us has a separate *atman* even though our scriptures tell us that when this apparently separate *atman* is covered with the body, it is called the *jivatma* but this *jivatma* is the same as the Paramatma—meaning to say it is not an isolated entity. This lives on even after the body dies since it has never been isolated from the whole so there is no question of going back. It simply slips into what it was, like the water in the bottle returning to the water of the pool when the bottle is broken. This consciousness of people has incredible powers. It can increase order in the world and make it as we wish it to be. If a number of individuals concentrate and wish for the same thing, it has even greater force. That is why we say that communal prayer has more power. The all-absorbing topic of the day is how to control the climatic changes which are being increasingly felt all over the world. If enough people had a burning desire to change the situation, they would do far better if they got together and meditated on this topic, willing the minds of people to change and thus stop the terrible effects we have brought upon ourselves. This would be far more effective than holding conferences and reading papers.

The human consciousness (as our scriptures have always told us) is a crucial factor in making up this universe. Sub-atomic particles settle down from their constant erratic movements and take on solid shapes only when we observe them. Since we are totally connected with everything and every creature in this universe, for each of us to strive to better oneself without regard to what happens to others is the most foolish thing that we could do. Human suffering stems from this very fact, that we have cut ourselves off from our roots and have condemned ourselves to a life of isolation. This was not how ancients wanted us to live. The greatest of the Vedic hymns keep this in view. *Loka samastha sukhino bhavantu*—Let the whole world be happy. Despite the various attacks on her culture and constant efforts to bring her religion down, India has always stuck to this slogan —*Loka samastha sukhino bhavantu.*

The cosmic vacuum was the original cause of creation of the universe, life and our thoughts. Our achievements are only reflection of its infinite wisdom. Can any human being subsisting in the endless ocean of consciousness claim originality or individuality.

Mandukya Upanishad

There is no parallel to Him,
Whose glory is truly great.

Yajur Veda

Loka Samasthath Sukhino Bhavantu!

ॐ

Pavanaaya Namaha!

CHAPTER XI

Desha and Kaala
(Space and Time)

In religion, India is the only millionaire—the one land which all men desire to see and having seen once by even a glimpse, would not give that glimpse for all the shows of all the rest of the globe combined.

Mark Twain

Lead me into that state of eternal light,
That light that shows the way to,
Perpetual, undecaying and immortal bliss,
May my heart turn towards the love,
Of the resplendent Lord,
The source of all light,
Speed fast, then O mind! And unite with the source of eternal bliss.

Rig Veda

Time is the most mysterious of god's powers. We really don't know how or why we calculate time. It has always been one of

Nature's untameables. Even though the mind has created it, the mind cannot understand it.

Time finds no place in Advaita Vedanta though space gets some prominence. Space is a positive entity. It is a product. On the contrary, time is a non-entity. It is not a product. In reality, there is nothing like time. Advaita Vedanta says that it is purely a mental concept. In the absence of any activity or event, there cannot be any mental concept of time. With the occurrence of more than one event, the mind constructs the concept called "time". After the dissolution of the cosmos and before the next creation starts, the Brahman alone remains. No events occur in that non-functional state. This is a timeless condition. Time exists as a concept due to the occurrences of many events taking place between creation and dissolution. The intellect conceives of these events as a series happening in time! When the universe does not exist, time does not exist. Even when it exists, it is not a real entity but merely a psychological concept!

Classical physics had always postulated that Time and Space were eternal realities. Space and time as independently existing realities were absolutes for Newton. He considered atoms to be the elementary building blocks of the universe. They were presumed to be absolutely solid, impenetrable, indestructible and unchangeable. He believed in the strictly causal nature of physical phenomena. So it was a big shock to the classical physicist to hear Einstein's theory of matter. Hardly had they recovered from this shock when came the second shock with his theory of relativity. Einstein and many of the scientists who came after him proved that time and space are relative. This is a shocking idea to us, bound as we are to our clocks and time schedules.

The fact that Time and Space are not eternal verities but convenient suppositions of the mind were well known to the *rishis*. They declared that human life is completely conditioned by the three *upadhis* (conditionings) known as *desha, kaala* and *nimitta*—space, time and causation. Everything we see in the world exists in space for a certain period of time and has a cause. This is how the mind works. Without these three *upadhis,* the mind cannot function.

Newton, as has been said, thought that both space and time were invariable and absolute verities but Einstein said that time and space are relative to speed. Distance varies according to speed. The faster you go the more slowly time seems to move. Speed is actually got by dividing distance (space) by time. This means that both time and space depend on motion. Time exists because things or events seem to happen. They move in relation to each other. What about space? It is only something which exists if something binds it on either side. We cannot think of space without anything inside it. Distance is a measurement of the space existing between two objects. Distance cannot exist without time. If all objects ceased to exist, there would be no space and no time since time cannot exist without space.

Einstein said that one cannot talk about space without bringing in time. All measurements involving space and time are devoid of absolute significance. The example of a pair of twins, who are twenty years old, is given. One twin goes in a spacecraft which goes at 9/10 of the speed of light. He returns to the earth when he is forty-six years old but finds that his twin has already turned eighty!

The same phenomenon is described in our Puranas, which shows that they were well aware of the fact that velocity reduces time. In the *Bhagavad Purana*, the king called Raivathan goes with his daughter, Revathi, to the world of Brahma and stays there only for the duration of a few minutes but when he returns he finds the whole world has changed and none of the people he knew existed any more. They were already dead and gone. Moreover, he finds that people have shrunk in size whereas he and his daughter were very tall. He could not find anyone who could match his daughter in size so as to be able to marry her. At last he found that the only man who could match her was Balarama, Lord Krishna's brother. There are many other instances which show us that the ancients were well aware of the fact that time and space and velocity are irrevocably bound together.

The moment we demarcate ourselves as belonging to a specified place and time, that moment we separate ourselves from our roots, thus bringing suffering on ourselves. We are the creators of time and space. When we bring energy to conscious awareness, through the act of perception, we create separate objects that exist in space through a measured continuum called time. By creating time and space, we create our own separateness.

As we have seen, Brahman alone is said to be *sat* or pure existence. Thus, the Brahman is beyond time. Hinduism does not declare the world to be *asat* or non-existent. The *jagat* or world is *mithya* and not *asat*. It is called *mithya* because it has a dependent and relative existence. It is not eternal and timeless but it exists on the substratum of the Brahman. The universe has a beginning and thus it also has an end. Time starts with the beginning of the universe and ends with its dissolution. Space is born with the origin of the universe and expands and contracts, finally dissolving with the dissolution of the universe. Thus, the universe is known as *mithya*. *Brahma Satyam, jagat mithya*

(Brahman alone is Real and the world unreal), is what our scriptures say.

Without change and movement nothing can exist even for a moment. The stars are revolving, the planets are rotating, the galaxies are moving, and the whole universe is expanding. This is applicable to the sub-atomic world also where every particle is constantly in motion. This movement is what gives rise to the illusion of space and time! The Sanskrit word for the world is *jagat*—that which is ever moving and ever changing. By giving the name *jagat* to the world, we can realise that the ancients knew this important fact. Vedanta declares that the world is not eternal. As long as it exists, it is ever changing. But it does not exist forever. It comes into existence at zero time and stays in position up to its maximum time. It has a definite span of life and then dissolves into the essence. This process of creation, maintenance and dissolution is repeated in cycles. Science supports this view that nothing in this universe exists forever.

Even though they denied any absolute existence to time, yet the *rishis* had their own method of calculating time since it is an obvious fact of our human life. Sanskrit has had words starting from micro seconds to millennia. They knew of light years. The lifespan of Brahma, the creator, is known as a *kalpa,* which is the longest period of time which we can think of—millions of light years. They also had words to describe the minutest period of time, less than the blink of an eyelid. They knew about atoms which were called *anus* and even particles which were called *paramanus.*

In order to aid their calculations, the *rishis* said that every cycle of creation has four *yugas* or eons which are known as Satya Yuga, Treta Yuga, Dwapara Yuga, and Kali Yuga. We are now in the Kali Yuga. By astronomical observations of planetary movements, the exact date of the Kali Yuga has been verified. Kali Yuga began in 3102 BCE in the month of February at 2 hours, 27 minutes and 30 seconds. The Western astrologer Bailey says,

> The calculations of the Brahmins are so exactly confirmed by our own astronomical tables that nothing but actual observation could have given so correspondent a result!

This means that the Kali Yuga began 5143 years ago.

The Mahabharata war began thirty-six years prior to the start of Kali Yuga when thirty-six years of Dwapara Yuga still remained. If we check this with the dates given by Western scholars for the Mahabharata war, we will see that their dates are quite absurd and unscientific.

Manusmriti and *Suryasiddhanta* state that one *kalpa* is a thousand *yugas*. Aryabhatta, the great Hindu astronomer of the 6th century, gives a slightly different account of the *yugas* which is simpler and more scientific.

He says that one *kalpa* is one thousand and eight *yugas*.

One *manvantara* or the age of one Manu (the universal patriarch and producer of the human race) is given in the *Suryasiddhanta* as seventy-one *yugas* while Aryabhatta says it is seventy-two *yugas*.

One *yuga* is said to be 4,320,000 years in the *Manusmriti* and Aryabhatta confirms this.

Both the older systems divided the *yuga* into four smaller *yugas* but Aryabhatta took them to be of equal duration, naming them as quarter *yugas*, the duration of each being 1,080,000 years.

From this we can see that Indian astronomers were able to calculate time from micro minutes to millennia long before European astronomers came to the picture.

Pure energy as it exists on the quantum level is not bound by time or space but exists as a vast continuum of fluctuating change which exists here and now. This moment, this tiny bit of time and space we are existing in now is the only truth and reality. The past is a dream and the future a fantasy. What exists is the present, which again has only a fleeting reality. Even as I am speaking this present which you and I think is real has already slipped into an irretrievable past and this future which I have been dreaming about has come and been swallowed up by the present.

What do we know about the exact meaning of the word "now"? If the past has already gone and future has not yet come then all that exists is "now". So how long does "now" last? What is the duration of "now"? If the past and future already exist then "now" is simply a moving finger agitating each pre-existing moment as it passes. Does this mean that the future already exists in some nebulous form which takes shape as we move towards it and as it gets focused upon by our consciousness? When we have something urgent to be done, ten minutes pass like one. If, however, we are waiting for someone to come then ten minutes appear to drag on forever.

Time and space cannot be cut up into units smaller than the smallest unit which is called minima. Parmenides, the Greek philosopher, came to the conclusion that Being consisted of only one thing or one unit. Of course this is something which the ancient *rishis* have always emphasised that Reality is only one. It cannot be divided and cut up into bits. Since space-time is a combined unit made up by the mind, it cannot be cut up into bits and this is what the mind tries to do all the time and thus gets frustrated.

The end of time is something we will never experience since it can only be experienced at the moment of death. The human being is the only one in the animal kingdom able to conceptualize past, present and future and thus the only being that is aware of the process of change, ageing, decay and death. This is why we are obsessed with death, mortality and the end of time.

Vedic astrology has always been sidereal or based on stellar positions. It determines the positions of the signs of the zodiac relative to the observable fixed stars. The old Western method employed a topical zodiac which determines the signs of the zodiac relative to the equinoxes and solstices. The sidereal zodiac takes the point of precession into consideration whereas the topical ignores it. Thus, if we know at what point in the sidereal zodiac the equinox occurs, we can determine the astronomical era and date, like the age of Aquarius. This is how Vedic seers determined the age of different planets. They used the most universal of all clocks, the stars. While such precessional changes are not noticeable in an ordinary human lifetime, in cultures that endure over centuries and millennia, they become obvious. From this we can gauge that the Vedic culture has emerged from the hoary past of the universe.

Now let us have a look at our ancient method of reckoning time. The Indian calendar has several types of time but the main one is sidereal, as has been pointed out. A sidereal month is measured not from one full moon to another but according to the moon's return to the same place among the fixed stars. Hence, a sidereal month has twenty-seven days. A sidereal year is marked by the time the sun returns to the same position in the fixed stars. A sidereal day is four minutes shorter than a regular day so there are 366 of them in a normal year. This orientation to a specific point in the sky causes the calendar to gradually slip backwards with the precession of the zodiac. In other words, the indication of the precession is built into the Hindu calendar by using sidereal time. A culture which employs sidereal time will find the position of the equinoxes to move back a week or so every 500 years, which is about seven degrees on the zodiac. This is why the Hindus celebrate the sun entering the sign of Capricorn on January 14th as this is an observable sidereal position whereas the Western topical calendar uses December 21st as the date of the winter solstice but this date is now actually in the sign of Sagittarius.

Now let us see what methods were used by our ancient people for calculating time. They knew about sundials but found that these could predict time only on sunny days and certainly not at night. So they made the ingenious devise known as water clocks, which did not depend on the sun. A small copper vessel with a small hole was floated in a big bowl of water. The water would filter into the vessel slowly and when it reached half an hour or one hour, as the case may be, the vessel would sink to the bottom. At that time a gong would be struck to denote the time and a bead would be shifted in an abacus. Anyone who wanted to know the time could come and count the beads on the abacus and have a good idea of the time. The Buddhist and Jain monks would use these water clocks to find out the amount of time they had to sit for meditation.

In Delhi and Jaipur, huge instruments were made in a place called "Jantar Mantar". These were positioned so carefully that one can find the correct time of day exactly to the minute by observing the shadows cast by them. Both these places have huge sundials and other instruments to gauge the position of the stars in the zodiac and so on. The kings who constructed these wanted to prove how accurate the Hindu almanacs and calendars were.

Today, we hear of the dawning of the age of Aquarius. What this means is that the point of the vernal equinox—the position of the sun among the stars on the first day of spring—is approaching the sign of Aquarius. This tilting of the earth on its axis is known as the precession and this changes at a rate of 50 seconds per year and completes a whole cycle of the zodiac in about 25,800 years.

One Vedic calendar goes back to 3000 years and another goes back to 6000 years. The western world could not believe or did not want to believe that the ancient *rishis* were such experts in astronomy that they could actually make such accurate calendars. They insisted that the Hindus must have stolen it from the Greeks. Actually, the opposite is true and the Greek calendar uses many of the words of the ancient Vedic calendar. The Western world had always taken Greece to be the source of all modern culture and now despite all evidence to the contrary, Western scholars do not want to believe that Vedic culture existed much earlier than the Greek.

Why does our new year start on April 14th? As you know, the earth revolves around its axis and around the sun. Our Vedic astronomers said that the earth's revolution round the sun starts from the fixed point known as *mesha sankranti rekha,* which is the Alpha Aries point. This is why our astronomical new year's day starts on *mesha sankranti,* which normally falls on April 14th. In Sanskrit it is known as *mesha vishuvath.* The Kerala New Year is called Vishu from the word *vishuvath*. As usual, Hinduism connects science with spirituality. The time of the change of the sign from *meena* to *mesha (mesha sankranti)* is known as *punya kaalam*, or an auspicious time, hence spiritual practices done on this day have extra power.

When the Vedic seers observed the stars, they saw a different orientation from what we see today. The points of the solstices and equinoxes fell among different stars than they do now. This is because of the slow changes in the Earth's orientation to the constellations according to the precession of the equinoxes. The Vedas present ancient astronomical positions which can give us the dates at which they existed. But Western scholars generally tend to distrust any astronomical data from the Hindus who they believed to be unscientific!

The *rishis'* knowledge of space as existing in the cosmos is amazing when you realize that these truths have only recently come into the vision of the modern scientists. The great sage Vasishta is supposed to have told Rama,

> Countless have been the universes that have come into being and then dissolved. In fact even now countless universes exist at this moment and it would be impossible to conceive them in our minds. However they can be immediately realised in one's own heart, for these universes are the creations of the desires that arise in the heart, like castles built in the air. Human beings conjure up this world in their hearts and keep on strengthening the illusion of reality during their lifetime. When they pass away, they conjure up the worlds beyond and experience those. Thus there are worlds within worlds just as there are layers within layers in a banana stem. Neither the world of matter nor the modes of creation are truly real, yet the living and the dead think and feel that they are real.

Ignorance of this truth helps to propagate and give a semblance of reality to this illusory creation!

From this we see that the ancient sages knew that our galaxy was only one, in infinite space in which many such galaxies like ours exist. These discoveries were very recent in Western science. However, in the ancient text called the *Devi Purana*, the Maha Devi takes Brahma, Vishnu and Shiva for a joyride in her chariot and they pass many galaxies and she points out to them that each one has its own Brahma, Indra and set of gods each busy with his own function. She explains to them that this galaxy is not the only one and that many such galaxies exist in her control! (This has already been told in another chapter.)

Now let us consider what the *rishis* knew about the age of the universe. Western religion has always claimed that the universe is only 6,000 years old but the *rishis* have always contented that our present cosmos is billions of years old and that it is just one of many such universes which have arisen and dissolved in the vastness of eternity. The birth of our solar system has been poetically described in the Puranas as has already been mentioned. The Puranas talk about the milky ocean, which is of course the Milky Way. Through the will of the creator, a vortex shaped like a lotus rises from the navel of eternity (Vishnu). It was called Hiranyagarbha, the shining womb. It gradually coalesced into our world, but it will perish some day billions of years hence when the sun expands to many times its present size, swallowing all life on the earth. In the end, as the Puranas proclaim, the ashes of the earth will be blown into space by the cosmic wind. It is only with the birth of the 20th century that we can understand this to be a beautiful simile for the fate of our planet!

Thus, Hindu astronomy is a much specialised system that requires precise astronomical observations and shows an ongoing knowledge of the exact placement of the planets and equinoxes relative to the fixed stars. Hence, the knowledge which the ancients had about Time and Space was indeed formidable.

> If I am asked which nation has been advanced in the ancient world in respect of education and culture, then I would say it was—India.
>
> *Max Müller, German Indologist*

> Distribute thy wealth to those who deserve it,
> And seek the love of God,
> The most precious treasure of life.
>
> *Sama Veda*

Loka Samasthath Sukhino Bhavantu!

ॐ

Achintyaaya Namaha!

CHAPTER XII

Vedic Astronomy and Astrology

I seem to have been only a boy playing on the sea shore diverting myself now and again by finding a smoother pebble or a prettier shell while the great ocean of truth lay before me.

Isaac Newton

The evolutionary energy of the Supreme Self created the universe, life and the mind. Its infinite intelligence has enchained us to the endless conundrum of cause and effect.

Mundaka Upanishad

In the solitary regions of green valleys,
And the confluence of the rivers,
The sages obtain divine intuition.

Rig Veda

Modern astrophysics and astronomy tell us that our Galaxy called the Milky Way or Akasha-Ganga, in Vedic terminology, contains approximately 100,000 million of stars. Each star is like our sun having its own planetary system. We know that the moon moves round the earth and the earth moves round the sun along with the moon. All planets move round the sun. Each of the above bodies revolves on its own axis as well. Our sun along with its family takes one round of the galactic centre in 22.5 crore years. All galaxies including ours are moving away at a terrific velocity of 20,000 miles per second.

The total kinetic energy generated by the galaxies moving at 20,000 miles per sec. creates an amazing sound and this acts as an umbrella and balances the total energy consumption of the cosmos.

The great 14th century scholar, Sayana, in his commentary on one passage in the *Rig Veda* says, "With deep respect, I bow to the sun, which travels 2,202 *yojanas* in half a *nimisha*".

What exactly does this imply? A *yojana* is about nine miles. A *nimisha* is 16/75 of a second. How much does this give us? 2,202 *yojanas* x 9 miles x 75/8 *nimishas* = 185,794 miles per second. Thus, Sayana, a Vedic scholar who died in AD 1387, calculated that sunlight travels at the rate of 186,000 miles per second and this information was gleaned from a hymn in the *Rig Veda* written at a time which we cannot even imagine. The amazing fact is that this happens to be the speed of light which has been calculated by modern physicists in the last century!

Western scholars might say that this is a coincidence. If so, the Vedic tradition is filled with such coincidences!

Some Western scholars have claimed that the Babylonians invented the zodiac of 360 degrees around 700 BCE, perhaps even earlier. Many claim that India received the knowledge of the zodiac from Babylonia or even later from Greece. However, in the *Rig Veda*, the oldest Vedic text, there are clear references to a *chakra* or wheel of 360 spokes placed in the sky. The number 360 and its related numbers like 12, 24, 36, 48, 60, 72, 108, 432 and 720 occur commonly in Vedic symbolism.

It might seem impossible for us to believe that the speed of light or the fate of our solar system could be determined without advanced astronomical instruments. How could the writers of old Sanskrit texts have known the unknowable?

In searching for an explanation, we first need to understand that these ancient scientists were not just intellectuals; they were practicing *yogis* who had sharpened their intuitive intellect to hitherto unknown heights.

The very first lines of the *Surya Siddhanta* say: "In the Golden Age a great astronomer named Mayan desired to learn the secrets of the heavens, so he first performed rigorous *tapas*. Then the answers to his questions appeared in his mind in an intuitive flash." In his *Yoga Sutras,* Patanjali Maharishi, the foremost of the great psychologists of India and the world, states that through *samyama* (concentration, meditation, and unbroken mental absorption) on the sun, moon and pole star, we can gain all knowledge of the planets and stars. The next *sutra* (couplet) clarifies this by saying, "Through keenly developed intuition, everything can be known."

Highly developed intuition is called *pratibha* in Sanskrit. It is available to those who have completely stilled their minds and are capable of focusing their attention on one object with laser-like intensity. Since their minds are totally under control, they are not limited to the fragments of knowledge supplied by the five senses. All knowledge became accessible to them. The traditional Hindu view is that pure consciousness contains all knowledge—past, present and future—and thus it is the very source of universal knowledge.

The *Surya Siddhartha* is the oldest surviving astronomical text in Hinduism. It is dated by Western scholars to the 5th or 6th centuries though of course the text itself claims to come from a much older tradition. It says that the earth is shaped like a ball and on the very opposite side from India is a great city where the sun is rising at the same time as it sets in India. In this city they claim that a race of *siddhas* or spiritual adepts live. If you follow these directions on the globe, you will find that Mexico lies on the exact opposite of India. The ancient *rishis* were obviously well aware of the great astronomers of Central America many centuries before the so-called discovery of America by Columbus. Today, we know that the Mayans and Incas were well ahead of their times in astronomy.

Vedic astronomers were also able to describe the different planets and stars and had names even for Uranus, which is only a recent discovery. They even predicted the length of time for Hailey's comet to reappear.

The star called Antares is said to be the 15th brightest in the solar system. However, Hindus call it *jyestha* or the biggest or eldest. It is only recently that it was discovered to be fifty times bigger than other stars! Indian astronomers had identified it seven thousand years ago!

Arundhati and Vasishta are the names of two stars found in the constellation known as the Big Bear, which was considered to be just one star by Western astronomers. Hindu astronomers had found that they were actually two stars revolving round each other and that is why they looked like one star. They called this couple Vasishta and Arundhati, after the great sage Vasishta and his wife Arundhati who were supposed to be an exemplary couple. On the first night of their wedding, south Indian couples are asked to go and take a look at these stars so that they could also have a perfect marriage.

Valmiki, the author of the *Ramayana*, is actually the first Indian astronomer and thus the first world astronomer. He clearly gives the correct positions of the stars at certain points in the life of Rama, around the year 5000 BC which have been verified by modern software procedure.

Many Hindus use a *mala* or rosary of *rudraksha* seeds or *tulasi* beads containing 108 beads in order to do their *japa* (repetition of the *mantra*). There is a scientific reason for using this particular number as there is in everything prescribed by Hinduism.

The diameter of the sun is about 108 times the earth's diameter. The distance between the earth and sun is approximately 108 times the sun's diameter. The distance between the earth and the moon is 108 times the moon's diameter. Incredible as it may seem, the *rishis* were well aware of these facts and that is why they declared the number 108 to be sacred. Had they given scientific reasons for this in those ancient times, nobody would have been capable of believing them. It is only now with the progress of modern science that we of the modern age can recognise these facts and begin to believe in the unbelievable intelligence of those amazing beings.

There is another reason why the number of beads in the Hindu rosary has 108 beads instead of 100. This *mala* represents the ecliptic, the path of the earth and moon across the sky. Hindu astronomy divides the ecliptic into four equal sections called *paadas* or steps. These *paadas* contain 27 stars called *nakshatras*. When you multiply 27 with 4, you get 108 and these mark the steps that the earth and moon take through the heavens. Each of these steps is associated with a particular planet and deity with which you align yourself as you turn the beads.

The 109th bead is known as the *meru* or *guru* bead and it comes in the very middle of the *mala*. When you repeat the *mantra* and turn the *mala* round in your hand, you will come to the central bead or the *guru* bead. Here we are supposed to stop and turn the *mala* round and continue reciting the *mantra* as you move the beads in the opposite direction. The *meru* bead represents the summer and winter solstices, when the sun appears to stop in its course and reverse its direction in a dramatic fashion. By using a *mala* in this way we are actually connecting ourselves with the cosmic cycles governing our universe! The *rishis* were well aware of the fact that the macrocosm (solar system) is mirrored in us (the microcosm). Actually it is said that there are 108 steps between our ordinary human awareness and the divine consciousness at the centre of our being. Each time we chant a *mantra*, we are taking another step towards our own inner sun!

Now the question arises how these people found out so much about the planets without any instruments. The reason is simple. "Instruments are only the extensions of a human being's inherent powers",—the power to see, to hear, or to accomplish things he wants done. For example, a telescope allows us to see distant objects like the planets; a microscope allows us to see tiny objects. Unless we have eyesight, neither of these instruments will work. However, when these powers are developed in oneself, then one has them at his or her command by the mere power of thought without the need for instruments. You must remember that the *rishis* were in perfect control of their minds. So if the *rishis* wanted to find out about the planets or about anything else, all they had to do was to concentrate on that object and they were able to find out everything they wanted. This of course is an infallible method and that is why their findings have never been refuted up to the present day whereas in the West one person would discover something and another person would come and refute it. Such things are going on even now.

The *rishis* were also able to intercept the electromagnetic waves and tune in to things which were happening in other places without using a radio or TV. They could also visit other planets in their astral bodies. It is only if we want to transport our physical bodies that we need rockets and spaceships but the *rishis* could travel in their astral bodies and thus they were able to find out many things about other planets. As has been said, the microcosm is only a reflection of the macrocosm and thus everything that takes place anywhere in the cosmos can be known by the human being. The sciences of parapsychology and telepathy are all very new to the modern mind but these phenomena were well known to the *rishis*.

Since the *rishis* were so good in astronomy, it followed that they were also very good in astrology. Our great seers could see into the future and make many predictions.

Astrology is the science of life and can predict the type of life which every human being in the world will undergo at certain periods of time. The planets under which we are born have given us all our characteristics, both physical and mental. Apart from this, every moment of our lives we are under the domination of some planet or other even though we may not know it. This is what makes us display erratic patterns of behaviour at certain times. Very often we are unable to account for the changes in our "moods" as we call it.

The earth is the recipient of impact from other planets. Vedic calculations are based on the moon because the moon is the closest planet revolving round the earth and draws all planetary energies towards the earth's environment. Vedic astrology understood that the moon is the fastest moving planet compared to the others in the invisible zodiac zone. Thus, Vedic calculations use the lunar month and not the solar.

It takes fourteen days for the new moon to reach its fullness. This phase is known as the white phase (*shukla paksha*). It then takes another fourteen days to proceed to the new moon state, which is the waning phase known as (*krishna paksha*) or the dark phase. There is an overlap of a day as the new moon and full moon appear on the fourteenth day. This double counting is overcome by subtracting one day to get a total of twenty-seven days in a lunar month. The moon thus takes twenty-seven days to circle the 360 degrees of the zodiac. Each of these twenty-seven points of the moon is represented by a star or *nakshatra* beginning with Aswini and ending with Revathi. These provide the moon with a different constellation for every day of the lunar month. It is a more scientific system and easier to compute than the twelve signs of the zodiac of the western astrological system, in which there is a change of sign for the moon every two-and-a-quarter days. While each of the twelve signs of the zodiac consists of a thirty degree section of the heavens, the *nakshatras* cover an area of thirteen degrees and twenty minutes. This means that every thousand years, the equinox would have to be moved back to another lunar constellation to adjust for the precession.

Each month of the Vedic calendar is named after one of these lunar constellations or *nakshatras* on which the full moon occurs. If we examine the *nakshatra* chosen to rule the month we find that they mark the beginning of their sign. These *nakshatras* begin with the one that marks the vernal equinox. The *nakshatra* marking the full moon of the winter solstice is thus mentioned as the first month of the year (Aswini). Everyone is born under a particular *nakshatra* or star. These stars have also been broadly delineated as possessing god-like, demonic or human tendencies. Of course these are only broad characteristics and our natures also undergo changes with the changing of the planets during our lifetime and even during the day or week or month.

This system is totally different from that adopted by Western astrology which bases its calculations on the sun. The sun takes thirty days to move from one zodiac zone to another and thus can give only limited information. The moon moves faster and has greater impact on life. Hence, Vedic astrology is more precise and goes into greater detail. Based on the moon's movement round the earth and the earth's movement round the sun, the astrologer can predict with amazing accuracy the experiences which will occur in the lives of people living on earth. Likewise each planetary movement causes definite changes in the earth's environment as well as in the lives of those who live on this planet. The astrologer can identify the dynamic movements of energies by observing the position of the planets at the time of birth in the zodiac.

Using the Vedic astrological system and the data available at the time of your birth, the astrologer can determine the birth star and ruling planetary periods. Such periods will bring specific experiences. The sum of these periods is 120 years, which is supposed to be the lifespan of a human being. The astrologer identifies all the energies inhaled by you with your first breath, which determines the qualities of your physical, mental and astral systems and thus predicts the highlights of your life. He then casts your horoscope from which he or any other astrologer can predict with a fair degree of accuracy the broad facts about your birth, the number of siblings that you have, your parents' status, academic status, marriage, career, success, health, accidents and death. Of course, the experience of the astrologer who reads the horoscope is also of great consequence.

The time of manifestation of the baby from the mother's womb will determine its inborn characteristics. This will show how the planets are positioned in the zodiac at the time of birth. Great importance is given in astrology in identifying the very first inhalation to determine the effects of all subsequent inhalations. But it is very difficult to get the exact four seconds of the time of a baby's birth. So the astrologer has to work around the time given by the parents about the time of the baby's first inhalation.

The horoscope can only give broad outlines of the things that will happen to the person. How these things came to be, is not known to the astrologer. Hinduism says that the time of birth as well as everything concerning a person is determined by his or her past *karmas*. In fact, we come into this world to work out the effects of our *karmas*. Even though the astrologer can predict the future of a person, he cannot say why it is so and certainly he cannot control it. The universal intelligence is the one which is always in control. We can predict the weather but we cannot control it. However, by knowing the type of weather it would be possible for us to take the necessary precautions like an umbrella if it is going to rain and a sun hat if it is going to be too sunny and so on. This is the way in which astrological predictions can help us in our lives.

04 THE SCIENCE CALLED HINDUISM

There is a form of Indian astrology, which keeps track of our past, present and future life. It is called *The Nadi Shastra*, and was written by great saints called *siddhas*. These leaves are known as *Brighu patrikas* in north India and Agastya Nadis in south India and they predict with an amazing degree of accuracy, the whole life history of any person who goes to consult the man who deciphers the leaf. People are astounded to see that everything about them has already been written on that particular leaf thousands of years ago.

You might wonder, as to how these *siddhas* who lived hundreds of years ago, could have known about our lives. This might seem miraculous to us but obviously these great sages connected themselves with that unified Field in which everything exists—past, present and future. It is really amazing to know that these leaves are not only found for Indian residents, but also for foreigners, and other nationals belonging to different religions and creeds. It is interesting to note that not everyone has a *Nadi* leaf, predicting his life. Only those who were related to these saints in their *poorva janma* (previous life) will have a *Nadi* leaf.

The history of *Nadi* astrology can be traced back to over 2000 years and above. It is said that the *siddhas* were perfected beings who could appear in different forms at different places. Most of them were great lovers of God, especially in his form as Shiva. Lord Shiva, pleased with their devotion, granted them incredible powers which enabled them to predict the past, present and future of all the people who came after them. The *siddhas* wrote their predictions on palm leaves, called "*Nadi* leaves".

These leaves were written in Sanskrit. The king of Tanjore, Serfoji II, was a true patron of art and sciences. So, he stored these palm-leaves in his palace library, called the "Saraswathy

Mahal". He also had them translated into the ancient Tamil script, called "Vatellezuthu". It so happened that the British acquired possession of these leaves during their rule, and later sold them to a few families through auctions. These families have carefully preserved the *Nadi* leaves, awaiting their moment of rendezvous with the intended recipients. These can be found in Tamil Nadu near the temple of Vaideeswaran and some other places.

Now this raises another interesting subject which again the scientists have proved for us. Are we capable of controlling our future? When our mind connects to the universal mind, which we call *chitta* in Hinduism, we are actually capable of controlling our future. This is because this *chitta* or unified field provides a holographic blueprint of the world for all time, past and future. So one who can tap this field can well predict the future. Thus we can conclude, as our scriptures tell us, that everything in the future already exists at some bottom rung level in the realm of pure potential and when we look into the future or the past we help to shape it and bring it into being by the simple act of observation, just as we do with a quantum entity in the present. Information transferred through sub-atomic waves does not exist in time or space but somewhere in the ever present. The past and present blur into one vast here and now and our brain picks up these signals and forms our own future. Our future exists in some nebulous state that we may begin to actualize in this very present. Again, we must remember that this field is the field of all possibilities and what actually happens, happens because we will it to happen, either consciously or subconsciously.

When we look at the history of the world and the stories of our epics, etc., we will see that aggressive forms of life seem to exceed in number and intensity than optimistic and peaceful life forms. This shows in our lives also. Negative and dominant thoughts seem to overwhelm optimistic feelings all too often.

The reason for this can be found in the organisation of the planets in our solar system. There are nine planets in the zodiac—the sun, moon, Mars, Mercury, Jupiter, Venus, Saturn and Rahu (Uranus) and Ketu (Neptune). Of these only Mercury, Jupiter and Venus discharge positive energy. The moon can be sometimes positive or negative depending on its position in the zodiac. The sun and Saturn dispel negative tendencies and Mars, Rahu and Ketu generate both negative and repelling tendencies. Thus, there are only three positive energy discharging planets while the remaining five planets discharge negative energy. This is why both in our external life and inward life, we find negative forces easily overcoming the positive. However much modern science may deny the effect of planets on our lives and scorn the astrologer as old-fashioned and unscientific, these facts cannot be denied. The only way we can overcome these evil forces is to increase the positivity in our own lives and begin to show compassion for everyone and every creature. This is the lesson of the Vedas. Of course the highest method is what is given in the Upanishads—to align yourself to the highest force in the universe—the Brahman and thus the planets can never harm you. The planets all exist in the level of space and time and the one who has gone beyond these and has become one with that Absolute will be above all the effects of the planets!

It is to be hoped that modern science will eventually come to realise that the planets are indeed emitting invisible energies, both positive and negative, from the electromagnetic field which pass through our bodies and give certain directions to our minds. If science accepted these facts then scientists would start to concentrate their minds on how to increase or decrease these energies in order to bring about a peaceful atmosphere both in the individual and the world. The ancients however had already discovered these facts and have given us certain methods how we can protect ourselves. These will be dealt with in the next chapter.

> The all-controlling, immortal wheel of the Universe,
> Is revolving in infinite space,
> Ten, yoked together draw it in this wide world,
> The wisdom of God, united with Cosmic Energy,
> Manages the whole Universe,
> On this Energy rest and depend,
> All regions and planets.
>
> *Atharva Veda*

> You grope in the darkness of ignorance seeking the elusive goal of your spiritual quest. But it lies deep in your own mind and becomes visible only to those who care to look inward.
>
> *Yajur Veda*

Loka Samasthath Sukhino Bhavantu!

ॐ

Varadaaya Namaha!

CHAPTER XIII

Scientists of Hinduism

Indeed if I may be allowed the anachronism, the Hindus were Spinozites more than 2,000 years before the existence of Spinoza; and Darwinians many centuries before Darwin; and Evolutionists many centuries before the doctrine of Evolution had been accepted by the scientists of our time and before any word like evolution existed in any language of the world.

Sir Monier Williams

Mayest thou O Lord of vitality, traversing through the misty Heavens,
Listen to our prayers.
Mayest thou O circumambient wind,
Listen to our invocations.
Mayest thou O crystal clear water-laden cloud,
As thou floatest around the towering mountains
Listen to our call.

Rig Veda

Spiritualism is the very basis of Hinduism and so it follows that our great scientists were also great spiritualists. Therefore, we can say that spirituality is the basis of Indian science. In India not only science but art, music and sculpture are all based on our spiritual roots and are thus aimed at taking us to the summum bonum of life which is the attainment of unity with the Absolute. India has produced countless scientists through the ages whose discoveries boggle the modern mind as to how they could have found out so much with absolutely no modern instrumentation. Of course in this book we will only be able to touch upon the lives of a few of these fascinating personages so that people can understand the depth of their intelligence and ability.

The scientists of India fathomed the secrets of creation only through their *tapasya* (austerities). Each one of them concentrated on one particular field of knowledge. The Vedic *rishis* had insisted that both *para vidya*—spiritual knowledge— and *apara vidya*—secular knowledge—were important. Later on, the scientists, who were indeed sages, who were responsible for giving us so much scientific knowledge, perfected their body, mind and intellect to serve as fine-tuned laboratories. Their inner light and divine grace was what enabled them to achieve so much in so short a span of life.

Western science even now cuts up Nature into different parts and probes into these various aspects as if they were totally unconnected. Western doctors also cut up the human being into parts and have specialists for the different parts—the nose, the eyes, the toes and so on. They like to believe that both the human being and Nature are a conglomerate of different parts and have shut their eyes to the fact that both these are actually wholes. It is better to treat the human being as an organic whole than as a collection of parts and the same applies to nature.

Medical science in Hinduism is known as Ayurveda. It is the science of life and health not of disease and death. It tells us how to remain healthy rather than telling us how to treat ourselves after we contact a disease. It makes use of nature and natural substances to create health. The sun, air, water, earth are all used for curing the body as well as a large amount of herbs which nature has provided us with. These sage-scientists were great botanists. They had an incredible knowledge of plants and herbs. In fact you will notice that all the plants associated with the worship of the great gods of the Hindu pantheon are actually herbs. The *tulasi* plant is connected with Vishnu and His *avataras* and has great medicinal properties. A decoction made out of its leaves gives great relief if taken at the onset of a cold. The *bilva (vilva)* leaf is essential in the worship of Shiva and this again has amazing curative properties. The fruits of this tree are a unique cure for all types of stomach problems. *Dhruva* grass, which is used in the worship of Ganesha, has great medicinal value. The juice of this grass if kept in the mouth is of great help in curing gum problems. Everyone was encouraged to grow these plants in their own garden so that common complaints could be cured by resorting to the herbs growing in their own backyard. The names of all these life-giving herbs have been detailed in the great books on Ayurveda.

Dietetics is a very new idea in the West but from ancient times it was said in Ayurvedic books, "Let food be your medicine and medicine your food." So they were well aware of the importance of a good, healthy diet in order to upkeep their health. They knew that *prana* or the vital breath of the universe was what kept the body in health and not the use of externally

Dhanvantari

injected medicines. *Prana* can only be revitalised by eating life-giving foods.

GREAT PHYSICIANS

O supreme Lord, Let eminent scholars, possessing the lustre
of spiritual knowledge,
Be born in our country.

Yajur Veda

DHANVANTARI

Born in 1000 BCE, Kashirau Divodas Dhanvantari, the king of Kashi, is hailed as the father of surgery in Ayurveda, which is the most holistic medical science in the world. Ayurveda or "the science of long life" forms a part of the *Atharva Veda*. Dhanvantari's teachings and surgical techniques were compiled by his foremost pupil, Sushrut, in the *Sushrut Samhita,* which has survived over the ages. Dhanvantari laid great emphasis on the study of anatomy using cadavers. He described how a dead body should be preserved so that it could be used by his students who were learning surgery. He made his students practise internal surgery with the use of many different things like gourds, watermelons, etc. in lieu of the foam materials which are used today. He also invented twenty sharp and one hundred and one blunt instruments to be used in surgical operations. Some of his surgical procedures included removal of stones, skin grafting and repairing a mutilated nose (rhinoplasty). The German scholar, Jurgen Thorwald was greatly impressed by the successful operations performed by Indian village surgeons exactly as described thousands of years ago in the *Sushrut Samhita* and said, "Nowhere in the world do we find such a conception."

Dhanvantari gave a detailed description of the removal of stones from the bladder and urethra by perineal incisions.

Dhanvantari also made contributions in the fields of physiology and anatomy, as well as pharmacology (*dravya vignana*), materia medica and therapeutics (*chikitsa vignana*). Some of his findings have led modern scholars to call him a molecular biologist. He gave a complete theory of drug composition, the molecular structure, psycho-chemical properties and the therapeutical action of food and drugs. He based these on the ancient Nyaya system (one of the six systems of Indian philosophy), of *paramanus* (molecules) and *anus* (atoms).

He was the first to cite the haemopoetic or blood-forming factor in the *yakrut* (liver) and the role of both liver and spleen in the formation of blood. He prescribed goat liver for anaemia and night blindness. Many such original discoveries can be listed which originate in ancient India coming from Dhanvantari and his disciples.

SUSHRUT

Sushrut compiled the teachings of his *guru* Dhanvantari in the *Sushrut Samhita*. During his era, surgery formed a major role in general medical practice. It was known as *shalya-tantra*. Sushrut details many surgical procedures in obstetrics, orthopaedics and ophthalmology. He describes a method of removing cataracts known today as "couching". This method was successfully practiced amongst Indian surgeons till the first half of the 20th century. Sushrut introduced the concept of anaesthesia, using intoxicants such as wine and cannabis. He was the first to do plastic surgery. His method of replacing a broken nose is known as rhinoplasty and was in vogue till the beginning of the 20th century. The concept of plastic surgery came to the West only after the First World War.

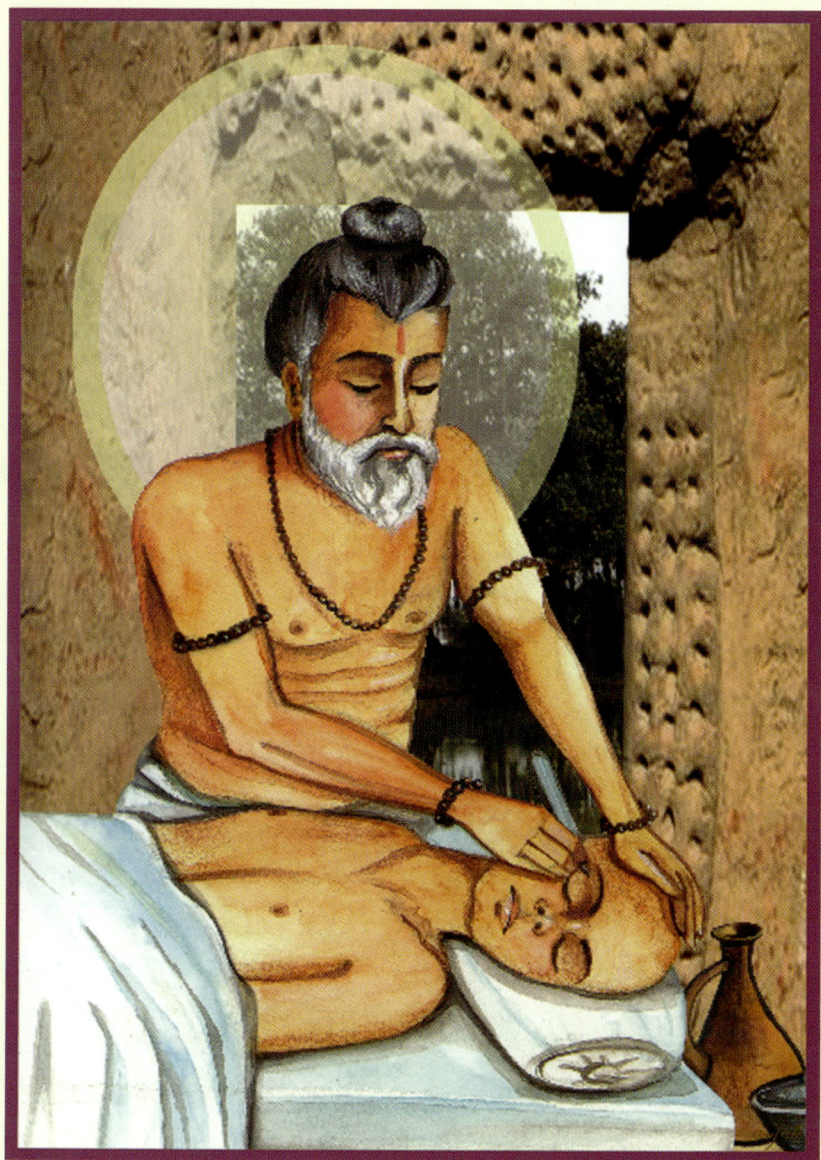

Sushrut

The details he gives of human embryology are mind-boggling. These observations are done today only by using microscopy, X-rays and ultrasound. He mentions that the foetus develops seven layers of skin, naming each layer and the specific diseases that may affect that layer in adulthood. He was aware of diseases due to genetics and mentions congenital defects acquired from parents.

Besides trauma involving general surgery, he gives an account of the treatment of twelve varieties of fractures and six types of dislocations which would confound orthopaedic surgeons today. He meticulously detailed both pre-and post-operational procedures. He even showed methods of treating scars after the wound had healed.

> No single surgeon in the history of science has to his credit such masterly contributions in terms of basic classification, thoroughness of the management of disease and a perfect understanding of the ideal to be achieved.

His excellence in surgery and original insight in all branches of medicine render him the most versatile genius in the history of medical science. The examples cited here remind us that these great souls of Ayurveda practiced an astonishingly scientific, sophisticated and advanced art of medicine as early as the third and second millennium BCE. Several millenniums later, so-called modern medicine is retreading these beaten paths! Sushrut attributed his inventions to the excellence of his *guru* Dhanvantari and divine grace invoked by his personal *sadhana*.

CHARAK

Charak has been cited as India's most outstanding medical practitioner. *Char* means to move about. Therefore, it appears that Charak was a wandering teacher who practised and propagated his knowledge by constantly travelling from village to village to relieve human suffering.

Four thousand years ago, the *rishi* Agnivesh compiled an Ayurvedic treatise called the *Agnivesha Samhita*. Around 800 BCE, Charak redid this *Samhita* which became renowned as the *Charak Samhita*. Its fame spread beyond the borders of Bharatavarsha. By 987 CE, it had been translated into Persian and then to Arabic. Al Beruni, the noted Arabic physician, confessed that his chief source of medicines was this Arabic edition. The famous Arab physician Serapion often referred to Charak as 'Sharak Indianus' in his medical treatise.

The *Charak Samhita* consists of 120 chapters in eight sections. His work has deeply impressed many modern physicians. Dr. George Clarke of Philadelphia observes,

> If modern physicians would stop the use of modern drugs and chemicals and treat their patients according to the methods of Charak, there will be less work for the undertakers and fewer chronic invalids in the world!

The human body is composed of the *panchamahabhutas* or the primary five elements—earth, water, light, air and space. The body's constitution is based on the three *doshas* or humours known as *vata, pitta* and *kapha,* which refer to the quantity and quality of air, bile and phlegm which is present in the system. When their equilibrium is disturbed, disease sets in. Two thousand years before Harvey, the concept of blood circulation was well known in Ayurveda. Charak described the heart as the controlling organ of blood circulation. He said that the body is composed of *dhamanis*—big and small vessels—which supply nutrition to the tissues and remove waste products from them.

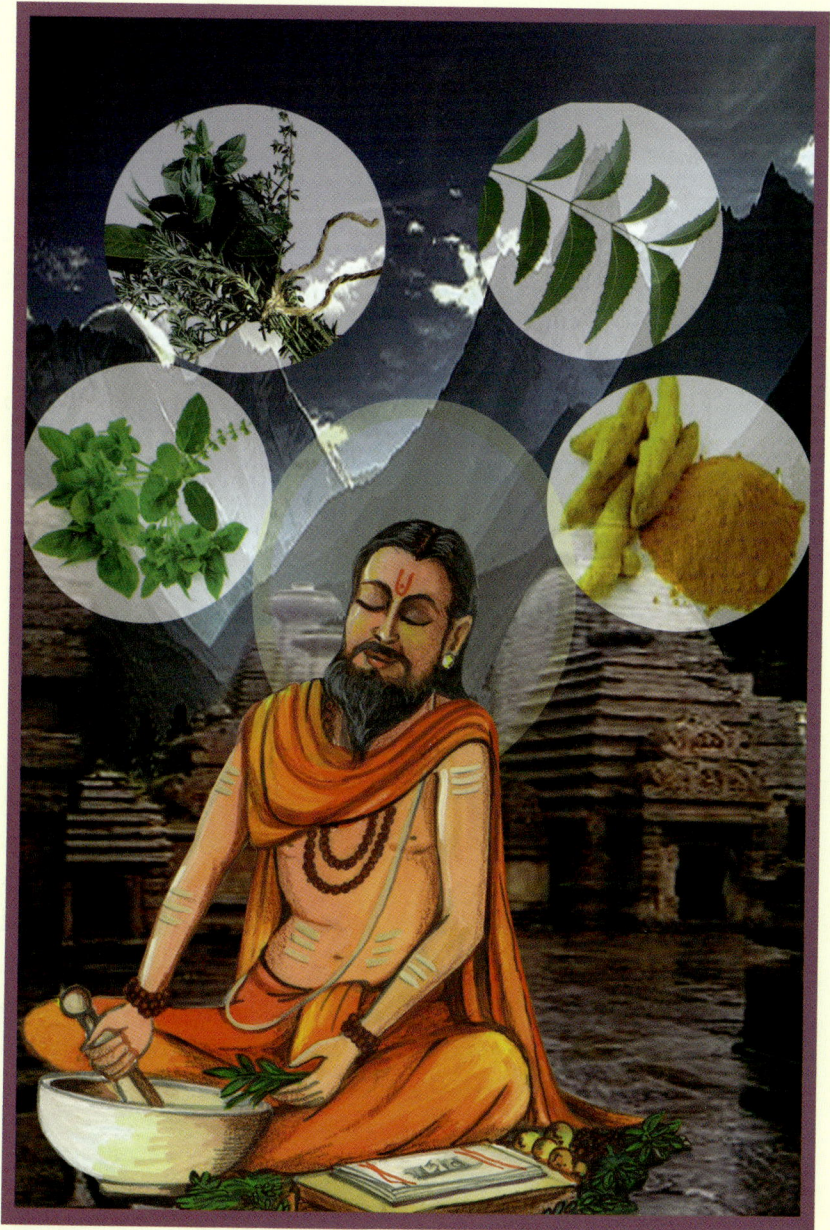

Charak

He refuted the theory that germs were the only cause for disease. Different types of germs may flourish in the body only if favourable conditions prevail. He attached great importance to the digestive fire or *jadaragni* within us to maintain vitality, energy and *ojas*. He clearly described the digestive process and its end products which are remarkably similar to those discovered by western science now. He said that when the digestive fire was either increased or decreased, disorders would result.

His treatment consisted of a system of *Mahakashayas,* each having ten herbal preparations for various diseases. The *Pancha Karma* treatment which has become so popular now was given to rejuvenate and cleanse the body. Charak treated the patient as a whole rather than just a specific disease. In addition to medications, he stressed the importance of diet, daily activity, and seasonal activity in the long-term health of an individual. He laid emphasis on prevention rather than cure. This was Ayurveda's unique approach to the understanding and treatment of diseases which Charak followed faithfully.

He discussed the nature of epidemics which can totally destroy a locality. He listed four contributing factors such as polluted air, water, place and time. He also said that the root cause of epidemics was mankind's unrighteous behaviour (adharmic) acts. He was well aware of water-borne diseases and advocated drinking only boiled water during the rainy season. He gives a fascinating account of visible *krimis* or parasites and microscopic *krimis* in the blood. In the absence of microscopes, his account of microbes will confound modern microbiologists.

He said, "These (microbes) are very minute and can be observed with a *yantra* (instrument)." We are left to wonder if he foresaw the discovery of the microscope! He was the first to identify and name such microbes. He even typified their symptoms, itching, needle-like piercing, pain and an electric current-like effect. Such accuracy without a microscope is only possible for a *Brahmanishta rishi* or one in a state of cosmic consciousness. This would enable him to observe the minutest functions of the body right down to the cellular level.

Inoculation against small pox is something which was only practised in the 19th century in Europe but we find that during Charak's time, this was already in vogue. This was done by making four scratches on the forearm of the person with a special instrument and introducing the pus from a smallpox sporé into the scratches. This was then bandaged and left for a few days. Every morning and evening, four pots of cold water were poured on the person's head to keep the fever in check. This treatment was most successful and during smallpox epidemics, in which normally forty out of hundred died, the number was reduced to two out of hundred.

Charak also showed how to plan, construct and equip hospitals including mental and obstetric hospitals. He gave minute details on accommodation, bathrooms, toilets, disinfection, medicines, equipment and security. He even considered kitchens which had to be warmed in winter. His hospitals included a section where healthy people could undergo rejuvenation therapy such as *Pancha Karma* thrice a year.

Charak laid great emphasis on the physician's integrity and control of the senses, including observance of *brahmacharya* (celibacy). According to him, medical practice was not for the fulfilment of any desire or gain but solely for the sake of removing suffering from humanity.

A physician who fails to enter the inner body of the patient with the lamp of knowledge and understanding can never treat him. Above all the doctor should be compassionate.

His excellence can be attributed mainly to his personal *sadhana* (spiritual discipline) which no doubt endowed him with many *siddhis* (miraculous powers). This gave him the phenomenal ability to document the medicinal qualities of thousands of plants and minerals during his lifetime without experimentation. It is said that due to his *sadhana,* he was able to converse with plants as he walked through the forests. The plants would let him know their medicinal properties which he would tell his pupils who were following behind him, who in turn noted them down.

Anatomy: God pierced the seven openings in the head. He made these ears, these nostrils, eyes and mouth through whose surpassing might in various forms bipeds and quadrupeds can complete their journey of life.

Atharva 10.2.6

Medicine: Just as light hangs between earth and firmament, so does Munja (a healing medicinal herb) cure fever and dysentery.

Atharva 1.2.4

O patient suffering from urinary disease, just as the water of the flooded ocean rises and flows into streams so have I unclosed the orifice of thy bladder so that your urine can come out unchecked.

Atharva 1.3.8

These veins serviceable like maidens, which run their course
clothed in blood must now stand quiet like sisters who are
brotherless and bereft of power.

Atharva 1.17.1

O patient we control your jaundice with the seeds of Shuka
trees and other strong healing medicines.

Atharva 1.22.4

O woman from thee we banish and expel the cause of sterility.
We lay this apart and far removed to another place.

Atharva 3.23.1

The herb named Rohini is the healer of broken bones.
Arundhati is the wound healing herb. Heal thou this wound.

Atharva 4.12.1

If some flesh consuming germ, entering my raw, cooked, half
cooked, or thoroughly cooked food hath injured me, let the
germs with their wives and offspring be destroyed so that I
may be free from disease.

Atharva 5.29.6

PSYCHOLOGY

PATANJALI

There are actually three *rishis* known as Patanjali but here we
are concerned only with the great Yogacharya (master of *yoga*),
who wrote the *Yogasutras*, commonly known as *Patanjali Yoga
Darshana*. He is the greatest and most ancient psychologist in
the world. Even today there is none greater than him. His works
have been famous from ancient times. *Yoga* has been expounded

Patanjali

in the *Rig Veda*, Upanishads, and Puranas. However, it was Maharishi Patanjali who gave it a concise form in his *Yoga Sutras*.

The word *yoga* comes from the Sanskrit word *yuj*, to unite or join or merge. The union of the *jivatma* with the Paramatma is known as *samyoga*.

The word *yoga* is commonly bandied about in the modern world and does not have the right connotation. It is actually what is known as Hatha Yoga in India and is concerned with the perfection of physical health and purity with the aid of eighty-four *asanas* (postures) and *pranayama* (control of *prana* through breath).

Patanjali *yoga* is also known as Raja *yoga* and focuses on controlling the mind by the will and aims to eliminate all sources of disturbances in the mind whether external or internal, thus making it responsive to the spiritual reality within. Unlike modern psychologists who think of the ego and the libido as the basis of all mental disturbances, Patanjali explores all the facets of the mind and makes it go on the evolutionary path which is open to all human beings. Instead of degrading the human being into his animal origins, he uplifts him to his spiritual status. This *yoga* is known as *ashtanga yoga* since he divides the process into eight parts which he calls limbs.

These limbs are:

1. *Yama:* These are the disciplines that apply to everyone and are five in number.

    a. *ahimsa* (non-violence in deed, word and thought).

    b. *satya* (truth).

    c. *asteya* (refraining from taking what belongs to others).

    d. *brahmacharya* (celibacy).

    e. *aparigraha* (detachment).

2. *Niyama:* These are the disciplines that one places on oneself.

   a.   *shoucha* (purity).
   b.   *santosha* (contentment).
   c.   *tapas* (austerity)
   d.   *swadhyaya* (study of the scriptures).
   e.   *Iswara pranidhana* (total surrender to God).

3. *Asana:* It is the third limb of *ashtanga yoga* and means postures. The main reason for practising *asanas* is to be able to master a posture so that one can comfortably stay in it for three hours without discomfort and be able to practise meditation without disturbance to the body.

4. *Pranayama* (control of the *prana* through breath). *Prana* is the vital air or life force. Regulation of *prana* induces steadiness of the body and mind and promotes peace. *Pranayama* also purifies the subtle nerve channels known as *nadis*. This is done by a method of controlling the breath. Many different types of breath control are given but they should be practised with caution. While practising, it must be kept in mind that the object of *pranayama* is the control of *prana* and not the mere control of breath. There is a close connection between *prana* and breath, which enables one to manipulate pranic currents by manipulating breathing.

5. *Pratyahara* (withdrawal of the senses). This is the control of the five senses by the mind and diverting them inwards away from their respective objects.

These five are the external limbs of *ashtanga yoga.* The next three are the internal limbs.

6. *Dharana* (contemplation and concentration). The mind is made to fix itself on the object of contemplation until its movements cease. It becomes one with the essential nature of

the object and can move no further. It has to be brought back again and again whenever it strays from the path.

7. *Dhyana* (meditation).This is an extension of *Dharana*. Here there is an uninterrupted flow of the mind towards the object of meditation. The practitioner masters this stage only if she or he succeeds in completely eliminating all distractions.

8. *Samadhi* (superconscious state).This is an advanced state of *dhyana* in which the mind totally submerges itself in the object of meditation and nothing else remains. In other words the mind and the object becomes one.

Patanjali Yoga is often combined with other systems of liberation. Even the Buddhists took it up.

The theory of evolution was well known to Patanjali long before Darwin came into the picture. The manifestation of latent powers is the reason why species evolve. This idea has been well expressed in a few words by Patanjali in the second aphorism of the fourth chapter of his *Yoga Sutras*. Vivekananda comments on this in his book on Raja Yoga. "The Evolution into another species is caused by the in-filling of nature."

Kapila, the father of Hindu Evolutionists, explained this theory for the first time through logic and science. Nature is filled not from outside but from within. Nothing is superadded to the individual soul from outside. The germs are already there, but their development depends upon their coming in contact with the necessary conditions requisite for proper manifestation. We sometimes see a wicked man suddenly become saint-like. There are instances of murderers and robbers becoming saints. Vedanta says that the moral and spiritual powers that remained latent in them have been aroused, and the result is a sudden transformation. None can tell when or how the slumbering powers will wake up and begin to manifest. The individual soul possesses infinite possibilities. Each soul is studying, as it were, the book of its own nature by unfolding one page after another. When it has gone through all the pages, or, in other words, all the stages of evolution, perfect knowledge is acquired, and its course is finished.

When we read a book and we feel interested in a particular page or chapter, we will read it over and over again and will not open a new page or a new chapter until we are perfectly satisfied with it. Similarly, while going through the book of life, if the individual soul likes any particular stage, he will stay there until he or she is perfectly satisfied with it; after that he will go forward and study the other pages. One may read very slowly, and another very fast; but whether we read slowly or rapidly each one of us is bound to read the whole book of our life and attain to perfection sooner or later. This is the great and beautifully re-assuring teaching of Hindu psychology. No one is cast beyond the pale or damned to eternity.

The father of Western psychology, Freud had only read the pages of the book of life referring to our lower nature, which passes through each stage of animal life from the minutest bioplasm up to the present stage of existence. Patanjali, the father of Indian psychology, showed us the pages which deal with moral and spiritual laws thus encouraging the human being to go forward to find his or her highest potential within our own psyche.

Loka Samasthath Sukhino Bhavantu!

CHAPTER XIV

Astronomy and Mathematics

Aryabhatta is the master who after reaching the furthest shores and plumbing the inmost depths of the sea of ultimate knowledge of mathematic, kinematics and spherics, handed over the three to the learned world.

Bhaskaracharya

VARAHAMIHIR

Astrology or *jyotisha* is one of the oldest sciences and has its roots in the Vedas. In the history of Indian astrology, Varahamir stands unparalleled. He was the son of a Brahmin called Adityadas and lived in Avanti (Ujjain). Both father and son were ardent devotees of the sun as their names would imply. Varahamihir was born in 499 CE and passed away at the age of 88 in 587 CE. Therefore, he lived later than Aryabhatta. He wrote many books of which the *Panchasiddantika* deals with five principles of ancient astronomy. Had it not been for him, the details of the five ancient systems would have been lost. The *Vivahapatal* and *Yogayatra* deal with the auspicious times for marriage and journeys as their names imply. The *Bruhajjataka* deals with individual horoscopes and is still regarded as the most authoritative work on the subject.

The *Bruhat Samhita* is his last work which is the most celebrated. It has 106 chapters and 4,000 *shlokas* which includes everything pertaining to planets, asterisms and the signs of the zodiac. One portion deals with architecture, sculpture, geography, iconography, econometrics, auspicious signs in human beings and animals like horses, elephants, cows, dogs, goats, etc. It also deals with omens, water divining, and methods of making swords, perfumes and cosmetics. It has chapters dealing with the science of precious stones, botany, etc. He is the earliest authority on Vaastu Shastra, the science of architecture. He describes in great detail the many ways in which to build houses, temples and make sculptures. He gives the types and dimensions of dwellings for different members of society, from palaces for kings to officers, royal astrologers, preceptors, physicians and laypeople. He has detailed twenty types of temples and even suggests auspicious types of flowers and trees to be grown near dwellings and temples. His genius is brought out in these details.

He had a profound knowledge of astronomy. He was the first who declared the shape of the earth to be spherical. He wrote, "All things which are perceived by the senses are witness to the fact of the globular shape of the earth and refute the possibility of its having any other shape." The famous Arab Indologist, Al-Beruni frequently referred to two Indian astronomer-astrologers—Varahamihir and Brahmagupta—as excellent astronomers who spoke only Truth.

When acute water scarcity hit Gujarat in 1980, the scholars went through the *Bruhat Samhita* and discovered a few simple methods given by Varahamihir to detect underground water.

Aryabhatta

1. If there is a termite hill in the east, near a Jambu tree, then sweet water will be found two heads deep to the right of the termite hill.

2. Sweet water which will not dry will be found 3¼ heads deep and three arm lengths in the south from a Nagoda tree, shading an anthill.

Many such methods are given in the book which has been found to be absolutely correct. He also gives details on the method of constructing tanks and ponds for storing water for long periods!

His uncanny methods of locating groundwater veins could not possibly have been discovered in a human lifetime, solely by physical digging. It is much more likely that his revelations sprang from the insight he acquired through meditation and other *sadhanas* similar to the Ayurvedic *rishis*.

He was the first to construct a simple ingenious water clock. It was a bowl made from copper or coconut shell with a small hole at the bottom placed in a larger vessel filled with water. The size of the hole allowed water to seep in, sinking the bowl about once every half an hour—60 times in 24 hours. Every time it sank, a gong was sounded and a bead moved in a type of abacus, indicating the total time. (This has been detailed in the chapter on Time.)

ARYABHATTA

Aryabhatta is the greatest astronomer and mathematician of ancient India. He gave theories which were "discovered" many centuries later by Western scientists. He was the first to gift algebra to the world. He cites his date of birth with astonishing accuracy in his famous work, *Aryabhatiya*.

When sixty times six years and three quarters of a *Yuga* had elapsed of the current *Yuga*, I had passed twenty three years since my birth.

This means that in the year of Kali Yuga 3600, he was twenty-three years old. The Kali year 3600 corresponds to 499 CE. So he was born in the year 476 CE in Pataliputra, modern Patna in Bihar which had the famous university of Nalanda.

Aryabhatta was designated as the head of this university where a special observatory existed for studying astronomy. He was known as Ardubarius in Europe in the middle ages. Though he wrote two books, only the *Aryabhatiya* has survived. He wrote it at the age of twenty-three. It deals with astronomy and mathematics and is the first Indian text to record the most advanced astronomy in the history of ancient science.

He gave the value of "pi" as 3.1416 and this is the same as we use today. Yet, even this value he calls *aasaana* or approximate.

Aryabhatta gave two methods of computing the sine table. He also gave the theory of solving indeterminate equations.

He knew that the earth was spherical and that it rotated. The period of 1 sidereal rotation of the earth in *Aryabhatiya* is given as 23 hours, 56 minutes and 45.1 seconds. The modern value is 23 hours 56 minutes and 45.091 seconds.

He determined the length of the solar year from the heliacal risings of some bright stars at an interval of 365 and 366 days. The year according to him is 365 days, 6 hours, 11 minutes. 29.64 seconds!

This value of the solar year is nearer to the modern value than that of Ptolemy.

Based on his own observations, his astronomical constants differ from those of other astronomers and are more accurate than that of previous astronomers.

The epicycles of the planets given by earlier astronomers, including Ptolemy are fixed in value. Those given by Aryabhatta vary from place to place and yield better results.

His divisions of time can be seen in the chapter on Space and Time.

He gave the correct method for calculating the celestial latitude of both superior and inferior planets.

His book is perhaps the earliest text on astronomy to use the radian measure of 3,438' for the radius of the circle.

He was the first to describe the true theory of the cause of the lunar and solar eclipses—that they were due to the shadow of the earth and moon. He also said that the moon was inherently without light but was illuminated by the sun.

His theory of the earth's rotation and orbit round the sun was 1,000 years before Copernicus put forward his heliocentric theory.

There was no doubt that he was a genius in both astronomy and mathematics.

According to Georges Ifrah, at the beginning of the 6th century CE, Aryabhatta had perfect knowledge of zero and the place value system to calculate the square root and cube root, since these two operations could only be carried out by using the place-value system with nine distinct numbers and a tenth sign which performed the function of zero.

In fact, the discovery of 0 is one of the greatest contributions of India to the world. In one of the Vishnu temples inside the Gwalior Fort, the figure of "0" is seen for the first time. The deep calculations made by Indian astronomers would have been impossible without the use of "0". This is an abstract concept and Hindus were experts in abstractions. The concept of the

Brahman is purely an abstract one. Therefore, they were quick to realise the need for something which was absolutely nothing on which the whole edifice of the universe as well as of Mathematics could be constructed. India was the first to start using the digits from 1 to 9. From India it travelled to Arabia and when it went to the West, they called it the Arabic numerals but actually they came from India as the Arabs themselves admitted. Europe was still using the heavily structured Roman numerals which made Arithmetic very clumsy and difficult. When these Indian numerals came to Europe in the 3rd century, the Roman Catholic Church denounced it as being the work of the devil and it did not come into vogue in Europe till a couple of centuries later. This is an example of the deep distrust and dislike the Church had to accept anything which was new. This is why western science lagged so far behind India in those days.

The method of graduated calculations was documented in the *Pancha-Siddhantika* (five principles), in the 5th century but the technique is said to have come from the Vedas. In fact, the first reference to astronomy is found in the *Rig Veda*.

The value of *pi* was also calculated by Budhayana (6th century). He also explained the concept which is now known as the Pythagorean Theorem.

Quadratic equations were explained by Sridaracharya in the 11th century.

The largest number used by the Greeks and Romans was 10 to the power of 6 whereas Indians used numbers as big as 10 to the power of 53, with specific names as early as 5000 BC.

Even now the largest number used in mathematics is Tera 10 to the power of 12.

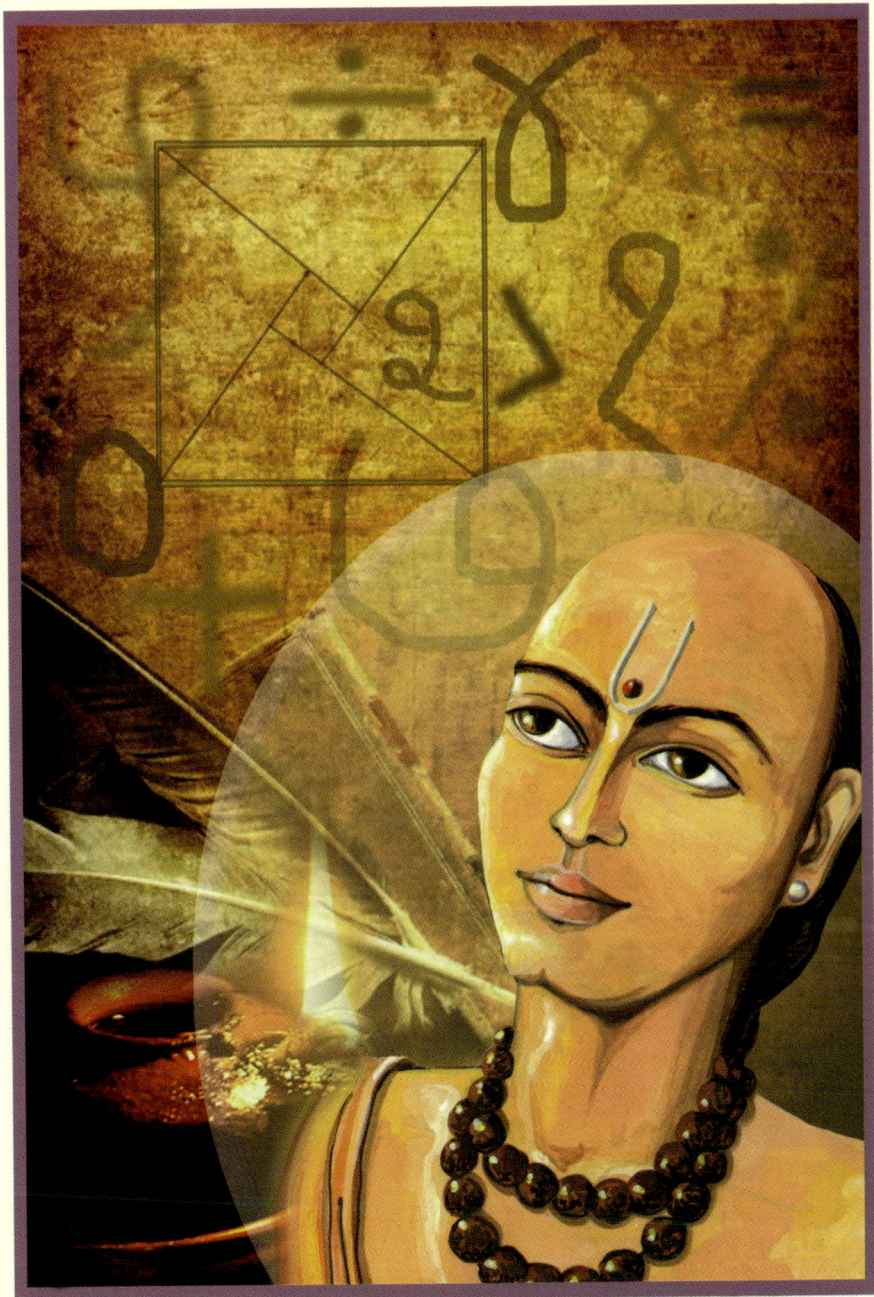

Bhaskaracharya

Astronomy:

The aforesaid constellations in the heavens, the mid-regions, observed in waters and on earth, on the mountains and in all quarters as the moon passes by them, revealing them, may they all be peaceful to me.

Atharva 8.9.2

The Lord's joy manifests through the splendorous beauty and serenity of his creations.

The supreme bliss of this divine love is felt within the soul that is pure and receptive to the sanctity of God's boundless love. It kindles the innermost self of devotees.

Sama Veda 547

BHASKARACHARYA

Bhaskara, son of Maheswara, was born in 1114 CE. It was his father who taught him mathematics. From the time of Aryabhatta, mathematics came to be incorporated into astronomy, which also required knowledge of geometry, trigonometry, arithmetic and algebra. Bhaskara's son, Lakshmidhara and grandson, Chanagadeva also became renowned astronomer-mathematicians. Bhaskara's first work, which he wrote at the age of thirty-six, was *Siddhanta-Shiromani* which is divided into four sections called *Bijaganit, Grahaganit, Goladhyaya* and *Lilavati*, named after his daughter. These works are considered to be unparalleled. He was the first to discover gravity, five hundred years before Newton.

The *Lilavati* deals with mathematics, addition, subtraction, division, squaring, cubing, extraction of square and cube roots. He gives names to all the main numbers in this work.

His *Bijaganit* is a systematic and complete treatise on Hindu algebra till the modern times. His greatest contribution was the method of solving problems of indeterminate equations of the second degree. For these he gave both algebraic and geometrical solutions.

The *Grahaganit* and *Goladhyaya* deal with the astronomy of heavenly bodies based on the Suryasiddhanta. In the third chapter, he describes the situation of the earth, unsupported in space and how beings exist on the surface of this spherical earth. He deals also with the circumference, surface area and volume of the earth using *pi* as 3.1416. He calculates the length of the sidereal year—the time taken for the earth to revolve round the sun as 365.2588 days. The modern value is 365.2563 with a difference of only 3.5 minutes!

The 5th chapter looks at the mean motions of the sun, moon and planets. The 6th and 8th chapters show how to calculate sunrise by calculating the lunar crescent, how to find out the relative lengths of days and nights in different seasons and latitudes. It also teaches how to find the latitude of a place.

The next three chapters deal with eclipses and another chapter deals with astronomical instruments used for observing heavenly bodies. At the end he concludes that intelligence is a better tool than all instruments!

The period between Aryabhatta and Bhaskara is considered to be the golden age of astronomy in India. However, Bhaskara's works are unparalleled. He was so thorough that he left no room for improvement.

His last work at the age of sixty-nine was *Karanakutuhal*. This is used even today to make calendars. However, his *Lilavati* is the most acclaimed of his works. It is said that a person adept in the *Lilavati* can even compute the exact number of leaves on a tree!

Panini

There is an interesting story in connection with his daughter Lilavati. When he made his daughter's horoscope, he found a bad omen in it. If her marriage did not take place at a certain specified time, she would become a widow. At the time of her marriage, he made an instrument to know the exact time. He floated a small vessel, something like a cup with a hole at the bottom in a vessel filled with water. The water would slowly start filling the cup and at the auspicious moment, the cup would sink. He placed the device in a room and warned her not to touch it. However, curiosity prompted her to go near and look into it. A pearl from her nose-ring fell into the cup and caused it to sink. Hence, the marriage took place at an inauspicious time as he had foreseen in the horoscope and Lilavati became a widow. Bhaskara realised that however brilliant an astrologer may be, he can only predict the postion of the stars. He cannot control them! Control is by another law—the law of Karma. However, to console his daughter and give her eternal fame, he named his masterpiece after her.

Bhaskara was the last of the great astronomer-mathematicians of ancient India. After his time, wave after wave of foreign hordes started invading and desecrating and destroying the land. Such a war-torn land was not the place for genius to flourish. But by this time Bhaskara's fame had spread to all parts of the then known world like Arabia and Persia.

PANINI (GRAMMARIAN)

Sanskrit is a language which has a very intricate type of grammar. Of course many books had been written on Sanskrit grammar but Panini (520–480 BC) is unequalled in his work. He was mentally retarded as a child and was expelled from the Gurukula or school where students resided along with their tutor and learnt the Vedas. His *guru* showed him that the line of intelligence was missing from his palm. Panini was so incensed with this that he took a knife and carved the line on his palm. He then went to the Himalayas and performed intense *tapasya*. Shiva, the great *guru,* was pleased with him and taught him the knowledge of Sanskrit grammar. Shiva rattled His *damaru* (small hand drum) fourteen times. Each sound became a Sanskrit *sutra.* Panini created a new method of Sanskrit grammar from these *sutras.* He listed about 1,700 basic elements of grammar and 4,000 rules of pronunciation, which made Sanskrit a most precise and scientific language, unequalled in the world. Everyone soon came to follow Panini's grammar which was much easier to learn. His famous work is known as the *Ashtadhyayi,* composed of eight chapters. In 1959 when John Backus, the inventor of the world's firtst computer language, was studying the grammar of many of the world's languages, he discovered that the rules described in the *Ashtadhyayi* were as mathematical and precise as his computer language and was the best to be used for computers.

Panini divided Vedic literature into two parts—'Dhrusta', which includes the four Vedas and 'Procta', which includes Brahmana, Kalpa and Sutras. His work on Sanskrit grammar has remained unsurpassed to this day.

OTHER SCIENCES

Ancient India was also far advanced in metallurgy. The esoteric knowledge of how to stop iron from rusting is something which modern science is still to discover. The huge iron pillar in Delhi was made a thousand years ago and is still shining as if it was made the previous day. A similar rust-proof pillar is to be seen in Bangalore which was made by the tribals to welcome Sri Adi Shankaracharya more than two thousand years ago.

For many thousands of years, India was the only country to know how to extract zinc out of ore. This is a very difficult process and was known only to the Indians. The Chinese came and learnt this technique and the British took it from the Chinese. It was only in 1543 that the scientist called William Chapier made the first zinc extraction plant in England. Until that time, zinc could be got only from India.

The ancient art of making exquisite figures out of copper and bronze is still to be found in the city of Tanjore in Tamil Nadu. This was an ancient method in which they used wax to make the mould and then poured the hot metal into that and then encased it in mud and heated it on the fire. When the mud-covering was broken, the wax would have already melted and the beautiful figure would stand revealed. We find a wealth of beautiful figures of the gods in Tanjore.

Ancient India was also famous for its wonderful temple architecture. The science was known as "Vaastu" and it is a unique form of construction since it takes into consideration the cosmogony of the universe. Everything is connected to the different directions.

Generally, temples are located in places where the earth's magnetic waves pass through. They are located strategically at places where the positive energy is abundantly available from the magnetic wave distribution of the north/south pole thrust.

The main idol is placed in the center, known as "Garbhagriha" or "Moolasthan", over a copperplate inscribed with some *yantra* (very often the Sri Yantra). The copper absorbs the earth's magnetic waves and radiates it to the surroundings. Thus a person, who regularly visits a temple and makes a clockwise *pradakshina* (circumambulation), of the sanctorum, receives the magnetic waves which are being beamed all over the temple and thus get absorbed by his or her body. This is a very slow process but Hinduism encourages daily visits to a temple which will allow the body to absorb more energy. The sanctum sanctorum is completely enclosed on three sides so the effect of all the energies is very high in here. The lamps radiate the heat and light energy.

The ringing of the bells and the chanting of *mantras* produce sound energy. The fragrance from the flowers and the burning of camphor gives out chemical energy. The effect of all these energies is activated by the positive energy that comes out of the idol. Thus, visits to the temple also have a scientific reason.

During the time of the great Tamil king, Raja Raja Chola, many extraordinary temples were made both in Tanjore, which was his capital, and places abroad. The Cambodian king invited him to send his artisans and architects and the famous temples of Angkor Wat in Cambodia were all built by Hindu craftsmen. The temple to Vishnu called Borobodur in Java was also built by Hindu artisans. These temples are not only unique in their architecture but were also made in such a way that the main temple was on the same line of longitude as the main temple in Tanjore. Moreover, the temple door to the sanctum was constructed in such a way that the sun's rays fell straight to the foot of the deity during one or other of the equinoxes.

The same phenomenon can be perceived in the Buddhist cave carvings at Ajanta and Ellora. These caves are about seventy feet above the ground level and were all carved with the most incredible sculptures of gods and demi-gods from the inside of the cave where there is hardly any light. The caves seem to be in horse-shoe formation and each cave was oriented towards some specific direction in order to be able to see a certain star or planet. The figure of the Buddha in the main stupa was so designed that the sun's rays would fall on him during the summer solstice. These types of designs show the astonishing knowledge they had about cosmogony and cosmology. These caves are dated at 200 BC.

Till the 18th century, India was the world leader in the making of cottons. They dyes which were used were purely natural and had brilliant colours. However, the British learnt the techniques and started making their own cottons and of course India lost heavily because of this since the British used machines while the Indians were still using handlooms. Silks were also produced in India from ancient times. The exquisite silk cloth from Banaras and Kanchipuram is still not to be found anywhere else in the world.

The English word "navigation" is derived from the Sanskrit word, *navagatih* or ship. The word "navy" also comes from the Sanskrit word *nav* (boat). The art of navigation was first started in the river Sindhu. When Vasco Da Gama came along the shores of Africa in his search for India, he found some Indian merchants were already there before him with ships which were three times the size of his own. He was frightened to cross the ocean without keeping any land is sight as he had been doing, so the Indian merchants escorted his ship across the ocean. Europeans still thought the world was a "tabula raza" or a flat table and were frightened of falling off the edge! So Vasco da Gama reached modern Goa with the help of the Indian sailors. Despite all this, the West still believes the Portuguese to be the greatest of all ship-builders and navigators.

Ancient Hindus were also noted for the different types of games they played. Chess is known as Shatranj or Ashta Pada in

Sanskrit and was a game normally played by kings. Snakes and ladders and cards were also common.

The world's first university was in Takshashila, modern Afghanistan, which was a part of India in 700 BC. Records show that over ten thousand students from all over the world came to study there and more than sixty subjects were offered. The University of Nalanda in Pataliputra (modern Patna in Bihar) was constructed in the 4th century and was one of the greatest achievements of ancient India in the field of education. The construction of this university is credited to Chanakya, who is famous for his treatise on political science known as *Arthashastra*. Of course, the official language of the university was Sanskrit.

> Omniscient, you are unknown,
> Origin of all, you are self-existent,
> Lord of all, you are without a master,
> Though one, you divide into all forms.
>
> *Raghuvamsa, Kalidasa*

Loka Samasthath Sukhino Bhavantu!

ॐ

Sarva-darshitaaya Namaha!

CHAPTER XV

Mantras and Yantras (Symbols)

Truth is within us, it takes no rise,
From outward things, whatever you may believe,
There is an inmost centre in us all.
Where truth abides in fullness, and around,
Wall upon wall, the gross flesh hems it in,
This perfect, clear perception—which is Truth.

Robert Browning "Paracelsus"

The *rishis* were experts in the science of sounds known as phonetics. Sound is the softest but the most powerful form of energy in the universe. The *mantras* are sounds denoting the various gods and have a great scientific basis. The letters of the *mantras* constitute an alphabet of forms in a capsule of form, sound and power. They denote that formless Absolute which is beyond all forms yet is the cause of all forms. Hence, our gods are the outcome of this great science—the science of sounds giving rise to forms. In fact we say that our world is the outcome of sound giving rise to forms.

We all know that most whirling objects produce a lot of sound. We also know that the earth is whirling on its own axis with the moon round it and it is hurtling round the sun at a great speed. Every star in our milky way is actually a sun with its own planets gyrating round it. In fact these galaxies are moving at 20,000 miles per second and they create an amazing sound.

The sound thus generated cannot be heard by the normal human ear but it was heard by the *rishis* and they said that this was the sound of *Aum*, the cosmic hum of the creator. This was the original sound which led to the formation of the universe. This discovery is attributed to the great sage Vishvamitra and he is also the seer of the great *mantra* known as the *Gayatri*. This *mantra* has amazing propensities for taking us to higher levels of consciousness. Its greatness is only just being recognised by the Western world.

The *Gayatri Mantra* is chanted thus:

Aum bhur, bhuvah, swar,
Tat Savitur varenyam,
Bhargo devasya dhimahi,
Dhiyo yona prachodayat.

The first three words of the *mantra* are *bhur, bhuvah* and *swar* and these stand for the three spheres. *Bhur* stands for the earth sphere, *bhuvah* points to our galaxy with the sun at the centre, and *swar* for the super galaxies which exist beyond ours. All these create sounds and the *Gayatri Mantra* includes all this in its sphere of influence and hence it includes the totality of the energy generated in the universe and beyond it. Thus, it has great force if used with faith and correct pronunciation. From this we realise how much the *rishis* knew about phonetics and cosmology!

The earth (*bhur*), the planets (*bhuvah*), and the galaxies (*swar*) are moving at a very great velocity and the sound thus produced is *Aum* (the name of formless God). That God (*tat*), who manifests Himself in the form of the light of the sun (*savitur*) is worthy of respect (*varenyam*). We should, therefore, meditate (*dhimahi*) upon the light (*bhargo*) of that deity (*devasya*) and also chant *Aum*. May He (*yo*) guide our intellect (*dhiyo)* in the right direction (*prachodayat*).

Aum is also known as the *pranava*. It is a primeval sound, which is the most important symbol in Hinduism to denote the Supreme. In fact it is the Supreme in the form of sound. Every *mantra* has to be preceded by *Aum*. The Vedas also start with this sound. It is the most well known and important *mantra* for meditation. It is the first of the cosmic sounds out of which everything else came. Later on, other religions realised the importance of *Aum* and called it as *amen* and *ameen*.

A *mantra* is actually a particular vibration of the original throb of the cosmos and represents the sound body of one particular god in the structure of consciousness. *Mantras* are chanted during rituals in order to invoke the appropriate deity. Many *mantras* are given in Hinduism which balance the positive and negative tendencies of the planets and promote a steadying effect on human life. All the gods have their own *mantras* which when used continuously will draw the power of that particular god to oneself. According to this ancient science, mind is the fastest form of transport and sound is the softest yet the most powerful form of energy in the universe. When the mind chants these powerful sounds or *mantras* in order to achieve some definite purpose, certain specific changes will start to occur.

For long eras, the *rishis* transmitted knowledge from mouth to mouth and from ear to ear. Written transmission through birch-bark or palm-leaves or home-made paper came much, much later.

Symbolism plays a great role in Hinduism. Apart from sound forms like the *mantras,* it also makes use of mathematical symbols called *yantras* and *chakras* to denote the Supreme and to bestow auspiciousness on the user. *Mantra* is the sound form of the deity and *yantra*, the form pattern. In their anxiety to bring that formless and eternal Being into the vision of the ordinary human being, the *rishis* used their genius and captured the formless and wordless Supreme into these mathematical symbols. This made it easier for the common people to imagine the Infinite. It would be impossible even for the greatest mathematician to work without the help of numerals for Arithmetic. Algebra has to use numerous signs which are incomprehensible to the common man. The problem would get more complex as the numbers become larger and larger. If it is so difficult to do mathematics with finite numbers, imagine how difficult it would be to comprehend the Infinite without the help of symbols!

The word *yantra* is derived from the root *yam*, to control, and has been freely used in ancient India for any contrivance. The word actually means a machine or an instrument. Ancient India had produced many accessories for scientific activities, such as surgical instruments and laboratory equipment in medicine known as *pakayantras*. Many *yantras* used in astronomy are described in astrological works. In the *Mahabharata,* we hear of the *Matsya-yantra,* which is a revolving wheel with a fish on top, which Arjuna had to shoot in order to win Draupadi in the *swayamvara* (marriage by choice of the bride).

More interesting references are made by Valmiki, in the *Ramayana*, to *yantras* on the field of battle, the continuity of which tradition we see later in the *Arthashastra* (political science). The *Arthashastra* of Kautilya is one of the books on statecraft which throws a flood of light on that epoch. This work of 300 BCE being a treatise on statecraft, speaks of *yantras* in connection with battles, and also with architecture to some extent. The

Arthashastra is an ancient text which forms our most valuable document on the subject of *yantras*.

Valmiki claims that the fortifications of Ayodhya included equipment in the form of *yantras*. At one point Rama asks his brother, Bharata, whether the fort was equipped with *yantras*. Lanka, as a city built by the great architect, Mayan, was naturally full of *yantras*. The city even had a special chamber filled with *yantras*.

In the *Bhagavad-Gita*, Lord Krishna says that the human being is a *yantra* (instrument) in the hands of God who sits in the human heart and makes him act. Being enveloped in *maya*, the person deludes himself into believing that he is a free and competent agent.

The *yantras* used for spiritual practices are a little different. The formless radiance emanating from the Infinite emits rays of definite forms and weaves them into the features of the various gods. The *yantras* and *chakras* are the lines of light that make the form patterns of the gods. One can contemplate on the Absolute as a mass of ineffable light but if one wants to see the actual form of one's favourite deity, the light has to be codified into a definite pattern of rays and this codification is exactly what the *rishis* proceeded to do. This type of *yantra* is a geometrical figure drawn with lines, circles, squares and triangles. Due to its mathematical precision, it is a powerhouse of cosmic energy. Within its concrete form it encloses the uncontrollable power of the deity that it is meant to represent. It limits the limitless into a figure of lines and triangles. It creates a field of power that lives, breathes and moves with life, and within which the power of the divine can be invoked. These forms have always existed in the etheric sphere but we, with our limited vision, are unable to perceive them. The *rishis* drew them out of the vast ocean of consciousness that holds within it all conceivable forms.

The forms we see in nature are only their gross representations and rest on the subtle forms given by the *yantras*.

If one goes to a typical south Indian house one can see many strange drawings outside the house as we enter. These are known as "*kolams*" in south India. The "*rangoli*" designs we see in the North are similar to these. These have existed in India from immemorial times and they have obviously been drawn from the depths of the human psyche. They are symbolic representations of unseen forces. If we look carefully at many flowers we will see this incredible mathematical figure. This is known as the golden ratio and is found all around us—in the flowers, in the sea shells and the forms taken by desert sand when the wind blows through them. In India as I said they have been preserved from time immemorial and are used even today in many traditional houses. We don't know who drew them and why. All we know is that they are considered to be auspicious and most traditional homes have them. Now of course since so many people dwell in apartments these are used only for auspicious occasions. All these designs go to make up the sacred geometry of the Hindus. Modern technology has actually proved the existence of such designs. They are all made with the vibrations of sound which is the original source of all creation as has been said. With the help of something called a tonoscope, sounds made by the human voice can be viewed as turning into these incredible shapes. When the pitch is higher the form changes. If any Indian looks at these forms, he or she will be struck by the fact that they are strikingly similar to the *kolams* and the *rangolis* which we are familiar with. This again proves what our ancient *rishis* have always reiterated that all the forms which we perceive here have their source in a subtle field which the physical eyes are unable to see. Hence their prayer, "*asato ma sat gamaya*"—"Lead me from the unreal to the real."

The mystic power of *yantras* has been narrated in many sacred books. Lord Shiva explains to his consort Parvati, in the *Shiva Mahapurana*, that a *yantra* is as essential to the worship of the gods as a body is essential for living beings and oil to oil lamps. A *yantra* is helpful in every field of life, to attain success in one's profession, to acquire wealth, to get peace, to bring good luck, to get rid of tensions, to ward off diseases and to progress in meditation. By keeping a potentised *yantra* in a sacred place in one's house and worshipping it daily, one can fulfill all desires and attain all goals.

The focal point of a *yantra* is always the *bindu* or centre. It represents the point or nucleus, or seed from which creation has evolved and into which it will return. It also represents the union of the two dual principles of the universe, Shiva and Shakti—Consciousness and Energy. It can be called the point of contact between the creator and his creation. It is the drop that swells into the ocean of pure Consciousness. It is the cipher by which everything else is deciphered.

Most *yantras* make use of many forms. The circle is a primal form. Even our earth is in the form of a circle. It represents the cycle of timelessness, which has no beginning and no end. It denotes eternity and points to the eternal cycle of birth, existence and death. Space cannot be circumscribed by anything less than three lines so the next form used in the *yantra* is the triangle. The square denotes the terrestrial and physical world that is to be transcended. It is the substratum on which the *yantra* rests. The lotus is a flower that responds only to the call of light. It raises its head when the sun rises and closes its petals when it sets. The flower opens out petal by petal and this signifies the gradual unfolding of the latent spirituality in us. This is why the symbol of the lotus holds an important place in all the *chakras*, which are also *yantras*.

The *chakra* or wheel signifies the constant and dynamic circulation of the power of the Infinite. The perfect lines of beauty, harmony and symmetry with which the Master Mathematician designed the universe are caught in the lines of the *chakras* and *yantras*.

The Sri Chakra is a *yantra* which is known as the king of all *chakras*. It is the most potent and famous of all *yantras*. The Sri Chakra is also known as the Sri Yantra and is the most complex figure used for worship, devotion and meditation. It has been in use for thousands of years and its origin is unknown. It contains all other *chakras* within it as the Divine Mother goddess contains all other gods and goddesses within her. By worshipping the Sri Chakra, one can worship any of the other gods or goddesses. The central figure is composed of nine interlocking triangles. Every triangle is connected to the others by common points and this is the reason why it is so difficult to make a perfect drawing. If one tries to change the size or position of one triangle, we will be forced to change the position of many other triangles and this will end in total confusion.

Modern mathematicians are astounded by the beauty and symmetry of this incredible figure, the secret of which they have still not been able to fathom.

After making a few attempts at drawing this figure, it becomes obvious that it is not as easy as it looks. Given the fact that this is one of the oldest and most recognizable of the sacred geometry of the Hindus, one would assume that a correct method for drawing this legendary figure would be easy to find. But this is not so. The two most famous methods which are normally used are not very precise. Many modern techniques have been tried but after a careful scrutiny of all the figures, one realizes that they are all different! Was there an original geometrical figure that had been distorted with time? This mystery is still to be solved. Now let us see how the *chakra* is made.

The *bindu* or dot is considered to be the navel of the Sri Chakra. The *bindu* becomes the triangle and the triangle expands into the eight-sided figure, then to a ten-cornered figure and so on. Thus, the *bindu* or dot of the primary triangle transforms itself through a series of lines, triangles, circles and squares to the fully formed shape of the Sri Chakra. The vibrations that emanate from the Sri Chakra are so positive that even a person who sits near it, is subtly influenced by it. Adi Shankara, the founder of Advaita Vedanta, installed the Sri Chakra in all the temples that he visited or established all over India.

These *yantras* and *chakras* are normally made out of certain types of metals like copper, silver and gold. During some types of *pujas* or rituals, they are also made on the floor using various coloured powders like rice, turmeric and vermilion. Now let us examine how scientific the use of these metals was.

Modern science has found out that it is possible to generate heat and magnetic waves by channelling energy or electricity through copper coils. The "sim card" in a mobile phone is only a small compact, flat piece of very thin copper. By applying electrical charges to the card, we can store millions of data in the form of sounds and visuals. Even more amazing is the fact that you can use this sim card in another mobile phone to reproduce the same information even after many years.

Thus, modern science has at last discovered that they can transform letters, words and pictures into sounds and these frequencies can later be changed back into letters and words!

This is something our *rishis* had discovered ages ago and the *yantras* are their contribution to humankind to enable them to get spiritual benefits. The *rishis* knew that metals like gold, copper and silver are the best for conducting electrical charges. Thus, they made these *yantras* out of these three materials. These plates act like the printed circuit board of a computer. They also had symbols to represent different sounds of the universe, which were incorporated into the *yantras*. The priest then charged the *yantras* by mentally chanting the *mantras* and thus used the bio-currents generated in their own bodies and transmitted the desired message onto the metal plates. At the same time they also touched certain objects like wet flowers and leaves, and transferred the invisible energies on the metal plate through their touch.

When energy is passed through a copper coil, the metal becomes a magnet. Similarly, when the priest or the devotee constantly repeats this process over a period of time, the metal will be transformed into a cosmic magnet which is called a *yantra*.

Nowadays it is common for people to buy these *yantras* and keep them in their houses or wear them as talismans. But it must be understood that unless the spiritual energy in the *yantras* has been activated, it will not be of much use to them. Of course the person who has it can also activate the *yantra* by constant repetition of the *mantra* and by touching and handling the thing with some intention or *sankalpa* in the mind.

The *rishis* dissected the human personality and made different sciences which would raise it to its highest potential. Along with the process of using the *yantra*, the *rishis* also formulated the technique known as *Tantra*. *Tantra* is a mental science—a meta-psychology or method of exploring the mind and developing the range of one's perception. In fact, it can be called the science of personality. *Tantra* declares that enlightenment is available to every type of personality—spiritual or sensual, theistic or atheistic, weak or strong. All human emotions like fear, passion, hatred, love and anger are energy forces. If controlled they can enable us to experience higher realities. The human psyche is actually a field of all possibilities. The Supreme according to *Tantra* is Adi Shakti, or the Divine Mother, who possesses the ultimate personality. She is the supreme expression of the totality of manifest existence. The aim of *Tantra* is to replace the limited human personality with an unlimited divine one. *Tantra* also teaches that by using the name (*mantra*) and imagining the form of any deity, it is possible to attain the nameless and formless Brahman. *Mantra*, the sound and *yantra*, the form, are both to be used in the path mapped by *Tantra*. *Mantra* is the energy that moves the vehicle or *yantra* according to the path as prescribed by *Tantra*. The best *yantra* is the human body. The divine already resides within this body and if certain tantric rites are performed, the individual will be able to reach his or her full divine potential. The Highest Self is said to be a priceless gem locked in a chest that is buried in mud. Tantric disciplines consist in clearing the mud of our petty, negative desires and opening the treasure box in our brain to expose the gem of self-awareness.

The universe, including our own bodies, has evolved out of the *Shakti* or energy of Pure Consciousness which is known in *Tantra* as Shiva. Although Shiva and *Shakti* have momentarily parted in order to create the world, they are forever striving to unite in the human body in order to experience the cosmic unity from which they evolved. The whole aim of *Tantra* is to attain this cosmic union. Thus, *Tantra* insists that every experience that comes to the individual, whether good or bad, should be accepted gratefully. The universe is a manifestation of *Shakti*, the divine mother so everything that takes place in the universe is also divine. Tantric *sadhana* is also used for procuring material benefits since they are the foundation on which the whole spiritual structure stands.

Our body contains invisible sound transmitters and receivers. When sound waves exceed a certain range, our ears are no longer able to hear them. However, we hold within us the ability to hear these sounds which are constantly coming from the etheric sphere. This is how the ancient *rishis* heard the Vedic *hymns*. With meditation and *pranayama* (breath control) and the use of *mantras* and *yantras*, the body will acquire the capacity to hear these sounds. Think how powerful we can be if we integrate our mind with cosmic sound. Sound is very powerful and we have heard of the great singer, Mario Lanza whose voice could shatter a crystal chandelier hanging ten feet away!

However, *Tantra* is a difficult path which has to be learnt only from a proficient *guru* who has mastered the techniques otherwise it might have dangerous consequences.

In order to invoke the power of the deity and activate the *mantra*, the priest or the practitioner also needs to use symbols made with the hand which are known as *mudras*. The *mudras* are made by pressing the thumb to the tips of different fingers and thus invoking the energy residing in our body. The tips of the fingers contain many nerves which go directly to certain parts of the body. These *mudras* are a kind of sign language, which is understood by the body which makes it react in a certain way. From all these facts we can see that the *rishis* explored every method (all of them scientific) by which the human being could surmount the obstacles on his spiritual path and enable him or her to attain union with the divine. The Western world is yet to discover the truths of *Tantra* and many of the methods used by the *rishis*.

Hinduism also uses many concrete symbols. The *swastika* is an ancient symbol that is to be found all over the world but its source is India. The name comes from the Sanskrit word *svasti* (well-being) and *asti* (is). It is a symbol for bringing good fortune, good luck and well-being.

The right-handed *swastika* is one of the 108 symbols of the God Vishnu as well as a symbol of the sun-god, Surya. The rotation of its arms towards the right indicates the course taken daily by the sun. Interestingly, this is a symbol for the sun among Native Americans also.

The left-handed form of the *swastika*, which is called *sauvastika*, is sometimes considered to be evil since it represents night, black magic and the Goddess Kali. However, it is the form most commonly used in Buddhism. Strangely enough, this is the symbol that Hitler used for the Nazi movement.

Puja is a ritualistic method of worshipping the gods. It aims at the accomplishment of some intention or desire. All *pujas* have a scientific basis. Hindus do *pujas* in their houses and also in the temples and many of us can certify that these produce the desired effect. How is this possible? The *samkalpa* or intention is what shapes the end product. It is mentally made by us when the *pujari* (priest) asks us to touch the plate in which the flowers, which are to be used for *puja*, are kept. When our mind makes a strong *samkalpa* or intention, it has the effect of actually being able to change the future! This is the very basis of all miracles. Sometimes we find that the doctor pronounces the patient to be incurable and the patient recovers, sometimes due to the latter's own strong desire to live and sometimes due to the prayers of others. So in any *puja*, it is our *samkalpa* that ensures the result. No doubt our *samkalpa* can be enhanced by the spiritual quality of the *pujari*.

Every aspect of the *pujas* which are conducted in temples have very great scientific meanings behind them and give great benefits to those who participate in them and take the *prasad* (offerings to the deity), which is distributed to all those who are present. This *prasad* is filled with positive vibrations. At the end of the *puja*, the consecrated water is sprinkled on the heads of the people who are gathered there and a few drops are also given to them to sip. This water has amazing power.

Water is the best conductor of spiritual vibrations and hence water is used in all *pujas*. Even Christian churches have holy water. The consecrated water in temples known as *charanamritam* (nectar of the Lord's feet) is the water that has been poured over the deity to the chanting of *mantras*. A Japanese scientist has recently proved that the molecules of water undergo a drastic change and attain a high degree of coherence when positive vibrations are passed through them. Our ancient scientists, the *rishis*, were well aware of this fact. Hence, this *charanamritam* has a very strong effect on the person who drinks it. Even the Hindus themselves do not realise that this is not just any water but water that has been potentised with *mantras*. The molecular structure of this water is totally different from ordinary water which has not been treated.

When we take our bath, we are again asked to chant a certain *mantra*. By repeating this *mantra* which has positive vibrations, the negative qualities of the water are removed.

The same case applies to the food we eat. We are told to chant certain *mantras* and circle the food with water held in our palms and then sprinkle some of that water on the food and drink the rest. It is only now that modern scientists have come to realise that this chanting and sprinkling of the water produces untold benefits.

The *rishis* knew many esoteric truths which are only recently being discovered by scientists but again since these scientific facts are interwoven into the daily life of the Hindu, we fail to realise how scientific they are. The *rishis* implanted a spiritual seed in every action of the human being and thus Hinduism is more a way of life than a religion. The life of a true Hindu is spiritualism put into practice. If we follow the rules set forth by the *rishis* for a good life, we will find that every one of them had a scientific basis and were meant to take us to the fulfilment of a perfect life.

Let us look at the way Hindus greet each other. They fold their palms together and utter the word *namaste*. The two palms are placed together in front of the chest and the head is bowed when saying this word. Sometimes the eyes are closed. The scriptures enjoin five forms of traditional greetings for Hindus and this is the one which is most commonly used. *Namah+te* means "I bow to you or my greetings or prostrations to you." It also is a way of saying, "May our minds meet." When we bow our head, we extend our love with humility. This greeting has a deep spiritual meaning. This is the action we make when we go to the temple. When we do the same action when meeting a person, we are recognising the fact that the body which stands in front of us is the temple of God, the outer covering of the Divine Spirit and thus we are greeting or prostrating before that Divine Spirit and not just the gross form of flesh and blood. When we salute another person with this feeling, the very act will take us to spiritual heights of communion with the divine and inspire a feeling of love in the other person.

This action of holding the palms together with the tips of the fingers touching each other stimulates the nerve endings, which are connected to various parts of the body. Scientific studies have shown that the pressure points on our palms are connected to every organ in the body and if stimulated regularly, we can keep up our health very easily. The *mudras*, like joining the forefinger with the tip of our thumb and sometimes with the middle fingers, as has been mentioned, are all capable of activating certain points and *chakras* in the body, thus making us more alert and alive.

In olden times, every Hindu used to use a dot or some other mark in the centre of his or her forehead. This point is actually the *ajna chakra* (third eye), which is the seat of intelligence. When we meet a person, our eyes are immediately drawn to the dot in the middle of the other person's forehead. The other person will have a similar experience and thus each will be able to draw the best from the other since they are both concentrating on the third eye. Thus, even this cosmetic and perhaps insignificant aspect of Hinduism has a scientific basis.

In south India, when Hindus go to a Ganesha temple you will find them catching their ears with opposite hands and bobbing up and down in front of the idol of Ganesha. This exercise has recently been discovered to have amazing health benefits since the lobes of the ears contain a number of nerves, which stimulate the brain centres. The act of going up and down also greases the knees and elbows and keeps them supple.

The first thing that a Hindu is supposed to do when he or she gets up is to touch the earth with the fingers and repeat a certain *mantra* to the earth goddess, *Vishnu patnir namasthubhyam, padasparsham kshamaswame.* "O thou consort of Vishnu, please forgive my transgressions on thee."

There are two important reasons for this. One is to remind us of the great duty we owe to the earth—our very first mother. We ask her forgiveness for stamping on her, digging her and performing all the hundreds of dreadful things we are doing to her now. Another reason is that this small insignificant act actually gives our body the earthing it needs. The poles within our body need to be earthed when we wake up and this act does just that.

Thus, every action which the Hindu is supposed to do from the time he gets up to the time he goes to bed has some scientific basis.

In olden days it was the custom to light a lamp daily before the altar of the Lord. In some houses it is lit twice a day at dawn and dusk. All auspicious functions commence with the lighting of the lamp, which is kept lit throughout the occasion. Light symbolises knowledge. The Lord is *chaitanya* or the light of all knowledge. Hence light is worshipped as the Lord Himself. The question may be asked as to why we should not light an electric bulb instead of an oil lamp. That will also remove darkness. But as in all things in Hinduism, the traditional oil or ghee lamp has a symbolic and therefore spiritual significance. The wick stands for our ego and the oil or ghee for our negative tendencies both inherited and acquired. When we light the lamp, we pray that our negative tendencies and enmity to others, etc. should be removed. When the ego is touched by the light of spiritual knowledge, the negative tendencies slowly exhaust themselves as the oil becomes less and less. This daily affirmation by the mind has the effect of imperceptibly eradicating negativity. Western psychology has come to recognise positive affirmations as one of the best methods of treatment. Moreover, ghee has the power to purify the environment when it is lit.

The Western mind considered Nature, God and man to be totally unconnected. The *rishis* on the other hand realised that these three are actually interconnected and what affects one part will affect every other part. If Nature is defiled, man will have to suffer, which is what is happening to us now.

Every thought and action of the human being has a deep impact on the universe as a whole. Thus, the *rishis* insisted on the deep consideration to be shown to nature. Nature or Prakriti is not inert matter to be used and misused according to our pleasure but she is a pulsating, living being and has to be treated with all consideration and love. Only then will she yield her resources to the human being.

> When the mind is detached from memory, perception gets total clarity. It gives correct and complete knowledge beyond which nothing remains to be known.
>
> The yogic mind abides in total silence. In supreme silence the mind is liberated from the world of change to rest in unbounded consciousness.
>
> *Patanjali Yogasutras*

> He who knows the first vital thread,
> Binding all things formed in shape, colour and words,
> Knows only the physical form of the universe, and knows very little of that,
> But he who goes deeper and perceives the string inside the string,
> The thin web binding separate life forces with the cords of unity,
> Knows the real entity.
> Only he knows truly the mighty omnipotent and omnipresent God,
> Who is within and beyond all formulated entities of the vast universe,
> Penetrate deeper to know the ultimate truth.
>
> *Atharva Veda*

Loka Samasthath Sukhino Bhavantu!

ॐ

Satchidanandaaya Namaha!

CHAPTER XVI

Goals of Hinduism

Find the eternal object of your quest within your soul,
Enough have you wandered during the long period of your
quest!
Dark and weary must have been the ages of your search in
ignorance,
And groping in helplessness,
At last when you turn your gaze inward, suddenly you realise
that the
Bright light of faith and lasting truth was shining around
you.
With rapturous joy, you find the soul of the universe,
The eternal object of your quest.
Your searching mind at last finds the object of the search,
Within your own heart.

Yajur Veda

He whom they call in the Vedanta as One Person, pervading
both worlds,
Whose title "Lord" applies to no other,

For whom the seekers of deliverance search within their vital
breaths,
Who is found with ease through the yoga of devotion,
May He, the Absolute Lord, lead you to the supreme good.

Shiva Purana

Finally, it must be noted that what has made the Hindu culture
so scientific and why it has lasted for so long is because the basis
of all Hindu scientific genius is its spirituality. Many civilizations
have come into existence in some small region of the world and
perished in the course of time. The Hindu culture alone has
existed from the dawn of time, unparalleled and retaining its
inherent values through the ages. As has been pointed out,
spirituality is the very basis of Hindu culture and great care was
taken by all the *rishis* and saints of India to ensure that a touch
of spirituality was injected into every type of human endeavour.
Human excellence depends on the development of true cultural
values which are human values. As mentioned in the
Introduction, Hindu culture which is known as the Sanatana
Dharma is based on *dharma,* which is the cosmic law of
righteousness and hence it can be called the first human culture.

Hinduism has four goals of life known as Purusharthas. These
four goals are the pursuit of *dharma* (righteousness), *artha,*
(pursuit of material possessions), *kama* (pursuit of pleasure),
moksha (pursuit of enlightenment). These are the great human
values which Hinduism has always concentrated on inculcating
in society. It has always been ready to accept any activity which
strives to increase these values.

The four Purusharthas are like the four wheels of the chariot
of the human body. They collectively uphold it and lead it. Each
influences the movement of the other three, and in the absence
of any one of them, the chariot comes to a halt.

Now let us examine these goals. We will find that they cover the whole gamut of human life. The pursuit of wealth and pleasure has not been overlooked in Hinduism but it will be noticed that they have been bound on one side by righteousness and on the other side by a desire for liberation. Righteous methods of gaining wealth and pleasure are encouraged in Hinduism since these two are basic needs of the human being. That is why Narayana, the Lord who is responsible for the maintenance of the world order, is married to Lakshmi, the goddess of wealth and auspiciousness. If the methods used for gaining wealth and pleasures are righteous, even they will lead to *moksha* or liberation. This is what Hinduism declares. If the right path is chosen, the correct goal will be reached!

This again is a scientific approach to life as is found in the whole religion and as we have seen in the previous chapters. It is not easy to reach the goal of enlightenment. The entire energy of the system should be focussed on that goal if success has to be assured. Even in mundane affairs, we find that the artist, scientist, engineer, doctor or dancer who puts her whole heart and soul into her art or work, is the one who is likely to succeed. If this is so for the material world, how much more would it be for the spiritual?

The main message of Hinduism is that of *satya* and *ahimsa*—truth and non-violence. Look on everything as divine and thus you can never hurt or harm anything either in nature or in the human being. Thus, the Hindu has never wanted to conquer or control anything except his own mind. India is unique in accepting people of all religions and giving them asylum. Recently when China overran Tibet, India was the only country who gave an asylum to the Dalai Lama and allowed the Tibetans to come and settle down on Indian soil without let or hindrance and allowed them to practise their own religion—Buddhism.

Thus, you find that India has never invaded any country in the last ten thousand years of its history. This is the best accolade that can be given to this culture and one which shows its uniqueness.

Now the time has come for every Hindu all over the world, regardless whether they were born Hindus or have accepted the faith as their own, to see that this ancient religion and way of life should be kept alive. It is up to the Hindus to protect their country and their faith as the Westerners tried to protect their faith when they first came to India. We should also inculcate our faith and spread the ideals of this wonderful *dharma* all over the world in as systematic a manner as the Westerners sought to suppress it during the 19th and 20th centuries. As can be seen from a reading of this book, all original thought in India perished with the advent of the British along with the use of so many great scientific techniques which had their origin in India. Just as the Indians of those times were enticed to view their own culture as outdated and ape Western culture so now we have to produce a new generation who will be proud of their culture and who will be happy to share it with other noble-minded souls.

The whole world is really bound to support this ancient religion and to see that its scriptures are kept intact for future generations. The only liberation for humanity from its bondages is to follow the ancient tenets found in the Vedas and the Upanishads and listen to the voice of the great *rishis*, exhorting us to look to the divine within us and see it everywhere so that the world can live in true love and compassion for the whole of the whole universe and for the creatures that live in it.

As Annie Besant said,

If the Hindus do not maintain Hinduism, who shall save it?
If India's own children do not cling to her faith, who shall
guard it? India alone can save India, and India and Hinduism
are one.

Let us close this book with the great Vedic prayer for universal
peace.

Aum swasti prajabhyaam, paripaalayantaam,
Nyayena margena, mahimahishaha,
Go brahmanebhyam shubamastu nityam,
Lokaasamstaa sukhino bhavantu,

May all people be happy,
May the kings rule the earth righteously,
Let animals and men of wisdom be taken care of,
May everyone be filled with auspiciousness.

Kaale varshatu parjanyaha,
Prithivi shashyashaalini,
Deshoyam kshobharahitaha,
Satjanaath santu nirbhayaaha.

May rains come at the proper time,
May the earth produce all types of grain,
May countries be free from famine,
May good people be free from fear.

Sarveshaam swastir bhavatu,
Sarveshaam shantir bhavatu,
Sarvesham poornam bhavatu,
Sarvesham mangalam bhavatu,
Sarve bhavantu sukhinaha,
Sarve santu niraamayaaha,

Sarve bhadraani pashyantu,
Ma kaschid dukhabhav bhaveth.
Aum Shanti! Shanti! Shantihi!

Let the whole world enjoy good health,
Let the whole world enjoy peace,
Let the whole world enjoy prosperity,
Let the whole world be filled with auspiciousness.
May all creatures be happy,
May everybody be free from disease.
May all see only auspiciousness in everything,
Let not any sorrow prevail.
Aum Peace! Peace! Peace!

Truth, eternal order, that is great and stern,
Consecrations, austerity, prayer and ritual uphold the earth.
May she, queen of what has been and will be, care and provide
vast space for us.

                                                        Atharva Veda

Loka Samasthath Sukhino Bhavantu!

Bhaktavatsalaaya Namaha!

CHAPTER XVII

Poems by Vanamali

How fortunate am I to be born a Hindu on this holy soil,
Breathing the perfumed air, saturated by the breath of
countless sages,
Drinking in the sight of this sacred river,
This incredible mountain,
Listening to the chants of the ages,
Washed down the river of time,
Floating across the Ganga,
Bells ringing, conchs blaring,
The sound of *Aum*, echoing down the corridors of time,
Thrilling me to the very core,
Urging me not to waste even a small precious moment,
Charging me to go forward,
Searching for my ephemeral self,
Which all the time resides in me,
My constant companion,
My lover of a thousand ages,
My child, my father, my mother, my beloved.
My one and only Me,

The eternal Me,
Nothing else exists,
There is no Thou,
Only I, I and again I.

ॐ   ॐ   ॐ

O to be in India when the monsoons come,
To feel the rain on your face, and the mist in your eyes,
To smell the earth with heaving bosom,
To bow before the lashing waters,
To laugh with the thunder and gurgle with the stream.
To flinch when the lightning hits your eyes.
To listen bemused to the orchestra of the night.
To be in India—to be an Indian!

ॐ   ॐ   ॐ

When will I be able to roam over the Himalayas,
The cradle of our civilization,
To be young and free and clamber over the snowy mountains,
To feel my Mother's pulse rushing in my veins,
To feel her spirit raising me to the heights,
To plumb the depths of her beauty,
To unveil the secret of her eternity,
To roam wild over her mountainside,
To plunge into the depths of her waters,
To rejoice that the eternal spirit of the rishis,
Courses through my veins,
To be free, to be a seeker,
To be an Indian!

ॐ   ॐ   ॐ

Himalaya!
Thy name is a blessing and a boon,
Walking through the forest of Devatarus—the trees of the
gods,
I sit sometimes immobile, meditating on thee O mighty
Himalaya!
To think of thee is to be blessed!
To live in thee is grace supreme,
To die on thy chest is liberation!

ॐ   ॐ   ॐ

O Ganga!
Thou art not a river,
Thou art a goddess,
Coursing through the Milky Way of stars,
Washing the feet of Vishnu.
Falling on the matted locks of Shambu,
Beguiled by Bhageeratha,
Gushing down the gorges of the Himalayas.
Rushing through the plains,
To defile the purity of your waters in the salty ocean.
In order to bless this land, the land of your choice.
O Ganga! Thou ethereal goddess,
Blessed am I to have thy darshana every morning!

ॐ   ॐ   ॐ

How fortunate am I to be born on this holy land,
Where countless sages and avataras have trod,
Where the very air is fragrant with the perfume of their holy
feet,
Where sacred rivers and streams gush in ecstasy to reach the
ocean,
Where every stone is a linga in disguise,

Where every cow is a holy animal,
Where one can lie on the earth and say,
This is my land, the holy land.

ॐ   ॐ   ॐ

Love lies in the heart of the sun,
You cannot see it but you can feel its heat,
Soaking through you, filling you with warmth,
It reveals itself in the eyes of the person before you,
Even though you might never have seen him before.
It shines through the twinkling gaze of your child,
Who looks at you as if you were the end and the all.
It enters your heart unattended,
Ready to reveal itself, ready to care for you,
If you allow it.
All the love you get in the world is the love of god for you,
The love of you (the human) for god!
There is no other love—there is no other love.

ॐ   ॐ   ॐ

However many births I might take,
May I still be born a Hindu,
As a tulsi leaf or lotus flower,
On the soil of India,
How many births have I gone through,
As leaf and worm and reptile—animal and brute man,
Before being born a Hindu on this sacred soil.
My Mother, Supreme!
I take thy sacred dust and place it reverently on my head,
I am replete with thy love, thy compassion,
Mother allow me to serve you till the end of my life.
Take my hand Mother and lead me to liberation.

ॐ   ॐ   ॐ

There is a divine romance flowering in the hearts of all,
An aroma of the Spirit, creeping into our souls,
A mystic sound emanating from our hearts,
Prepare yourselves O daughters and sons of this soil,
The dawn is about to break!

Loka Samasthath Sukhino Bhavantu!

ॐ

List of Mantras

ॐ *Ganeshaaya Namaha*	Salutaions to Lord Ganesha
ॐ *Vishvasmai Namaha*	Salutations to the one who is Everything
ॐ *Dharmaaya Namaha*	Salutations to the Eternal Law
ॐ *Bhutatmaaya Namaha*	Salutations to the Self in every creature
ॐ *Vishvaaya Namaha*	Salutations to the one who is everywhere
ॐ *Shaswataaya Namaha*	Salutations to the Eternal
ॐ *Vishvakarmaaya Namaha*	Salutations to the maker of all things
ॐ *Aprameyaaya Namaha*	Salutations to the Immeasurable
ॐ *Shantidaaya Namaha*	Salutations to the giver of Peace
ॐ *Paramatmaaya Namaha*	Salutations to the Supreme Self
ॐ *Purushottamaaya Namaha*	Salutations to the Supreme Person
ॐ *Sarvatjnaaya Namaha*	Salutations to the All-Knower
ॐ *Twashtaaya Namaha*	Salutations to the Immortal Craftsman

ॐ *Anaghaaya Namaha*	Salutations to the Flawless One
ॐ *Pavanaaya Namaha*	Salutations to the Purifier
ॐ *Achintyaaya Namaha*	Salutations to the one Beyond Thought
ॐ *Varadaaya Namaha*	Salutations to the giver of boons
ॐ *Sundaraaya Namaha*	Salutations to the Beautiful One
ॐ *Sarva-darshitaaya Namaha*	Salutations to the All-seeing One
ॐ *Satchidandaaya Namaha*	Salutations to the one who is Existence-consciousness-bliss
ॐ *Bhaktavatsalaaya Namaha*	Salutations to the lover of his devotees

ॐ

Glossary

aranya	pertaining to the forest
asana	a seat
acharya	teacher
adharmic	unrighteous
Aditi	mother of the gods
advaita	non-dual
agni	fire
ahamta	sense of mineness
ahara shuddhi	purity of food
ahimsa	non-violence
ajna chakra	the chakra between the brows
akasa	sky (space)
amavasya	new moon day
anadi	that which has no beginning
ananda	bliss
anandamaya kosha	the sheath of bliss
ananta	that which has no end
annamaya kosha	the sheath of food
anu	atom
apah	the element of water
apana	the breath which is exhaled
apara vidya	scientific knowledge

apas	water
apaurusheya	not the work of man
aric	wise man; sage
artha	wealth
asaana	approximate
asat	non-existence
ashrama	spiritual retreat
ashtanga yoga	the yoga of eight limbs by Patanjali
asti	beingness
asura	demonic being
atma(n)	the divine spirit in the human being
Aum	the initial sound of the cosmos
avaidika	contrary to *the Veda*
avatara	incarnaton of God
avidya	ignorance
avyakta	that which is not clear
Bhakta	devotee
bhakti marga	the path of devotion
bhakti yoga	the yoga of devotion
bilva/vilva	type of leaf important in the worship of Shiva
bindu	dot
braahmana	Brahmin; a member of the highest class
brahamanda	a supergalaxy
brahma-muhurtam	time between 3 and 4 a.m.
brahmacharya	continence
brahmajnana	knowledge of the Brahman

brahmanishta rishi	sage who is established in the Brahman
brahmarishi	sage who is a knower of Brahman
briha	large
chaitanya	light of divine consciousness
chakra	wheel
chandas	metre used in poems
Chandogya	one of the Upanishads
charanamritam	sanctified water which has been poured over the deity
chikitsa vignana	knowledge of treatments
chit, chitta, chid	highest level of the mind
chitta shuddhi	purification of the mind
chitta vritti nirodha	to steady the wavering mind
da-ma	compassion
daa-na	charity
darshana	point of view
desha	country
deva	shining one (god)
dhamanis	veins and nerves that supply food to the body
dharma	universal law of life and righteousness
dharmic	pertaining to dharma
dhatu	nerve
dhruva	a type of grass used in worship of Ganesha
dosha	one of the three problems of the body

dravya vignana	pharmocology
dwaita	duality
gada	mace
gayatri	name of a metre; famous hymn to the Sun-god.
gotra	lineage coming from a *rishi*
gotra rishi	rishi whose name was given to the lineage
gotra-pravartakas	founders of the Brahmanical clans
guna	one of the three strands of nature
guru	spiritual preceptor
homa	fire ceremony
ishta deva	favourite deity
itihasa	epic
jadaragni	fire of digestion
jagat	world
jagrita	waking state of consciousness
japa	repetition of god's name
japa yoga	the yoga of the repetition of the mantra
jijnasu	enquirer on the path of truth.
jiva	the life principle
jivatma	the embodied soul
jnana	wisdom
jnana kanda	volume on wisdom
jnana marga	the path of wisdom

jnani	the man of wisdom
jyestha	elder
jyotisha	astrology
kaala	time
Kali Yuga	name of the present epoch
kalpa	lifetime of Brahma, the creator
kama	passion
kapha	phlegm; on of the three *doshas*
karma	action; bonds accruing from action
karma kanda	volume or portion pertaining to action
karmic	pertaining to the bond created by our action
krimis	germs; parasites
krishna paksha	dark half of the lunar month
kurma	tortoise
laya	state of dissolution
lila	play
loka	world
lokasamgraham	for the maintenance of the world
mahakashayas	herbal concoctions used in Ayurveda
maharshi	great sage
mahavakyas	the great sayings of the Upanishads
mala	necklace
mamta	mineness
manava-dharma-shastra	book describing the duties of a human being

mandala	mystic drawing
mandukam	frog
mantra	a spiritual formula
mantra-drashta	the person to whom the *mantra* was revealed
manvantara	an epoch ruled by a Manu
matsya	fish
matsya-yantra	an instrument using the fish symbol
maya	the illusion of a separate world; appearance; the phenomenal world
meena	an astrological sign
meru	mythical peak
mesha	astrological sign and the name of a month
mesha sankranthi	the day preceding the month called Mesha
mesha sankranthi rekha	the alpha aries point from which the earth starts its rotation round the sun
mesha vishuvath	Hindu new year
mithya	that which does not exist
moksha	liberation from mortal coils
mudra	mystic design made by the fingers
muladhara chakra	energy whorl found at the base of the spine
Mundaka	name of an Upanishad
nadi	a nerve
nadi shastras	palm-leaves on which people's horoscopes are found
nakshatra	star

nama	name
namaste	folding the palms together as a salutation
Narasimha	the incarnation of Vishnu as half-human and half-lion
nav	boat
navagatih	navigation
neti, neti	not this; not this
nimisha	second
nimitta	cause
nirukta	etimology
ojas	physical spleandour
padaas	steps
pakayantras	laboratory instruments
pancha bhutas	the five elements in Nature
pancha karmas	the five types of cleansing in Ayurveda
panchamahabhutas	the five great elements
papa	sin
para vidya	knowledge of the Absolute
paramanu	molecule
Paramatma	the supreme Soul
patrika	palm-leaves on which horoscopes were written
pitta	bile; one of the three *doshas*
poorna	totally full
poorva janma	previous birth
prajnanaghanam	filled with consciousness
Prakriti	Nature

pralaya	flood
pramaana	infallible knowledge
prana	vital breath; life-force
pranamaya kosha	the sheath of breath around the body
pranava mantra	the *mantra Aum*
pranava swaroopa	the form of *Aum*
pranayama	the technique of breath control
pranic	pertaining to the *prana* or life-force
prarabadha karma	results of action done in a previous life
prasad	left-over of offerings to God
prasna	enquiry
pratibha	highly developed intuition
Prithvi	the earth
puja	ritualistic worship of god
punya	spiritual merit
punya kaalam	auspicious time
puranic	pertaining to the Puranas
puranic rishis	the sages responsible for writing the Puranas
Purusha	the Supreme Person
rajas	activity, passion; one of the three modes of Nature
renu	particle
rik	hymn from the *Rig Veda*
rishi	great sage
rudraksha	seed of a tree which is important for Shiva
rupa	form

sabda-pramana	Vedic hymns
sadhana	spiritual practice
samadhi	super conscious state
samans	hymns of the *Sama Veda*
samhara	dissolution
samyama	unbroken mental absorption
samyoga	union of the jivatma with the Paramatma
Sanatana Dharma	the real name for Hinduism; the ancient law of righteousness
sandal	sandalwood
sandhya	that time when day changes to night and night to day
sannyasins	renunciates who wear ochre robes
saptarishis	the seven sages
sat	existence
sat-chid-ananda	existence-consciousness and bliss; attribute of Brahman
sattva	quality of purity; one of the modes of Prakriti
satyam	truth
sauvastika	left-handed form of the Swastika
shad-darshanas	six schools of Hindu philosophy
Shakti	force, power of the goddess
shalya-tantra	surgical procedures
shastra	scriptures
sloka	couplet in a poem
shrishti	creation
sruti	that which was heard

shruti siras	the head of the Vedas (refers to the Upanishads)
shukla paksha	bright fortnight of the lunar month
shunya	zero; nihil
siddha	perfected being
siddhi	supernormal power
smriti	that which is recollected, the second and third portion of the Vedas
sadhana	spiritual discipline
sthiti	status quo
sushupti	state of deep sleep
svasti	auspiciousness
swapna	dreaming state
swara	pitch
swastika	a symbol of auspiciousness
swayamvara	marriage by choice of the bride
tamas	sleep; inertia; one of the three modes of *Prakriti*
tantra	an esoteric type of yoga
tantric	pertaining to tantra
tapas; tapasya	austerity
tejas	spiritual effulgence
tulasi	the holy basil
turiya	state of superconsciousness
upadhis	conditionings of the mind (space time and causation)

vac	sound; speech
vaidika	pertaining to the Vedas
vaidika dharma	rules of behaviour given by the Vedas
Vamana	incarnation of Vishnu as a dwarf
Varaha	incarnation of Vishnu as a boar
vata	element of wind in the body (one of the *doshas*)
vayu	air
Veda	the four holy books of the Hindus
Veda Vedya	that which is to be known through a study of the Veda
Vedic	pertaining to the Vedas
vel	spear (weapon used by Lord Subramania)
vidya	knowledge
vijnanamaya kosha	the intellectual sheath of the human being
vishuvath	the start of the Hindu year
Vyakarna	grammar
vyakta	perceivable to the senses
vyoma	transcendental space
yajna shalaas	places where *yajnas* are held
yaj	to worship
yajnas	fire ceremonies
yakrut	liver
yam	to control
yantra	instrument, spiritual design

yoga	spiritual practices to attain union with the Divine
Yoga Sutras	aphorisms given by the sage Patanjali
yogi	one who practices yoga
yojana	about a mile
yuga	an epoch
yuj	to unite

ॐ

Bibliography

Capra, Fritjof, 1976. *The Tao of Physics,* Fontana.

McTaggart, Lynn, 2003. *The Field,* Harper Collins.

Mukundcharandas, Sadhu, 2011. *Rishis, Mystics and Heroes of India,* Swaminarayan Aksharpith, Ahmedabad.

Panda, N.C., 2005. *Maya in Physics,* Motilal Banarasidass, Delhi.

Saraswati, Sri Chandrashekharendra (Shankaracharya of Kanchi Kamakoti Peetham), 1991. *The Vedas,* Bharatiya Vidya Bhavan, Mumbai.

Vidyalankar, Pandit Satyakam. *The Holy Vedas,* Clarion Books, Delhi.

Hari Aum Tat Sat